REFRESHED ◆ REVISED ◆ UPDATED

Hachette CHILDREN'S

Yearbook & Infopedia 2024

hachette INDIA

First published in 2023 by Hachette India
(Registered name: Hachette Book Publishing India Pvt Ltd)
An Hachette UK company
www.hachetteindia.com

1

IMAGE COPYRIGHT INFORMATION: FRONT COVER: DROUPADI MURMU: Wikimedia Commons: GODL-India: https://commons.wikimedia.org/wiki/File:Droupadi_Murmu_official_portrait,_2022.jpg; Author: President's Secretariat; PRIME MINISTER NARENDRA MODI: Press Information Bureau; SAM ALTMAN: Wikimedia CC Attribution-Share Alike 3.0 Unported; Attribution: Amos Ben Gershom/Government Press Office; https://commons.wikimedia.org/wiki/File:Isaac_Herzog_meeting_with_Sam_Altman,_June_2023_(GPOABG244).jpeg; MAHENDER SINGH DHONI: image courtesy Neeraj Jha; XI JINPING 2019: Wikimedia CC Attribution 2.0 Generic license: https://commons.wikimedia.org/wiki/File:Xi_Jinping_2019.jpg; Author: Officia do Palácio do Planalto; extracted from file: 2019 Audiência com o Presidente da República popular da China, Senhor Xi Jinping.jpg; KING CHARLES: https://commons.wikimedia.org/wiki/File:Charles_III_2023_Coronation_(cropped).jpg: Open Government Licence v3.0; DEEPIKA PADUKONE: Wikimedia CC Attribution 3.0 Unported license; Attribution: Bollywood Hungama; Source: http://www.bollywoodhungama.com/news/parties-and-events/ranveer-singh-deepika-padukone-promoting-bajirao-mastani/ranveer-singh-deepika-padukone-promoting-bajirao-mastani-4/; LIONEL MESSI: Wikimedia CC Attribution 4.0 International license; Attribution: Tasnim News Agency; https://commons.wikimedia.org/wiki/File:Lionel-Messi-Argentina-2022-FIFA-World-Cup_(cropped).jpg; RISHI SUNAK: https://commons.wikimedia.org/wiki/File:Portrait_of_Prime_Minister_Rishi_Sunak_(cropped).jpg: Open Government Licence v3.0; HARMANPREET KAUR: Wikimedia GODL: Press Information Bureau on behalf of President's Secretariat, Government of India under the ID 112631 and CNR 101165; Attribution: President's Secretariat (GODL-India); VIKRAM-S: Attribution: Indian Space Research Organization (GODL-India); Wildfire: PD; Author: Mike McMillan/USFS; PIXABAY: Olympic rings; climate-change; elephant; robot and space; **BACK COVER:** CHANDRAYAAN 3 Attribution: Indian Space Research Organization (GODL-India); The remaining photographs and illustrations are sourced from the public domain.

The copyright details and credits for the photographs in the book are on page 224, which is to be considered as an extension of the copyright page.

RESEARCH AND CONTENT WRITING: Aishwarya Rajak; Aliza Ajith; Debangana Mishra and Nandini Dang.

ISBN 978-93-5731-271-4

Hachette Book Publishing India Pvt. Ltd
4th & 5th Floors, Corporate Centre
Plot No. 94, Sector 44, Gurugram 122003, India

MIX
Paper from responsible sources
FSC www.fsc.org FSC™ C043100

Typeset and design by Syed Salahuddin

Printed and bound in India
by Manipal Technologies Limited

CONTENTS

CONTENTS

1 NEWS INDIA

OCTOBER 2022

'Blue Flag' for two more beaches in India

In October, the Ministry of Environment, Forest and Climate Change announced that two more Indian beaches, Minicoy Thundi and Kadmat, both of which are located in Lakshadweep, have received the 'Blue Flag' certification. It is an international eco-label given to the cleanest beaches and 10 other beaches in India have this label. The programme is developed and operated by the Foundation for Environmental Education, and it is headquartered in Copenhagen, Denmark. The Blue Flag label is given to beaches, marinas and boating operators to promote sustainability and environmental awareness.

Hyderabad wins World Green City award

Hyderabad emerged as the overall winner and the winner in the category of Economic Recovery and Inclusive Growth at the International Association of Horticulture Producers World Green Cities Awards 2022. The event was organized in South Korea on 12 October. Hyderabad outperformed cities like Paris, Mexico City, Montreal, Fortaleza and Bogota.

NOVEMBER 2022

FIRSTAP, India's first sticker-based debit card

IDFC First, in collaboration with the National Payments Corporation of India, launched FIRSTAP, India's first contactless debit card in sticker format. The sticker-based debit card increased customer convenience as it is much smaller than a regular debit card and the sticker can be pasted on a wide range of devices such as mobile phones, identity cards and tabs. Transactions can be made easily and without the hassle of carrying debit cards or scanning QR codes.

Tamil Nadu's first biodiversity heritage site

Tamil Nadu declared an area of 193.215 hectares in Arittapatti and Meenakshipuram villages in Madurai district as the first Biodiversity Heritage Site (BHS) in the state under section 37 of the Biological Diversity Act, 2002. The area's biological significance is evident by the presence of several lakes and natural springs, and birds like falcons and eagles as well as animals like pangolins that pronounce the biological diversity of the place. The rock-cut temples and Tamil Brahmi inscriptions, among other things, enhance the value of the place further by marking its historical significance.

Hanle Dark Sky Reserve

The Dark Sky Reserve at Hanle village in Ladakh is the country's first night sky sanctuary. In a night sky sanctuary, there is no loud source of light or any form of light pollution, resulting in total darkness which makes sky observation easier. Settlements around the reserve will also observe some rules to maintain zero or minimal light pollution. The area identified for the Dark Sky Reserve comprises the six hamlets of Bhok, Punguk, Khuldo, Shado, Naga and Tibetan Refugee habitations within the Changthang Wildlife Sanctuary. Established in 2001, the Indian Astronomical Observatory, at an elevation of approximately 14,764 feet, will now be the centre of the night sky sanctuary.

Vikram-S is launched successfully

India's first privately built fuel rocket, Vikram-S, was developed by Hyderabad-based Skyroot Aerospace Pvt Ltd. It was launched by ISRO from the Satish Dhawan Space Centre in Sriharikota. Apart from the launch, ISRO also assisted with the infrastructure for testing and integration operations. The rocket was launched as part of Mission Prarambh to mark a new beginning as private sector organizations begin taking part in India's space journey which was entirely dependent on ISRO until now. The rocket is named after Indian physicist and the Father of the Indian space programme, Vikram Sarabhai. Vikram-S, a single stage, sub-orbital vehicle, was launched mainly to test the prototype of the technology used in the Vikram series of space vehicles that will be launched later.

Border conflict at Yangtse

On 9 December, Indian and Chinese forces faced each other in a conflict along the Line of Actual Control (LAC) in Yangtse which is nearly 25 km away from Tawang in Arunachal Pradesh. Around 300 to 400 soldiers from China's People's Liberation Army transgressed the LAC to gain access to a peak that allows a broader view of the region. However, their advance was soon checked by the Indian Army who called for reinforcements to drive back the Chinese troops.

Project Vaani

With funding and additional tech support from Google, IISc Bangalore and ARTPARK have collaborated to develop Project Vaani. It is a digital project that will map the diversity of Indian languages by collecting speech- and text-based data from 1 million people across 773 districts of India. The district-level plan has been made because in India the dialects differ across districts. Apart from further developing technologies like automatic speech recognition, speech-to-speech translation and natural language understanding, the project also attempts to remove linguistic barriers currently present in technology and make it more accessible.

The world's first intranasal Covid vaccine

On Republic Day, Bharat Biotech released iNCOVACC, an intranasal Covid-19 vaccine which was approved both for primary doses and heterologous booster doses. iNCOVACC works by stimulating a local immune response in the nose and throat. Intranasal vaccines eliminate the need for needles, making them easier to administer without the help of a trained healthcare worker. They are also easier to store and transport, which makes them particularly advantageous for low-income and remote areas.

IIT Madras develops BharOS

BharOS is an open-source, free operating system (OS) developed by IIT Madras and funded by the government. This project is a step towards a self-reliant India, aiming to promote the use of locally developed technology. It does not come with any default apps because it aims to enhance the user's control over the technology. BharOS is currently being used by organizations that have stringent privacy requirements and handle sensitive information. It offers Native Over the Air (NOTA) updates, which can be automatically downloaded and installed on the device, to keep the devices secure.

Kisan Drone Yatra

Prime Minister Narendra Modi inaugurated the 'Kisan Drone Yatra' in different parts of the country. He virtually flagged off 100 kisan drones to modernize farms across India. Drones can assist in crop assessment, land record digitization and pesticide spraying to make these

processes efficient. To promote drone use on farms, the government will provide 50 per cent subsidy on drones for scheduled castes and tribes, women farmers, farmers in northeastern states and small or marginal farmers.

FEBRUARY 2023

Upgrading villages through the 'Vibrant Villages Programme'

The 'Vibrant Villages Programme' was first announced in the 2022 Budget as part of the Centre's efforts to raise the standard of living in areas along the border of China. Under this programme, 2,967 villages have been chosen from 19 districts, including Sikkim, Arunachal Pradesh, Uttarakhand and Himachal Pradesh. The focus of the scheme will be on improving infrastructure for healthcare, water supply, power supply, roads and tourist attractions. The Cabinet has approved ₹4,800 crore for the programme, of which ₹2,500 crore has been earmarked for road infrastructure.

MARCH 2023

India's vision for 6G

Prime Minister Narendra Modi unveiled the 6G vision document with plans to design, develop and deploy 6G network and technologies by 2030. The document has been carefully prepared by the 22-member innovation group led by Telecom Secretary K. Rajaraman and the Technology Innovation Group on 6G (TIG-6G). The government plans to implement 6G in two phases. According to the document, it will focus on new technologies such as terahertz (THz) communication, tactile internet, radio interfaces, AI for connected intelligence, new encoding methods and waveform chipsets for 6G devices.

Bollywood meets Hollywood at NMACC

On 30 March, India witnessed the star-studded inauguration of its biggest yet cultural centre for performing and visual arts. The centre, whilst being a medium for promoting Indian heritage and culture, is a platform for outreach and literacy programme, learning and competitions, and for the world to come showcase their artistry while enjoying India's. Armed with a Grand Theatre, a Studio Theatre, the Cube and an Art House, NMACC is geared for multi-disciplinary exhibits of international standards, including globally celebrated Broadway shows.

APRIL 2023

Country's first 3D-printed post office

The first-of-its-kind post office has been constructed in Bengaluru's Cambridge Layout in Halasuru using 3D printing technology. The project has been undertaken by Larsen & Toubro, which has experience in constructing 3D-printed buildings, including India's first 3D-printed building in Kanchipuram, Tamil Nadu. With the help of a robotic printer, this printing technology deposited concrete layer-by-layer in accordance with the 3D model drawing input.

India's first water metro

The Kochi Water Metro was inaugurated as the first public boat service in India integrated with a metro rail network. The boats used are battery-powered, air-conditioned and disabled-friendly. Each boat can carry 100 passengers. The project will expand to cover 76 km with 78 boats. Operating in the backwaters, the water metro will connect 10 nearby islands with Kochi's mainland, resulting in shorter travel times and more cost-effective transportation.

MAY 2023

Indian navy successfully test-fires BrahMos missile

The BrahMos supersonic cruise missile was test-fired from the Indian Navy's guided missile destroyer INS Mormugao. BrahMos Aerospace is a joint venture between India and Russia, which manufactures supersonic cruise missiles that can be launched from air, sea or land. The missile flies at three times the speed of sound and demonstrates the Indian Navy's formidable firepower. These missiles are also exported by India.

Kerala becomes the first fully e-governed state in India

At the 'Total e-Governance Kerala' event held in Thiruvananthapuram, CM Pinarayi Vijayan declared Kerala to be India's first fully e-governed state. Kerala has been successful in digitizing an extensive range of government services, ensuring prompt and transparent delivery to its citizens. The government has implemented the Kerala Fibre Optic Network (KFON) project, which has made internet access a citizen's right, as well as a single-window portal called e-Sevanam that offers an extensive array of over 900 services which would soon be extended to taluka-level offices.

JUNE 2023

NITI Aayog and the UN partner to accelerate sustainable development in India

NITI Aayog and the United Nations signed the Government of India -United Nations Sustainable Development Cooperation Framework (GoI-UNSDCF 2023–2027) in a bid to drive sustainable development efforts across India. The framework is built on four key pillars – People, Planet, Prosperity and Participation – which involves six outcome areas comprising health and well-being, environment and climate, quality education, economic growth and empowerment of individuals and communities.

JULY 2023

ISRO launches Chandrayaan-3

On 14 July, the Indian Space Research Organization (ISRO) successfully launched its third lunar mission. Chandrayaan-3 embarked on a month-long journey to the lunar surface with the help of ISRO's latest heavy-lift launch vehicle, Fat Boy LVM3-M4. The soft landing, which is believed to be the most challenging part of the mission, has been planned for 23 August. If Chandrayaan-3 completes its mission, India will become the fourth country to successfully orchestrate a soft landing on the moon.

STOP PRESS

North India's first nuclear power plant

A new nuclear power plant is set to come up in Gorakhpur, in the Fatehabad district of Haryana. This is north India's first nuclear plant, as the rest are concentrated in southern and western India. Union Minister of State for Science and Technology Jitendra Singh announced that the project was part of a push from the government to increase India's nuclear capacity.

Aam Aadmi Party gains national party status

The Election Commission granted national party status to the Aam Aadmi Party based on its performance in Delhi, Goa, Punjab and Gujarat. On the other hand, the Trinamool Congress, Nationalist Congress Party and Communist Party of India all lost their status as national parties due to their poll performances since 2014.

JITENDRA SINGH

ARVIND KEJRIWAL

ASHWINI VAISHNAW

India's first quantum computing-based telecom network

India's first quantum computing-based telecom network link was created in New Delhi, running between Sanchar Bhawan and the National Informatics Centre office. This network uses quantum principles to transmit information, providing higher security than traditional telecom networks. IT and Telecom Minister Ashwini Vaishnaw announced a ₹10,00,000 prize for ethical hackers who were able to break the encryption.

Truss resigns

In September, Liz Truss became the 56th prime minister of the United Kingdom, beating Rishi Sunak by nearly 21,000 votes. Amidst the inflation and cost of living crisis that had gripped the nation, Truss had introduced schemes that were not successful in facing the economic crisis. Instead of making clear plans for raising funds, Truss's government announced large borrowing schemes to aid tax cuts, a move which was not received well by the market or the public. The situation did not improve, and the pound continued to fall and reached its lowest level against the US dollar. She resigned on 20 October, after 45 days in office, making her the shortest serving British prime minister. Sunak succeeded her as the country's next prime minister.

China launches Kuafu-1

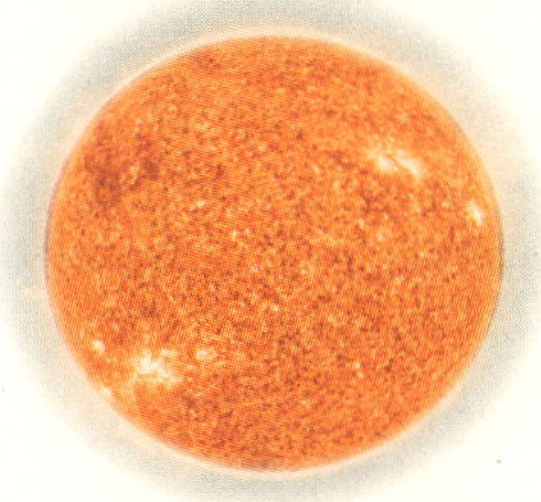

Named after a giant who chased the sun in Chinese mythology, Kuafu-1 is a space-based solar telescope called the Advanced Space-based Solar Observatory (ASO-S). It is positioned in an orbit 720 km above Earth, higher than the orbit of the International Space Station. The four-year mission will study the Sun, enabling scientists to gather information and view images of the Sun during 'solar maximum,' its most active phase. It will study the relationship between the solar magnetic field and two major eruptive phenomena: solar flares and coronal mass ejections. Both phenomena occur when the motion of the Sun's interior distorts its magnetic field, releasing a large amount of energy. This can result in the creation of a sudden flash of light (solar flare). The magnetic disturbances might also result in the release of solar matter into space. Both these phenomena may occur at the same time as well. Their interaction with nitrogen and oxygen creates auroras called Northern and Southern Lights.

Russo-Ukrainian War pushes 4 million children into poverty

On 17 October, the International Day of Eradication of Poverty, UNICEF reported that the ongoing war between Russia and Ukraine and the resultant crisis of inflation has resulted in 4 million children across Eastern Europe and Central Asia being pushed into poverty. The report studied data collected from 22 countries. The rising cases of child poverty in these regions could result in thousands of children dying before they complete their first year and many children dropping out of school this year. The UNICEF report also offers an outline of measures that will provide support to vulnerable children and help control the economic situation and bring down the number of children living in poverty.

Day of 8 billion

On 15 November 2022, the world's population reached 8 billion, crossing the 7 billion milestone after 12 years. According to the UN, the growth in population is attributed to increasing lifespan due to hygiene, nutrition, medicine and better public health, along with 'high and persistent levels of fertility in some countries'. In the next 15 years, by 2037, the global population will reach 9 billion, meaning that the increase in time to reach the next milestone indicates the slowing of the growth rate.

Convidecia Air

Pharmaceutical company CanSino Biologics developed the first inhalable Covid-19 vaccine. Convidecia Air is available in aerosol form and can be received as an 'emergency-use booster'. It can be taken by people who are above the age of 18 and have already completed their primary immunization six months ago. According to CanSino, Convidecia can effectively prevent the virus from spreading further since it can provide triple protection by inducing immunity at three levels – humoral, cellular and mucosal. The new aerosol version has the benefits of being painless and non-invasive over the intramuscular version.

FDA approves Tzield

On 17 November, the US Food and Drug Administration approved Tzield (teplizumab-mzwv). Tzield is a new drug that can delay the onset of stage 3 Type-1 diabetes in adults and stage 2 Type-1 diabetes in children aged eight and above. Tzield is administered by intravenous infusion. The infusion must be administered once, for at least 30 minutes, daily for 14 consecutive days to complete the treatment. While the new drug is a breakthrough and will prove helpful particularly for at risk

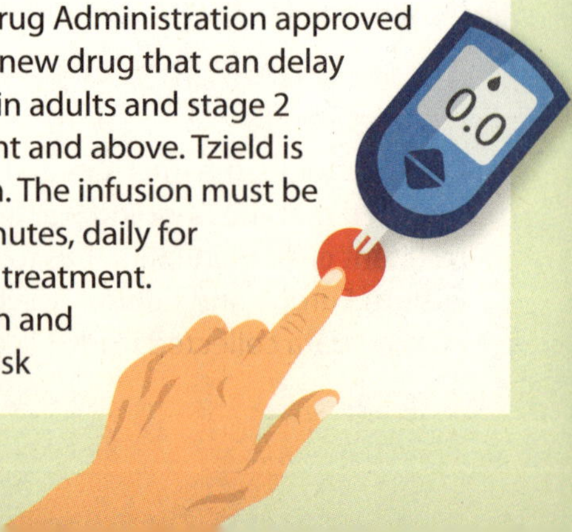

patients, it also has some side effects that may include a reduction in lymphocytes (a type of white blood cell), infections, rash and headache, among others.

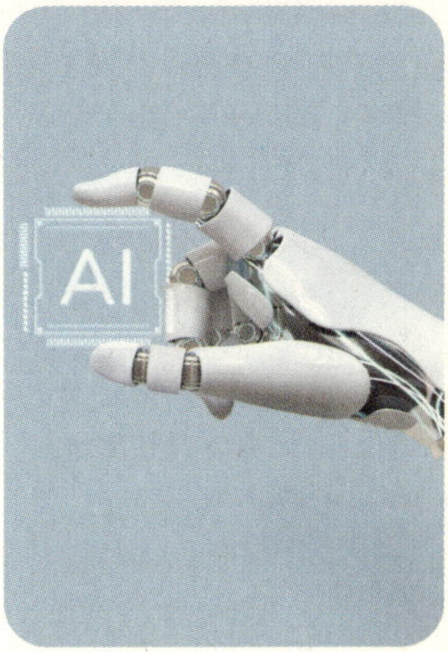

Google to launch new AI model that supports 1,000 languages

Google has announced a new project to build an AI model that can support 1,000 of the most spoken languages in the world. The model also aims to protect languages that are spoken by fewer people and are threatened by extinction in the future. Taking the first step, the company has already launched an AI model trained in 400 languages, referred to as the Universal Speech Model.

Iran banned from UN Commission on the Status of Women

Amidst growing concerns over the safety of women in Iran, the UN Economic and Social Council (ECOSOC) removed Iran from the Commission on the Status of Women (CSW) until 2026, when the country's membership term will end. The CSW was established in 1946 to defend women's rights and promote gender equality. Members to CSW are elected by ECOSOC for a term of four years. The resolution to expel Iran was put forth by the US. It was supported by 29 members of the ECOSOC, while eight members were against this resolution, among them Russia and China, and 16 members, including India, abstained from voting. The Iranian government's actions have been a cause of concern since September 2022. Mahsa Amini's death in September and the government's brutal response to the protests that followed Amini's death have drawn attention to the suppression of women's rights in the country.

EU recognizes the candidacy of Bosnia-Herzegovina

Bosnia-Herzegovina applied for membership to the European Union in February 2016. Leaders of the EU granted the country candidate status in December 2022 at a summit in Brussels. The EU's membership process has remained static for a long time with the last country that was granted membership being Croatia in 2013. However, the EU has reassessed its approach to forming alliances with eastern European countries amidst the ongoing Russia–Ukraine war. Bosnia-Herzegovina's candidacy has been approved after six years of application, but this does not guarantee the country a membership soon. The membership process is a long one and the country must ensure that it makes several economic and political changes as recommended by the EU.

Breakthrough in nuclear fusion energy

In an experiment conducted by the National Ignition Facility at the Lawrence Livermore National Laboratory (LLNL) in California, the energy output of the nuclear fusion was more than the energy put in. Experiments on nuclear fusion are taking place all over the world. However, this experiment is a breakthrough because it has manged to produce more energy than the energy put in for the first time. In previous experiments, the energy input was higher than net energy. The experiment at the National Ignition, a $3.5-billion experiment produces energy by using a high-power laser to heat hydrogen fuel. The successful outcome of this experiment takes scientists closer to develop a source of clean energy.

JANUARY 2023

Croatia joins the eurozone

At the beginning of 2023, Croatia became the 20th member to join the eurozone and adopt the euro (€) in place of the Croatian kuna. It is also the first country to join the Schengen area in 11 years. The Schengen area allows free movement of people, goods and services across borders. Croatia's membership in the eurozone will benefit its economic stability, by enhancing investment and trade, boosting tourism and reducing borrowing conditions on loans from the EU.

FEBRUARY 2023

The first woman astronaut from Saudi Arabia

Rayyana Barnawi is a biomedical researcher who will become the first woman from Saudi Arabia to go into space. Along with fellow Saudi native Ali Al-Qarni, she will embark on a 10-day missionto the International Space Station to conduct scientific experiments. They will launch off from the Kennedy Space Center in Florida on the SpaceX Falcon 9 rocket, becoming the second and third Saudi Arabians to go to space.

MARCH 2023

UBS–Credit Suisse merger

After Credit Suisse's stock plummeted due to loss of confidence, the Swiss government intervened to control the damage to the Swiss economy. It brokered a deal for UBS Group to acquire Credit Suisse at a knockdown price. Despite reluctance from UBS, they agreed to buy Credit Suisse for 3 billion Swiss francs in stock, assuming up to 5 billion francs in losses. This emergency rescue is the biggest banking deal of the last decade.

TikTok CEO testifies before US Congress

Shou Zi Chew, the CEO of TikTok, testified before a US house committee in a recent wave of governments expressing concerns over the power held by big tech companies. TikTok, which is owned by ByteDance, is a video hosting app which boasts 1 billion active monthly users. The committee questioned Chew on the company's relationship to the Chinese government and concerns related to data privacy and the safety of minors. The CEO defended TikTok's security measures and said that user data would not be accessible by any unauthorized foreign body.

APRIL 2023

India surpasses China to become world's most populous country

According to a United Nations report, India has overtaken China as the world's most populous country, with a population of 1.4 billion. China had held the status of the largest population since 1950, but experienced a decrease in fertility rate through implementation of its one-child policy. India currently comprises 17.5 per cent of the global population. The UN projects that India's population will continue to grow till its peak in 2064, before declining gradually.

Finland joins NATO

After more than 70 years of military non-alignment, Finland has joined the North Atlantic Treaty Organization (NATO). NATO is a political and military alliance between 31 European and North American countries. Finland's move was brought on by a need for increased security since the onset of the Russia–Ukraine war, as Finland shares a 1,340-km border with Russia. While Finland has gained significant military backing from this, it will lose out on considerable revenue from Russian trade and tourism.

MAY 2023

Erdogan is re-elected in Turkey for a third term

After two decades in power, Recep Tayyip Erdogan won the national election and extended his rule for five more years. The conservative politician beat out the leader of the opposition, Kemal Kilicdaroglu, with 52 per cent of the vote. Kilicdaroglu claimed that it was 'the most unfair election period in our history'. Erdogan's primary concern in his term is to deal with Turkey's economy, which is experiencing an inflation of around 40 per cent annually.

Scientists discover volcano in Norwegian waters

Scientists on the research vessel KronprinsHaakon have discovered an underwater volcano in the Southwestern Barents Sea off the coast of Norway. 'The Borealis Mud Volcano' is situated inside a 300-m-wide crater, and was found to be spewing mud, fluids and gas from the Earth's interior. Geologists believe that the crater was a result of a massive event 18,000 years ago, which abruptly released a large amount of methane.

JUNE 2023

New UN Security Council members elected

The United Nations Security Council held elections to elect five new, non-permanent members for 2023–24. Ecuador, Japan, Malta, Mozambique and Switzerland were elected and replaced India, Ireland, Kenya, Mexico and Norway. The council consists of 15 members, out of which five are permanent – Britain, China, France, Russia and the US. For years India has been at the forefront, demanding a change in the structure of the UNSC and claiming that it deserves a permanent position on the council as the current structure does not represent the geo-political realities of the 21st century.

JULY 2023

Hottest day in recorded history

According to scientists, 3 July 2023 was recorded as the hottest day in world history till date. The average global temperature reached 17.01 degree Celsius, causing heat waves across the globe. Even Antarctica, which is currently in its winter season, recorded startlingly high temperatures. A renowned scientist, Friederike Otto of the Grantham Institute for Climate Change and the Environment at Britain's Imperial College London, stated how this is not a milestone worth celebrating, but a 'death sentence for people and ecosystems'.

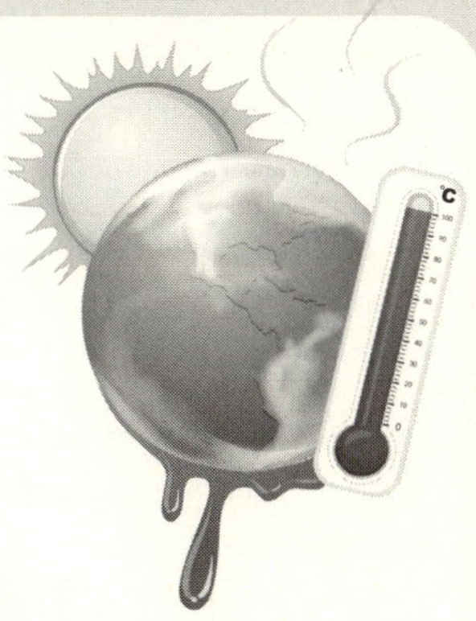

UN Security Council holds talks on risks regarding use of AI

The United Nations Security Council held its first formal discussion on AI in New York. With AI rapidly making advancements across several fields, governments around the world are considering how countries can monitor and regulate the use of the technology. Britain's Foreign Secretary James Cleverly chaired the meeting. He also announced that the UK will bring world leaders together for the first time to discuss the possibility of mitigating the dangers of AI and how to navigate the emerging technology.

STOP PRESS

Twitter rebrands to X

Twitter, one of the most widely used social media platforms in the world, was rebranded to 'X'. This rebranding took place as a part of the ongoing transformation of twitter into 'an app that can do everything'. Twitter was acquired by X Corp both to ensure freedom of speech and as an accelerant for X, the everything app, the company's owner, billionaire Elon Musk, recently said. He had purchased Twitter in October of 2022 for $44 billion after months of negotiation.

ELON MUSK

Protests in China

Since the Covid-19 outbreak, China initiated its zero-Covid policy to control the virus which relies on early detection, regular testing, quarantines at home or government facilities and sudden enforcement of lockdowns. However, China saw a dramatic increase in the number of Covid cases in November triggering more lockdowns. The protests began in Ürümqi but soon turned into a countrywide protest against harsh Covid-19 measures imposed by the government and also against the leadership of Xi Jinping.

Barbenheimer Craze Sweeps the Globe

Two of the highest grossing films of 2023, Greta Gerwig's Barbie and Christopher Nolan's Oppenheimer released on the same date – 21 July 2023. Although they covered vastly different topics, fans of both films actively debated against each other on the internet for months, even before the films were released! Theatres were flooded with shades of pink and black from the fans trying to honour the global trend of Barbenheimer.

PEOPLE TO REMEMBER

QUEEN ELIZABETH (21 April 1926–8 September 2022): The longest-serving monarch in British history, Queen Elizabeth acceded to the throne at the age of 25, in the year 1952.

SATYA PRAKASH SRIVASTAV (25 December 1963–21 September 2022): This Indian comedian, actor and politician was popularly known as Raju Srivastav. He participated in the show *The Great Indian Laughter Challenge* and the third season of *Big Boss*.

VANI JAIRAM (30 November 1945–4 February 2023): This celebrated playback singer held the moniker 'the Meera of modern India'. She won three National Film Awards and received the Padma Bhushan in 2023.

SATISH KAUSHIK (13 April 1956–9 March 2023): This Bollywood actor and filmmaker was a part of more than 100 movies, including *Mr. India, Ram Lakhan* and *Saajan Chale Sasural*. He was the recipient of two Filmfare awards.

SALIM DURANI (11 December 1934–2 April 2023): This Indian cricketer was known for his key role in beating England in the 1961–62 Test series, where he took 18 wickets. He was also critical in India's first Test win against the West Indies in 1971.

AL JAFFEE (13 March 1921–10 April 2023): This American cartoonist was known for his contributions to MAD magazine for 65 years. He holds the Guinness World Record for having the longest career as a comic artist.

RANAJIT GUHA (23 May 1923–28 April 2023): This Indian historian was a renowned scholar of subaltern postcolonial studies. He was respected for propagating an anti-elitist approach to historical studies in the 1980s.

BARRY JOCK ZONFRILLO (4 August 1976–30 April 2023): This Scottish chef, television presenter and restaurateur joined *MasterChef Australia* as a judge in 2019. He was also announced as a judge for *Junior MasterChef Australia* the next year.

S.P. HINDUJA (28 November 1935–17 May 2023): This British billionaire and businessman was the chairman of the Hinduja Group and the UK's richest man.

TINA TURNER (26 November 1939–24 May 2023): This American singer was known as the 'Queen of Rock and Roll'. In a career spanning half a century, she received 12 Grammy Awards and sold more than 150 million records worldwide.

AMA ATA AIDOO (23 March 1942–31 May 2023): This Ghanaian writer and academic was the first African woman to become a published dramatist. She won the Commonwealth Writers' Prize in 1992 for her novel *Changes: A Love Story*.

ANTHONY DOMINICK BENEDETTO (3 August 1926–21 July 2023): Also known as Tony Bennett, this American jazz and traditional pop singer had won many accolades, including 20 Grammy Awards, a Lifetime Achievement Award, and two Primetime Emmy Awards.

PADMA SHRI

Art: Jodhaiyabai Baiga, Premjit Baria, Usha Barle, Hemant Chauhan, Bhanubhai Chitara, Hemoprova Chutia, Subhadra Devi, Hem Chandra Goswami, Pritikana Goswami, Ahmed Hussain and Mohd Hussain, Dilshad Hussain, Mahipat Kavi, M.M. Keeravaani, Parshuram Komaji Khune, Maguni Charan Kuanr, Domar Singh Kunvar, Risingbor Kurkalang, Ghulam Muhammad Zaz, Rani Machaiah, Ajay Kumar Mandavi, Nadoja Pindipapanahalli Munivenkatappa, Ramesh Parmar and Shanti Parmar, Krishna Patel, Pareshbhai Rathwa, Raveena Ravi Tandon, Coomi Nariman Wadia, Kapil Dev Prasad, K. Kalyanasundaram Pillai, Mangala Kanti Roy, K.C. Runremsangi, Moa Subong, Neihunuo Sorhie, Shah Rasheed Ahmed Quadri, C.V. Raju, Ritwik Sanyal, Kota Satchidananda Sastry

Literature and Education: Radha Charan Gupta, C.I. Issac, Rattan Singh Jaggi, Anand Kumar, Antaryami Mishra, Prabhakar Bhanudas Mande, Ramesh Patange, Vishwanath Prasad Tiwari, Dhaniram Toto, Dr Janum Singh Soy, Mohan Singh, Prakash Chandra Sood, B. Ramakrishna Reddy

Medicine: Munishwar Chanddawar, Dr Gopalsamy Veluchamy, Dr Ishwar Chander Verma, Ratan Chandra Kar, Dr Nalini Parthasarathi, Hanumantha Rao Pasupuleti, Manoranjan Sahu

Public Affairs: Thounaojam Chaoba Singh, Narendra Chandra Debbarma (Posthumous)

Science and engineering: Modadugu Vijay Gupta, Khadar Valli Dudekula, Ganesh Nagappa Krishnarajanagara, Arvind Kumar, Prof. (Dr) Mahendra Pal, Bakshi Ram, Sujatha Ramdorai, Abbareddy Nageswara Rao

Social work: Bhiku Ramji Idate, Bikram Bahadur Jamatia, Ramkuiwangbe Jene, Hirabai Lobi, Moolchand Lodha, Gajanan Jagannath Mane, Uma Shankar Pandey, Palam Kalyana Sundaram, Karma Wangchu (Posthumous), Vadivel Gopal and Masi Sadaiyan, Sankurathri Chandra Sekhar, V.P. Appukuttan Poduval, Laxman Singh

Sports: S.R.D. Prasad, Gurcharan Singh, K. Shanathoiba Sharma

Trade and Industry: Rakesh Radheshyam Jhunjhunwala (Posthumous), Areez Khambatta (Posthumous)

Others: Animal Agriculture: Cheruvayal K. Raman, Patayat Sahu, Nekram Sharma, Tula Ram Upreti; **Archaeology:** S. Subbaraman **Spiritualism:** Dr Sukama Acharya, Kushok Thiksey Nawang Chamba Stanzin

PADMA VIBHUSHAN

Art: Zakir Hussain
Medicine: Dilip Mahalanabis (Posthumous)
Public Affairs: S.M. Krishna, Mulayam Singh Yadav (Posthumous)
Science and Engineering: Srinivas Varadhan
Others (Architecture): Balkrishna Doshi (Posthumous)

PADMA BHUSHAN

Art: Vani Jairam, Suman Kalyanpur
Literature and Education: S.L. Bhyrappa, Kapil Kapoor
Science and Engineering: Deepak Dhar
Social Work: Sudha Murty
Trade and Industry: Kumar Mangalam Birla
Others (Spiritualism): Chinna Jeeyar, Kamlesh D. Patel

65TH GRAMMY AWARDS

Record of the Year: 'About Damn Time' by Lizzo
Album of the Year: *Harry's House* by Harry Styles
Song of the Year: 'Just Like That' by Bonnie Raitt
Best new Artist: Samara Joy
Best Pop Vocal Album: *Harry's House* by Harry Styles
Best Rap Album: *Mr. Morale & The Big Steppers* by Kendrick Lamar
Best Rock Album: *Patient Number 9* by Ozzy Osbourne
Best Jazz Vocal Album: *Linger Awhile* by Samara Joy
Best R&B Album: *Black Radio III* by Robert Glasper
Best Country Album: *A Beautiful Time* by Willie Nelson

95TH ACADEMY AWARDS (OSCARS)

Actor in a Leading Role: Brendan Fraser for The Whale
Actress in a Leading Role: Michelle Yeoh for Everything Everywhere All at Once
Actor in a Supporting Role: Ke Huy Quan for Everything Everywhere All at Once
Actress in a Supporting Role: Jaime Lee Curtis for Everything Everywhere All at Once
Animated Feature Film: Guillermo del Toro, Mark Gustafson, Gary Ungar and Alex Bulkley for Pinocchio
Cinematography: James Friend for All Quiet on the Western Front
Costume Designing: Ruth Carter for Black **Panther:**Wakanda Forever
Directing: Daniel Kwan and Daniel Scheinert for Everything Everywhere All at Once
Documentary (Feature Film): Daniel Roher, Odessa Rae, Diane Becker, Melanie Miller and Shane Boris for Navalny
Documentary (Short Film): Kartiki Gonsalves and Guneet Monga for The Elephant Whisperers
Film Editing: Paul Rogers for Everything Everywhere All at Once
International Feature Film: All Quiet on the Western Front– Germany
Best Picture: Daniel Kwan, Daniel Scheinert and Jonathan Wang,Producers for Everything Everywhere All at Once
Production Design: Christian M. Goldbeck; Set Decoration: Ernestine Hipper for All Quiet on the Western Front
Short Film (Animated): Charlie Mackesy and Matthew Freud for The Boy, the Mole, the Fox and the Horse
Short Film (Live Action): Tom Berkeley and Ross White for An Irish Goodbye
Best Writing (Adapted Screenplay): Sarah Polley for Women Talking
Best Writing (Original Screenplay): Daniel Kwan and Daniel Scheinert for Everything Everywhere All at Once

SAHITYA AKADEMI BAL PURASKAR 2023

Powalmoni Aru Chichingar Duhxahaxik Abhijan *(Assamese)*: Novel by Rothindranath Goswami

Eroplaner Khata *(Bengali)*: Novel by Shyamalkanti Das

Gosaini Gwjwn Nwjwr *(Bodo)*: Short Stories by Pratima Nandi Narzaree

Kanjkan *(Dogri)*: Poetry by Balwan Singh Jamoria

Grandparent's Bag of Stories *(English)*: Stories by Sudha Murty

Hun Myaun, Tun Choon Choon *(Gujarati)*: Poetry & Stories by Rakshabahen Prahladrao Dave

Kotuk App *(Hindi)*: Short Stories by Suryanath Singh

Surakki Gate *(Kannada)*: Novel by Vijayashree Haldi

Jaann *(Konkani)*: Novel by Tukaram Rama Shet

Ol Katra, JholKatra *(Maithili)*: Poetry by Akshay Anand a.k.a. 'Sunny'

Perumazhayathe Kunjithalukal *(Malayalam)*: Novel by Priya A.S.

Chhand Dei Aanand *(Marathi)*: Poetry by Eknath Avhad

Bal Ekanki Natakharu *(Nepali)*: Play by Madhusudan Bisht

Jejenka Gapa Ganthili *(Odia)*: Short Stories by Jugal Kishore Sarangi

Sachi Di Kahani *(Punjabi)*: Short Stories by Gurmeet Karyalvi

Tabran Di Duniya *(Rajasthani)*: Memoir by Kiran Badal

Manavi *(Sanskrit)*: Novel by Radhavallabh Tripathy

Nene-Pete *(Santali)*: Short Stories by Mansing Majhi

Vanganmal Ji Shaadi *(Sindhi)*: Poetry by Dholan Rahi

Aadhanin Bommai *(Tamil)*: Novel by Udhayasankar

Vajrala Vaana *(Telugu)*: Short Stories by D.K. Chaduvula Babu

Mamta Ki Dor *(Urdu)*: Short Stories by Late Mateen Achalpuri (Posthumous)

*No award in Kashmiri language for 2023.
*The award in Manipuri language were not declared by July 2023.

PULITZER PRIZES

JOURNALISM

Public Service: Associated Press, for the work of Mstyslav Chernov, Evgeniy Maloletka, Vasilisa Stepanenko and Lori Hinnant

Breaking News Reporting: Staff of the *Los Angeles Times*

Investigative Reporting: Staff of the *Wall Street Journal*

Explanatory Reporting: Caitlin Dickerson of the *Atlantic*

International Reporting: Staff of the *New York Times*

Feature Writing: Eli Saslow of the *Washington Post*

Commentary: Kyle Whitmire of *AL.com*, Birmingham

Criticism: Andrea Long Chu of *New York Magazine*

Editorial Writing: *Miami Herald* Editorial Board, for a series written by Amy Driscoll

Illustrated Reporting and Commentary: Mona Chalabi, contributor, the *New York Times*

Breaking News Photography: Photography Staff of Associated Press

Feature Photography: Christina House of the *Los Angeles Times*

Audio Reporting: Staff of Gimlet Media, notably Connie Walker

BOOKS, DRAMA AND MUSIC

Fiction: *Demon Copperhead* by Barbara Kingsolver and *Trust* by Hernan Diaz

Drama: *English* by Sanaz Toossi

History: *Freedom's Dominion: A Saga of White Resistance to Federal Power* by Jefferson Cowie

Biography: *G-Man: J. Edgar Hoover and the Making of the American Century* by Beverly Gage

Memoir or Autobiography: *Stay True* by Hua Hsu

Poetry: *Then the War: And Selected Poems, 2007–2020* by Carl Phillips

General Nonfiction: *His Name Is George Floyd: One Man's Life and the Struggle for Racial Justice* by Robert Samuels and Toluse Olorunnipa

Music: *Omar* by Rhiannon Giddens and Michael Abels

OTHER IMPORTANT AWARDS

Radhavallabh Tripathy	Bal Sahitya Puraskar – 2023 (Sanskrit Language Book)
Sudha Murty	Bal Sahitya Puraskar – 2023 (English Language Book)
Pandit Ramkishan	Shatabdi Purush (Man of the Century)
Meera Syal	BAFTA Fellowship 2023
Georgi Gospodinov and Angela Rode	International Booker Prize 2023
Salman Rushdie	Peace Prize of the German Book Trade 2023
Amina Luqman-Dawson's Freewater	2023 Newbery Medal and Coretta Scott King Author Award
Sir David Alan Chipperfield	Pritzker Architecture Prize 2023
Magnus Gens	2022 Ig Nobel Prize in Safety Engineering for developing a moose crash test dummy
Tata Steel	2023 Steel Sustainability Champion by the World Steel Association
Mirabai Chanu	BBC Indian Sportswoman of The Year for 2023
Bharat Heavy Electricals Limited (BHEL)	Best Contribution in Solar Energy by the Central Board of Irrigation and Power in India 2023
Dr Manmohan Singh	Lifetime Achievement Honour by the India–UK Achievers Honours in London 2023
R. Vishnu Prassad	The most distinguished scientist of the year at the Indian Achievers Awards 2022
P.N. Mohan	The Green Crusader by IAA Olive Crown Awards 2023
Pench Tiger Reserve, Madhya Pradesh & Pench Tiger Reserve, Maharashtra	Tigers times 2 (TX2) award for doubling the population of wild tigers – January 2023
Satpura Tiger Reserve, Central India	TX2 award for Tiger Conservation Excellence – January 2023
Arundhati Roy	45th European Essay Prize
Nandini Gupta	Miss India 2023
Chennai Metro Rail Limited	Green World Award (UK) - 2023

ALES BIALIATSKI

In the news for: **Winning the Nobel Peace Prize 2022; Where:** **Belarus**

Human rights activist Ales Bialiatski won the Nobel Peace Prize 2022 alongside the Center for Civil Liberties in Ukraine and Memorial in Russia, organizations which work to uphold and protect human rights. He founded the Viasna (Spring) Human Rights Centre in Belarus in 1996. At the time, street protests following a rule that allowed the president authoritarian powers were brutally subdued by the authorities and many protestors were imprisoned. Viasna supported the imprisoned protesters and their families, and documented the torture and abuse faced by political prisoners. He actively works for the establishment of democracy and peace in his country.

ANDREA KRITCHER

In the news for: **Leading an experiment that achieved nuclear fusion ignition; Where:** **USA**

Andrea Kritcher is a design physicist and the principal designer for an experiment conducted at the Lawrence Livermore National Laboratory's Inertial Confinement Fusion program. In December 2022, a team of scientists successfully produced nuclear fusion ignition for the first time in history by firing 192 lasers at a miniscule target. The experiment is a breakthrough in the mission for a net-zero carbon economy, as it was able to achieve an energy break-even – meaning that it produced more energy than it consumed.

ANGELA MERKEL

In the news for: **Receiving the Nansen Award; Where:** **Geneva**

Angela Merkel, the former Chancellor of Germany, received the UNHCR Nansen Refugee Award in a ceremony held on October 2022 at Geneva. The Nansen award honours people or organizations for their outstanding service to refugees, helping them and protecting them. The award was established in 1954 in honour of the first UN High Commissioner for Refugees, Fridtjof Nansen, a Norwegian Arctic explorer and scientist who served from 1920 to 1930, the years following the Fist World War. He helped those displaced during the war to return to their homelands or become legal residents of countries that gave them refuge. During Merkel's leadership, the country welcomed 1.2 million refugees and asylum seekers in 2015 and 2016, when violence and conflict in Syria as well as other places had escalated. She was lauded for her compassionate leadership.

ANNIE ERNAUX

In the news for: Winning the Nobel Prize in Literature 2022; Where: France

Awarded to a total of 119 writers since the prize was established, Annie Ernaux is only the 17th woman to win it. The French writer is known to explore the issues of class, gender and memory in her writing. Her works include *A Man's Place, A Woman's Story* and *Years*. The Swedish Academy praised her for 'the courage and clinical acuity with which she uncovers the roots, estrangements and collective restraints of personal memory.'

BOLA AHMED TINUBU

In the news for: Being elected as president; Where: Nigeria

In May 2023, Bola Ahmed Tinubu took office as the 16th President of Nigeria, succeeding Muhammadu Buhari. Tinubu won 37 per cent of votes, which is the lowest of any Nigerian president since the country's transition from military to democratic rule in 1999. He has stated that his top priority is the security of the nation.

BOMMAN AND BELLIE

In the news for: Raising abandoned elephant calves; Where: India

Bomman and Bellie, in Kartiki Gonsalves's Oscar-winning documentary short film *The Elephant Whisperers*. The documentary was filmed in the Mudumalai National park and followed the couple from the Kattunayakan community as they nurtured an abandoned elephant calf named Raghu. It showed the deep and caring attachment that developed between the elephants and the community as they coexisted in harmony. The film also documented the challenges to elephant conservation efforts in India today.

DEEPIKA PADUKONE AND SHAH RUKH KHAN

In the news for: **Starring in *Pathaan*; Where: India**

Siddharth Anand's blockbuster film *Pathaan*, which hit theatres in January 2023, stirred up controversy before its release. The trailer contained clips from the song 'Besharam Rang', meaning 'shameless colour', featuring Deepika Padukone in a saffron bikini. This riled up religious groups, who called for the boycott of *Pathaan* in theatres. However, the film grossed ₹1,000 crore worldwide at the box office.

ELIZABETH MARUMA MREMA

In the news for: Pushing the Kunming–Montreal Global Biodiversity Framework at COP15; Where: Canada

As the UN's executive secretary of the Convention on Biological Diversity, Mrema led 195 countries to sign an agreement to conserve or restore nature on 30 per cent of the Earth's surface by 2030. Further, wealthier countries agreed to pay $30 billion to poorer nations annually to invest in biodiversity initiatives. This is one of the most significant environmental agreements of the decade, sealed in December 2022.

ELAHEH MOHAMMADI AND NILOOFAR HAMEDI

In the news for: Breaking the news of Mahsa Amini's death; Where: Iran

In September 2022, Mahsa Amini was arrested by the morality police for 'improper attire' and suffered police brutality. She was taken to the hospital brain dead and passed away within a few days. Like so many incidents of brutality in Iran, this too would have been buried if not for Niloofar Hamedi and Elaheh Mohammadi, the female journalists who covered the story at great personal risk. This was the beginning of a historical revolution in Iran fighting for the rights of women. Both journalists have since been detained. They were awarded the UNESCO Freedom Prize in 2023.

JACINDA ARDERN

In the news for: Resigning as PM; Where: New Zealand

In 2017, Jacinda Ardern became the youngest prime minister of New Zealand as well as the youngest female head of government in the world. After successfully serving the country for almost five years, she resigned in January 2023. During her leadership, she tackled several challenges, including the Covid-19 pandemic, natural disasters, an economic crisis and the anti-immigration-motivated terrorist attacks in two mosques in March 2019, which the leader described as one of the country's 'darkest days.'

JOYEETA GUPTA

In the news for: **Being awarded the Spinoza Prize; Where: Netherlands**
An Indian origin scientist has been awarded the Spinoza Prize, which is the highest distinction in Dutch science, often referred to as the 'Dutch Nobel Prize'. Joyeeta Gupta is a professor of Environment and Development in the Global South at the University of Amsterdam. Her research aims to build a 'just and sustainable world' by using governance to address climate change. The prize bestows €1.5 million to be used for scientific research and knowledge utilization.

KARL LAGERFELD

In the news for: **Being the theme of the Met Gala; Where: USA**
At the 2023 Met Gala, the most fashionable event of the year, the theme was Karl Lagerfeld. The German fashion designer worked with Chanel for 35 years until his death in 2019, but his impact on the fashion industry persists. The who's who of celebrities gathered at the Metropolitan Museum of Art to celebrate his legacy, dressed in pearls, crystals and cat costumes.

KING CHARLES

In the news for: **Being crowned as Britain's monarch; Where: UK**
In May, Charles III was crowned as Britain's king. Hundreds gathered in Westminster Abbey to watch the first coronation in 70 years. His wife, Camilla, ascended to the title of Queen. About 100 heads of state attended the ceremony, as well as the royal family and several celebrities. King Charles's succession marks a new era where British monarchy will have to fight for its relevance in public life.

LIONEL MESSI

In the news for: **Winning the FIFA World Cup; Where: Qatar**

At the 22nd FIFA World Cup in December 2022, Argentina's captain and star player Messi donned the number 10 jersey for the last time and bagged a long-awaited victory. Winning the FIFA World Cup seems a fitting end Messi's legacy, as the 35-year-old hinted at his imminent retirement. Millions of fans celebrated as the tense shoot-out against the French national team's prodigy Kylian Mbappé resulted in victory for the beloved Argentinian football icon.

LUIZ INACIO LULA DA SILVA

In the news for: **Winning the presidential election; Where: Brazil**

In 2022, a politically polarized Brazil voted in left-wing candidate Lula da Silva with a narrow 50.9 per cent of votes, beating out the far-right incumbent Jair Bolsonaro. Lula made an impressive comeback from his 580-day stint in jail on corruption charges, which 'blocked his candidacy' or 'prevented his participation' in the 2018 election. In contrast to Bolsonaro, Lula has pledged to reduce carbon emissions, achieve net-zero deforestation and halt illegal deforestation in the Amazon rainforest by 2030.

MARGRETHE VESTAGER

In the news for: **Challenging big tech companies; Where: Belgium**

Since 2014, Margrethe Vestager has been EU Commissioner for Competition Policy. She has resolutely held big tech companies like Google, Facebook, Amazon and Apple answerable to EU law. In 2022, Google was fined $4 billion for promoting it's own products over others on the Google search engine. Vestager's mission is to make big tech be more transparent about their operations. In May 2023, Vestager announced that she was working on a draft of a voluntary code of conduct for generative artificial intelligence. In the era of artificial intelligence, the need to introduce technology regulations has become even more apparent.

MAX VERSTAPPEN

In the news for: **Winning the Formula One World Championship; Where: Abu Dhabi**

At the Abu Dhabi Grand Prix 2022, Max Verstappen became an F1 World Champion for the second time. In his 15th winning race of the 2022 season, the Red Bull racer faced off against Ferrari rival Charles Leclerc. Verstappen began in 2016 at just 17 years old as the youngest ever F1 competitor. The Dutch racer's second win solidified him as an F1 legend who is here to stay.

MUTHAMIZH SELVI

In the news for: **Being the first Tamil Nadu woman to scale Mount Everest; Where:** **Nepal**

In May 2023, Muthamizh Selvi became the first woman from Tamil Nadu to scale Mount Everest. After a hike of 56 days, Selvi was honoured by the Tamil Nadu minister of Sports Development for her achievement. The 34-year-old mountaineer was supported by the state government, who provided financing of ₹15 lakh. Upon her arrival at Chennai airport, Selvi received a warm welcome from her supporters. The Virudhunagar native said that she hopes to scale six more summits in the future.

OLEKSANDRA MATVIICHUK

In the news for: **Winning the Nobel Peace Prize; Where:** **Ukraine**

Oleksandra Matviichuk is a lawyer who has worked for 20 years defending human rights. She heads the Centre for Civil Liberties (CCL), which jointly received

the Nobel Peace Prize in 2022, becoming the first Ukrainian body to do so. CCL documents and seeks to create accountability for war crimes in Russian-controlled regions. It has logged more than 2,60,000 war crimes since 2014. She is also central in an effort to establish a special tribunal to place Vladimir Putin on trial. In its tireless crusade for democratic change in Ukraine, CCL stands out as a remarkable model of civil society.

PENG LIFA

In the news for: **Sparking the anti-Covid restrictions protest; Where: China**

In October 2022, Peng Lifa hung large banners from the Sitong Bridge in Beijing criticizing Xi Jinping's rule and the stringent restrictions imposed during the pandemic. 'We are citizens, not slaves,' they read. Within minutes, images went viral before being censored. Prior to his revolt, Peng posted a manifesto on Twitter encouraging citizens to stand up against the government. Peng was taken into custody, but this act of defiance sparked one of the most significant protests in China. Protestors held up blank sheets of paper to symbolize the oppressive regime of silence under the Chinese Communist Party. Peng came to be called 'Bridge Man' and became an inspiration through his sacrifice.

PERUMAL MURUGAN

In the news for: ***Pyre*** **chosen for the International Booker Longlist; Where: India**

Originally published as *Pookkuzhi*, the novel's English translation *Pyre* by Anirudh Vasudevan was selected for the International Booker 2023 longlist, making it the first Tamil novel nominated for the longlist. *Pyre* explores the subject of caste. However, the novel didn't make it to the shortlist which was announced in April. Born in Tamil Nadu, Perumal Murugan has written novels, short stories as well as poetry. The writer is known for his honest portraiture of modern society. Following protests against his novel *Maadhorubaagan* in 2015, he announced that he is retiring from writing. The case was brought to court where the judgement was made in his favour.

RAHUL GANDHI

In the news for: **Bharat Jodo Yatra; Where: India**

Beginning in September 2022, Rahul Gandhi began the Bharat Jodo Yatra, where he walked accompanied by citizens from Kanyakumari to Kashmir, spanning 4,000 kilometres and 150 days. While Gandhi resigned as leader of the Congress Party in 2019, he remains its de facto head. Through his national march, he has managed to sway the largely unfavourable public opinion and gain a new following who are inspired by the message of unity.

RISHI SUNAK

In the news for: Becoming UK's first Asian-British PM; Where: UK

After Liz Truss resigned, Rishi Sunak, the Chancellor of the Exchequer in the Boris Johnson-led cabinet, became the Prime Minister of United Kingdom–the country's third prime minister in a span of two months. Sunak made history as the country's first Indian-origin and Asian-British prime minister. Born to immigrant parents who trace their roots to Punjab, Sunak rose to become one of the wealthiest politicians in the country. Coming into office during a serious crisis, stabilizing the economy was his first major goal as prime minister.

SALMAN RUSHDIE

In the news for: Being attacked on stage; Where: USA

In August 2022, the author of celebrated and controversial works such as *Midnight's Children* and *The Satanic Verses* was stabbed on stage at the Chautauqua Institution in New York, where he was set to deliver a lecture. Rushdie has been under threat since 1988, when Iran's then-leader Ayatollah Ruhollah Khomeini issued a fatwa calling for his execution, following which he spent about 10 years in hiding. The attack left him with multiple wounds and blindness in one eye, but the author has since recovered and plans to write a book about the incident. The culprit, Hadi Matar, pled not guilty to the charges.

SAM ALTMAN

In the news for: His position as CEO of OpenAI; Where: USA

OpenAI was formed in 2015 as an open-source company working to develop Artificial General Intelligence (AGI). It researches generative models of AI to benefit humanity. It is currently working with text, image and audio models, including GPT4, DALL-E and Whisper. Sam Altman was named its CEO in 2020. OpenAI gained widespread attention in December 2022, when it launched a free preview of ChatGPT, an AI chatbot. In 2023, Microsoft announced a multi-billion dollar investment in the company. As artificial intelligence becomes increasingly integrated into our everyday lives, OpenAI is posed to lead the way in setting ethical standards for this realm of technology.

NEWSMAKERS

SHEHAN KARUNATILAKA

In the news for: Winning the Booker Prize 2022; Where: Sri Lanka

Karunatilaka won the Booker for *The Seven Moons of Mali Almeida*. He is the second Sri Lankan to the win the Booker (the first being Michael Ondaatje in 1992 for *The English Patient*). Karunatilaka has also written songs, scripts and stories that have been published in popular magazines like *Rolling Stone* and *National Geographic*. He received global recognition when he won the 2012 Commonwealth Book prize for his novel *Chinaman: The Legend of Pradeep Mathew*.

VOLODYMYR ZELENSKY

In the news for: *Time* Magazine's Person of the Year; Where: Ukraine

The Ukrainian President has been making headlines for leading his country through the ongoing conflict with Russia. Earlier, it was believed that Ukraine will fall in less than three days if Russia were to invade it, but Ukraine has endured and continues to resist Russian military aggression. The liberation of the seized city of Kherson in November 2022 after months of Russian occupation was one of the defining moments of the war. *Time* magazine has named him the 'spirit of Ukraine' as well as the Person of the Year 2022. According to the magazine, identifying 'who' or 'what' has mostly affected the events that have occurred in an entire year 'can be agonizing'.

XI JINPING

In the news for: Winning a third term as president; Where: China

In March, Xi Jinping captured a third term as China's President, breaking precedent on the term limit. Jinping is Secretary of the Chinese Communist Party, which has ruled for nearly 75 years. Over the last decade, his control over the country has grown increasingly authoritarian. In his third term, Jinping will have to lead the country out of an economic slump resulting from his administration's zero-Covid policy. This year, Jinping has strengthened ties with Vladimir Putin. This relationship is crucial to Russia, which has suffered from sanctions imposed by Western countries in the wake of the Russia–Ukraine war.

Caricatures by Mistunee Chowdhury

ANNIVERSARIES

29 January **150th birth anniversary of JOHN D. ROCKEFELLER JR**

(29 January 1874–11 May 1960)

American philanthropist Rockefeller Jr was the son of the John D. Rockefeller, the founder of Standard Oil Company. In association with his father, he also founded the Rockefeller Institute for Medical Research (1901; now The Rockefeller University) and The Rockefeller Foundation (1913), among others. During both world wars, he was active with a number of organizations, including the National War Fund, raising funds for those actively serving in the armed forces. He also built the now famous Rockefeller Centre in the city of New York. The construction and funding of this project during the Great Depression in the 1930s helped create about 75,000 jobs when the people were facing unemployment and the country was going through an economic crisis.

12 February **215th birth anniversary of ABRAHAM LINCOLN**

(12 February 1809–15 April 1865)

The 16th President of the United States of America is also known as Honest Abe, the Rail-Splitter and the Great Emancipator. An abolitionist, Lincoln strongly opposed slavery and had been elected before the Civil War which was fought between the Union and the Confederacy. While the war was initially a struggle to keep the country together and to preserve its unity, it soon focused on emancipation. Lincoln's Emancipation Proclamation of 1862 declaring the freedom of enslaved Black people led the way for the 13th Amendment to the United States' Constitution which officially abolished slavery. Roughly a month before the Union's victory, Lincoln was assassinated by John Wilkes Booth in 1865. Lincoln is still regarded as one of the greatest and most popular American Leaders.

'Those who deny freedom to others, deserve it not for themselves.'

13 February **135th birth anniversary of** SAROJINI NAIDU
(13 February 1879–2 March 1949)

Also known as the nightingale of India for her brilliant poetry, Naidu was also active in politics. She studied at the University of Madras and later, King's College London and Girton College in Cambridge. In 1914, the Royal Society of Literature elected her fellow. She was also active in the India's fight for independence. She was not only the first Indian woman to become the President of Indian national Congress but also the first woman to become governor of an Indian state. She held the chair of the governor of the United Provinces (now Uttar Pradesh) from 1947 until her death in 1949.

3 March **185th Birth Anniversary of** JAMSETJI TATA
(3 March 1839–19 May 1904)

The founder of the Tata Group, Jamsetji Nusserwanji Tata was born in Navsari, Gujarat, in 1839. He studied at Elphinstone College in Mumbai and began his career in his father's exports firm. In 1868, he founded a trading company, which would eventually grow to become the Tata Group. Later in 1872, he shifted his focus to cotton manufacturing and opened a number of mills. He is also credited to have organized the country's first largescale ironworks, which became Tata Iron and Steel Company and has now evolved into Tata Steel. He also built the iconic Taj Mahal Palace Hotel in Mumbai, India's first luxury hotel. He established the J.N. Tata Endowment, which is still active, to offer support and encouragement to Indian students so they can pursue higher education.

9 March **570th birth anniversary of** AMERIGO VESPUCCI
(9 March 1454–22 February 1512)

Born in Florence, Vespucci was an Italian explorer who went on a number of voyages between 1497 and 1504. Vespucci's voyage of 1501–02 would become the most important historically and geographically as he discovered lands belonging to the 'New World'. Although Columbus had sailed to the New World earlier in 1492, Vespucci is believed to have identified these new lands as part of a separate continent. In 1507, Martin Waldseemüller suggested that the new lands can be named America after their discoverer Amerigo. Vespucci held the prestigious post of piloto mayor, which is Spanish for 'master navigator' from 1508–12 in Sevilla, Spain, where he died in 1512.

'Logic will get you from A to Z; imagination will get you everywhere.'

14 March 145th birth anniversary of ALBERT EINSTEIN (14 March 1879–18 April 1955)

One of the most famous names in modern science, Albert Einstein was born in Germany to a Jewish family. A theoretical physicist, he is credited for developing a number of theories and concepts, which have greatly enhanced our understanding of the physical world. His research includes the theory of relativity and the explanation of photoelectric effect for which he won the Nobel Prize in Physics in 1921. In the 1930s, when Hitler came to power in Germany and began to have Jews killed, Einstein moved to the USA. When he joined Princeton University, newspapers reported that the 'pope of physics' had left Germany, making Princeton the new Vatican.

7 April 135th birth anniversary of GABRIELA MISTRAL (7 April 1889–10 January 1957)

Chilean poet Gabriela Mistral was the first Latin American person to win the Nobel Prize in Literature in 1945. Her work represented the culture and traditions of a region that was not widely recognized back then. While she is known for her poetry and contribution to Latin American literature, she was also an educator and engaged in social activism. In 1925, Mistral was appointed as secretary of the Latin American section in the League of Nations in Paris.

2 May 505th death anniversary of LEONARDO DA VINCI (2 May 1921–23 April 1992)

'Painting is poetry that is seen rather than felt, and poetry is painting that is felt rather than seen.'

Italian polymath, painter, draftsman, sculptor, architect and engineer, Leonardo da Vinci is best known as a Renaissance artist whose most famous paintings include the Mona Lisa and the Last Supper. Da Vinci received no formal education apart from basic reading, writing and maths. However, his father recognized his talent for art and sent him to Andrea del Verrocchio, a famous Florentine artist at the time, to be his apprentice. Not just art, he was interested in a variety of subjects. Interestingly, he envisioned and created designs for bicycle, helicopter, submarine and even military tank long before these would come into existence.

3 June 100th Death Anniversary

FRANZ KAFKA (3 July 1883- 3 June 1924)

'A book must be the axe for the frozen sea within us.'

Kafka was born in Prague, Czech Republic, and wrote German language fiction. Some f his well-known works include *The Trial* and *The Metamorphosis*, in which the protagonist wakes to find himself turning into an insect, a story that has captured the imagination of generations. Kafka's writing is known for his dark humour and experimental style. He was employed at an insurance company and died of tuberculosis in 1924. Kafka's fame was mostly posthumous and is due largely to the executor of his will who refused Kafka's request to burn all his manuscripts.

29July 120th birth anniversary of JRD TATA (29 July 1904–29 November 1993)

Jehangir Ratanji Dadabhoy Tata, or simply JRD, is also regarded as the Father of Indian Aviation. He was the first Indian citizen to get a commercial pilot's licence in 1929, and also laid the foundation of the aviation industry in India by creating the country's first airline. He started Tata Air Mail, a courier service in 1932. Later Tata Air Mail evolved into Tata Airlines, which was India's first domestic carrier, and in 1946 the company's name was changed, once again, to Air India as it is known today. For his valuable contributions to the society, Indian industries and economy, he was honoured with the Padma Vibhusan in 1955 and the Bharat Ratna in 1992.

17 October **175th death anniversary of FRÉDÉRIC CHOPIN (1 March 1810–17 October 1849)**

Chopin was a Polish music composer and pianist who wrote over 200 pieces for piano. Chopin could play the piano by the age of six and soon after started formal piano lessons. He was only eight when he gave his first public performance at a charity concert and few years later, he performed before Alexander I, the tsar of Russia who was in Warsaw then. Chopin received formal training in music and was enrolled at institutions like the Warsaw Conservatory of Music. His last public performance was at the Guildhall in London, where he played for the benefit of Polish refugees as a gesture of patriotism. Chopin struggled with his health for a long time before his death in 1849.

'Do or die.'

14 November **135th birth anniversary of JAWAHARLAL NEHRU**
(14 November 1889–27 May 1964)

India's first and longest serving prime minister, Nehru was noted for his leadership and his vision for nation-building. Nehru was greatly influenced by Gandhi and joined the Indian National Congress led by the latter in 1919, becoming actively involved in politics and the freedom struggle. His political views and participation in civil disobedience movements led to his frequent arrests and imprisonments. Nehru was a strong advocate of secularism in the country and keeping a newly independent India diverse, was one of his major goals as a leader. He died of a stroke in1964.

30 November **150th birth anniversary of WINSTON CHURCHILL**
(30 November 1874–24 January 1965)

Winston Churchill served in the British army before he began his long career in politics. He served as prime minister twice – his first term lasted from 1940 to 1945 and his second term from 1951 to 1955. His first term coincided with World War II and saw him emerge as a successful wartime leader. Known for his remarkable oratory skills, he inspired Britain and the Allies to unite and fight against fascism. With his stirring speeches and V for Victory salute became the face of the British war effort. He alsoa noteworthy literary career. He won the Nobel Prize for Literature in 1953. Among other works, he has produced multi-volume books documenting both world wars.

14 December 225th death anniversary of GEORGE WASHINGTON (22 February 1732–14 December 1799)

He took part in the American Revolutionary War fought against the British Crown for the independence of the 13 Britain's colonies in North America. He was also a founding father and the first president of the newly independent United States. Washington's presidency saw many firsts, including the signing of the first US copyright law, the appointment of the first Chief Justice of the US Supreme Court and the establishment of the first national bank, the Bank of the United States. During his term as president, Washington signed a bill which established a permanent US capital for the future along the Potomac River. This city would later be known as Washington, D.C., after the first president of the country.

'It is better to offer no excuse than a bad one.'

24 December 500th death anniversary of VASCO DA GAMA (1460–24 December 1524)

A Portuguese explorer, Vasco da Gama was the first person to sail directly from Europe to India. Through his voyages, he discovered a maritime route from western Europe to the East via the Cape of Good Hope. He sailed across the Indian Ocean and landed in Calicut (now Kozhikode) in 1498. He would make two more voyages to India, the third voyage being in 1524 when the Portuguese empire appointed him as their Viceroy in India. He assumed his post on reac hing India in September but soon fell ill and died in December of the same year.

DEMOCRACY IN ACTION: THE INDIAN GENERAL ELECTIONS OF 2024

The general elections will be held in India in 2024 to constitute the 18th Lok Sabha. They will take place between April and May 2024. Citizens in India will vote to elect 543 Members of Parliament. They will represent the various constituencies throughout the country. The elections will choose the 15th prime minister of the country. Parties will put forward their candidates. But most of them are small and operate only in regional areas. There are six national parties – Bharatiya Janata Party, Indian National Congress, Communist Party of India (Marxist), Bahujan Samaj Party, National People's Party and Aam Aadmi Party.

The Main Coalitions: Multiple parties have come together to form various alliances to contest in the elections. Two alliances are the ones to have created the maximum buzz. The National Democratic Alliance (NDA) has 38 parties led by the Bharatiya Janata Party. Prime Minister Narendra Modi currently heads the NDA. The other main alliance is INDIA, which stands for Indian National Developmental Inclusive Alliance. Twenty-six parties are members of INDIA and they are led by Indian National Congress and Rahul Gandhi has been appointed as their leader.

Types of Elections in India: India has two types of elections: Lok Sabha elections and State Assembly elections. The Lok Sabha elects Members of Parliament who will make big decisions for the entire country. On the other hand, each state in India has its own Assembly elections whose winners are called Members of the Legislative Assembly (MLAs). MLAs make decisions for that particular state.

Understand the Election Process: There are many stages of the election process.

Campaigning: Before the elections, leaders and parties hold rallies to share their ideas and plans for the country. They use speeches, posters and even social media to tell people about their campaign and why people should vote for them.

Voting day: On this day, people who are 18 years old and above get to cast their vote. They go to election booths where an Electronic Voting Machine (EVM) is present. The EVM has a list of all the names and pictures of the leaders and parties from that particular area. Citizens choose their candidate by pressing the button next to the person's name.

Counting the votes: After everyone has voted, officials from the Election Commission of India count the votes. They tally up how many people voted for each leader and party to see who got the most votes. That person will become the Member of Parliament in the 2024 elections.

- There are 94,50,25,694 voters, according to the Election Commission. That means 94.50 crore people will be voting in the 2024 elections. In the first Lok Sabha elections in 1951, India had 17.32 crore registered voters.
- Rajiv Kumar is the current Chief Election Commissioner. He has two Election Commissioners under him – Anup Chandra Pandey and Arun Goel.

Last Time Around... • There were 8,039 candidates contesting for 543 Lok Sabha seats in the previous general elections in 2019.

- Bihar had the most number of NOTA (none of the above) votes. Two per cent of its total number of voters – 8,16,950 – opted for NOTA.
- The BJP-led won 353 seats. The BJP won 37.76 per cent of votes, while the NDA's combined vote was 45 per cent of the 60.37 crore votes that were polled. The INC won 52 seats. It failed to get 10 per cent of the seats needed to claim the post of Leader of the Opposition.
- In 2019, for the first time ever in Lok Sabha elections, candidates with criminal records were required to publish this information in newspapers and through television channels on three occasions during the campaign period.
- The voter-verifiable paper audit trail (VVPAT) was used in all polling stations in 2019. VVPAT is a device that dispenses a slip with the symbol of the party for which a person has voted for. The slip appears on a small window for seven seconds and then drops in a box. The voter cannot take it home.

In 2024... • Most political experts predict that the NDA will be winner and Narendra Modi will be back as the prime minister.

- This is not likely to affect financial growth or inflation in the country. According to economists at Barclays, these two factors are more influenced more by domestic economic conditions and global factors rather than changes in government.

INDIA AT G20 SUMMIT: FORGING PATHWAYS TO GLOBAL PROGRESS

The Group of Twenty is an international organization. Also known as G20, it is a group of 19 developed and developing countries along with the European Union. Representatives of other global bodies such as the World Bank, the International Monetary Fund and the Organisation for Economic Co-operation and Development also attend G20 conferences.

G20 Countries

The G20 countries are Argentina, Australia, Brazil, Canada, China, France, Germany, India, Indonesia, Italy, Japan, Mexico, Republic of Korea, Russia, Saudi Arabia, South Africa, Türkiye, the United Kingdom and the United States. The 20th 'country' is the European Union. It is represented by the European Commission and the European Central Bank.

The History of G20

G20 was formed in 1999 after a large financial crisis hit Asia. Initially, only seven countries – Canada, France, Germany, Italy, Japan, the United Kingdom and the United States – were part of the forum, and representation was restricted to only finance ministers and central bank governors. Slowly, other major countries were also invited to join, and the G20 was upgraded in 2007 to include heads of state and governments.

Since then, finance ministers and heads of the central banks of all member countries meet once a year. The goal of G20 is to ensure the strong economic growth of the countries as well as their financial security. They discuss matters of international finance and exchange of currency, and sign agreements on trade. Leaders of the member countries also discuss issues relating to climate change, energy, sustainable development, agriculture, health, environment and anti-corruption.

How G20 Works

G20 processes are divided into two tracks – the finance track and the sherpa track. These tracks run parallel to each other. Finance ministers and central bank governors of member nations are part of the finance track. They meet throughout the year. Sherpas, who are personal emissaries of leaders, lead the sherpa track. They also meet separately all through the year and discuss the agenda for the main summit. Working groups designed around specific themes operate within both tracks.

Along with these two tracks are engagement groups. They bring together civil societies, parliamentarians, think tanks, women, youth, labour, businesses and researchers of the G20 countries to discuss common goals.

India's G20 Presidency

There is no permanent presidency of the G20. All member countries get a chance to assume presidency for a period of one year. For the year 2023, India is the president.

India assumed the presidency of the G20 grouping from Indonesia on 1 December 2022. Since the group does not have a permanent leader, each country's presidency is supported by the previous, current and future holders of the post. This is together called the troika. Along with India, 2023's troika includes Indonesia and Brazil. Indonesia held the presidency in 2022 and the baton will pass on to Brazil in 2024.

India will host the 18th G20 Heads of State and Government Summit in September 2023 in New Delhi. The summit will be the culmination of a series of meetings held over the course of the year. Bengaluru, Chandigarh, Chennai, Guwahati, Indore, Jodhpur, Khajuraho, Kolkata, Lucknow, Mumbai, Pune, Rann of Kutch, Surat, Thiruvananthapuram and Udaipur will be the host cities for various meetings between December 2022 and February 2023.

Women empowerment, health, agriculture, education, culture, tourism and the ongoing war between Russia and Ukraine will be discussed at the 2023 summit. Topics like financial inclusion, digital economy and environment and climate sustainability will also be covered. The G20 summit is the highest-profile international gathering ever to be hosted by India. It offers a unique opportunity for the country to contribute to the global agenda on important global issues.

The 2023 Theme and Logo

The logo for the 2023 summit is based on the philosophy of Vasudhaiva Kutumbakam. It means one earth, one family, one future in Sanskrit, and has been drawn from the Maha Upanishad. This is also the theme of the 2023 edition of the G20. Vasudhaiva Kutumbakam affirms the value of all life – human, animal, plant and microorganisms – and their inter-connectedness on planet Earth and in the wider universe.

The theme also highlights Lifestyle for Environment (LiFE), which speaks about environmentally sustainable and responsible choices, both at the level of individual lifestyles and national development. The idea of LiFE is to take globally transformative actions that result in a cleaner and greener future. India's G20 presidency is focused on 'striving for just and equitable growth for all in the world as we navigate through these turbulent times in a sustainable, holistic, responsible and inclusive manner', an official statement said.

The colours of the logo – saffron, green, white and blue – are derived from the Indian flag. The seven petals of the lotus in the logo signify the seven continents. The lotus has been chosen specifically since it is India's national flower and because it represents growth amidst adversity, reflecting the turbulent times we are currently living in.

Setting the agenda

Indian Prime Minister Narendra Modi has asked for international leaders to cooperate to deal with global issues. He said that the challenges of 'climate change, terrorism and pandemics can be solved not by fighting each other, but only by acting together'. The prime minister also said that governments of different countries should not hamper the global supply of food, fertilizers and medical products. This note of caution was issued to avoid humanitarian crises.

Even though Russia is currently at war with Ukraine, it will attend the G20 meetings and the summit.

Why India Matters at G20

International eyes are set on India in this summit as the country has always been a voice for the poor and developing world in the international fora.

This historic role brings additional responsibilities as many non-G20 countries (particularly from the global South) look up to India to voice their concerns at the summit, whose decisions shape their economies.

India's Priorities at G20

The Indian government has several priorities in focus this year. The six major priorities are:

1. Green Development , Climate Finance and LiFE: India's focus is on climate change, with particular emphasis on climate finance and technology. India also wants to ensure just energy transitions for developing countries. The LiFE movement has also been introduced, which promotes environmentally conscious practices and is based on India's sustainable traditions.

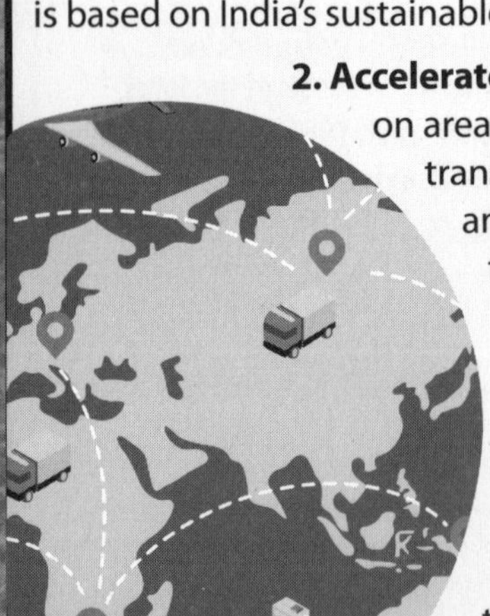

2. Accelerated, inclusive and resilient growth: Focus on areas that have the potential to bring structural transformation. This includes supporting small- and medium-sized enterprises in global trade, promoting labour rights and welfare, addressing the global skills gap and building inclusive agricultural value chains and food systems.

3. Accelerating progress on sustainable development goals (SDGs): India has, once again, committed to achieve the targets set out in the

2030 Agenda for Sustainable Development, with particular focus on addressing the impact of the COVID-19 pandemic.

4. Technological transformation and digital public infrastructure: Promotion of a human-centric approach to technology. There will also be increased knowledge-sharing in areas such as digital public infrastructure, financial inclusion and tech-enabled development in sectors such as agriculture and education.

5. Multi-lateral institutions for the 21st century: Efforts are being made to reform multi-lateralism and create a more accountable, inclusive and representative international system that is fit for addressing 21st-century challenges.

6. Women-led development: India has also emphasized inclusive growth and development with a focus on women empowerment and representation. This will boost socio-economic development and the achievement of SDGs.

200+

That's the number of G20 meetings India will hold under its presidency. The meetings will cover more than 30 workstreams.

For 2023, India has invited several countries who are not G20 member nations to be a part of the summit. The countries are Bangladesh, Singapore, Mauritius, Egypt, the Netherlands, Nigeria, Oman, Spain and the United Arab Emirates.

Three international organizations have been invited as guests as well – the International Solar Alliance, the Coalition for Disaster Relief Infrastructure and the Asian Development Bank.

COUNTDOWN TO PARIS OLYMPICS 2024

The next Olympics will take place in Paris, France, in 2024. It will be a 15-day extravaganza that will start on 26 July and end on 11 August. The Paris games will officially be called the Games of the XXXIII Olympiad. The last time the games were held in Paris was 1924 – exactly 100 years before next year's edition. The city was awarded the bid to host the games in 2017.

Over 10,500 athletes will compete in 32 different sports and 329 events.

'Games Wide Open' is the slogan for the Paris games, highlighting the spirit of equality and accessibility being chased in 2024. From the opening ceremony on the Seine being free to attend and the Marathon for all to there being only one slogan for the Athlete and Para-Athlete Olympic games, for the men and the women, this year's games are all about letting everyone experience the emotions and passion of the Olympics.

An Opening Ceremony Like No Other

The opening ceremony will take place on 26 July 2024. In the past, sportspersons from the competing countries would enter the major athletics stadium in alphabetical order, with the hosts being the last to enter. However, the 2024 games will break with this tradition.

This time, sportspersons will travel on boats in the River Seine. This will be a journey of six kilometres between the Pont d'Austerlitz and Pont d'lena bridges in central Paris. A total of **160 boats** from **206 countries** will carry the representatives of the participating countries. The parade will end in front of the Trocadéro area, where the final shows will be performed. The Trocadéro area is located right in front of the Eiffel Tower. The large complex is full of museums, sculptures, gardens and fountains.

The organizers are expecting at least six lakh spectators to attend the opening ceremony. This is 10 times more than the number of people that can fit in a usual Olympic stadium. This opening ceremony will be the largest ever held in the history of the games. Apart from the 10,500 athletes, 120 heads of government will also be attending.

What's New?

Breaking, sport climbing, skateboarding and surfing are the four new sports included in the Paris 2024 games. These are unusual picks since they have never been a part of the Olympics before.

Breaking is also known as break dancing. It is an urban dance style which is a part of hip-hop culture. Sport climbing has three disciplines: Speed, Bouldering and Lead. Speed is about how fast the athlete can climb. Bouldering is about climbing a boulder on a wall. Lead requires the athlete to climb a difficult route 20 metres high.

Surfing cannot be conducted in Paris since it doesn't have a beach. The competition will instead take place in Teahupoo, on the island of Tahiti. This island is part of French Polynesia located between Australia and South America.

Did you know?

The inclusion of certain sports depends on the host country? Karate, baseball and softball have been removed from the Paris games. They were a part of Tokyo 2020 because these three games are popular in Japan. They, therefore, attracted many Japanese viewers. However, they will be removed from Paris 2024 for the exact opposite reason: the French aren't interested in them.

The Torch Relay

Apart from being the world's greatest sports event, the Olympic games show that sport is a powerful medium to bring people together. The messages of peace and unity are everywhere, proving that rivalry is no barrier to respect or friendship.

The Olympic torch is lit by the rays of the sun in Olympia, Greece. This has been happening since the first games in Athens in 1896. The Olympic Flame will arrive in France after crossing the Mediterranean Sea. From Marseille on 8 May 2024, the Flame from the Paris 2024 Torch will open the celebrations. This will mark the start of an uninterrupted four-month celebration throughout France. It will travel thousands of kilometres, passed from person to person, on land and sea. On 26 July 2024, at the opening ceremony, the final torchbearer will ignite the cauldron with the torch. Only after this will the games be declared officially open.

The Olympic torch is designed a new by each host county. French designer Mathieu Lehanneur has designed the torch for the Paris games. It has been inspired by the three symbols of the upcoming games: equality, water and peacefulness. According to the designer, 'Equality is symbolised by perfect symmetry. Water is symbolised by the wave, relief, and vibration effects. Peacefulness is symbolised by the gentleness of the curves.'

The Paris 2024 torch is 70 centimetres tall and weighs 1.5 kilograms. It is champagne in colour and made from steel manufactured from recycled and renewable sources. Two thousand torches will be made that will be carried by 11,000 people.

The Logo

The official logo for the Paris 2024 games combines three iconic symbols representing both the Olympics and France – the gold medal, the Olympic flame and Marianne, a symbol of the French Republic.

The logo takes its shape and colour from a gold medal. Cut out of this gold circle is the shape of a white flame. It represents the Olympic flame, which burns throughout the event. A pair of golden lips show Marianne, which is a representation of the Goddess of Liberty that is often used as a symbol of the French Republic.

Marianne was added to the logo to demonstrate that the 'Games will be Games for everyone'. This is because the first Olympics in Paris held in 1900 was the first in which women were allowed to compete. 'Her face is also a homage to female athletes and a nod to history. It was in 1900 at the Olympic Games in Paris that women were first allowed to compete,' said the Olympic organizers.

Who are the Mascots?

Meet the Phryges, the mascots for the Paris 2024 Olympic Games. They have an important mission to accomplish: to show the world that sport can change everything and that it deserves to play a major role in society.

Phryges (pronounced fri-jee-uhs) are small Phrygian caps. Past mascots have usually been animals. But France wanted to do something different. 'We chose an ideal rather than an animal,' said

Paris 2024 president Tony Estanguet.

The Paralympics which will take place after the Olympics share the same mascot. 'The Paralympics mascot has a visible disability. It also sends a strong message: to promote inclusion,' said Estanguet.

The Phryges are in red, white and blue, the colours of the French flag. The golden Paris 2024 logo is placed across their chests. They also have a mischievous eye made of a 'cockade of France', a knot of ribbons that is the French national ornament.

What is a Phryge?

The mascots are based on Phrygian caps. They are a soft, conical type of cap in France. They have been asymbol of freedom throughout the country's history. Phrygian caps can be seen atop the head of the iconic figure Marianne in every town hall in France. Even coins and stamps in France have Phrygian caps on them.

Know Your Medals

Olympic medals aren't fully made with the same metals they're named after. The gold medals only contain about six grams of gold, and 92.5 percent of the medal is made of silver. The last time fully gold medals were awarded to winners was in 1912.

The medal sizes vary for each Olympic Games. The Winter Games medals are usually slightly bigger than the Summer Games ones. The medals must be between 70 mm and 120 mm in diameter. The thickness must be between 3 mm and 10 mm.

In terms of weight, the medals vary from 500 to 800 grams. The gold medal weighs a bit more than the silver medals. The bronze medals weigh the least. During the Tokyo Olympics, the gold medals weighed 556 grams, the silver medals were 550 grams and the bronze medals were 450 grams.

15 International Stars to Watch Out for

Katie Ledecky (USA, swimming): If she wins three gold medals in the pool, she will be the most successful woman in Olympics history. Katie Ledecky has won seven titles across London 2012, Rio 2016 and Tokyo 2020.

Stephen Curry (USA, basketball): Stephen Curry is one of the most famous faces in basketball around the world. This will be his first Olympic games, so fans will be excited to watch him play.

Rafael Nadal (Spain, tennis): Rafael Nadal has two Olympic gold medals to his name already. He won the singles title in 2008 and the doubles title in 2016. He has been injured for a few months now, so no one is sure if he will even participate. But the tennis tournament will take place on the red clay of Roland-Garros, the same field as the French Open. Since Nadal has won 10 titles there, he may give the Olympics a shot.

Yulimar Rojas (Venezuela, athletics): She made history in triple jump at Tokyo 2020. Rojas broke her own world record at the Olympics with a 15.67-metre mark. She is expected to do well in 2024 too.

Novak Djokovic (Serbia, tennis): The Serbian player loves to win and has broken several tennis records. He also holds the most number of Grand Slam wins in the men's category. But he hasn't won an Olympic gold medal yet, so he will surely play in Paris next year.

Shelly-Ann Fraser-Pryce (Jamaica, athletics): The Jamaican is widely considered to be the best female sprinter of all time. She has won three Olympic gold medals, four silvers and a bronze medal. She has also won 10 World Championship gold medals. Fraser-Pryce will be 37 years old in 2024, so the Paris Olympics could be her last.

Kylian Mbappé

Kylian Mbappé (France, football): Even though he and his team lost the football world cup final, Mbappé scored the maximum goals – eight – at the tournament. He has spoken about his dream of playing the Olympics and will play in Paris.

Hashimoto Daiki (Japan, artistic gymnastics): Daiki is a rising star in gymnastics. He has one world championship title and two Olympic medals. Daiki has also won three silver medals in a team event, floor exercise and horizontal bar at the world championships.

Faith Kipyegon (Kenya, athletics): She is going for a hat-trick at this Olympics in the 1,500-metre race. She recently set new world records over 1,500 metres and 5,000 metres.

Rory McIlroy (Ireland, golf): Golf returned to the Olympics in 2016. Since Tiger Woods will not be competing, McIlroy will be the favourite to win the gold medal.

Wang Chuqin (China, table tennis): China has won the maximum medals in table tennis in the history of the Olympics. Even though Wang Chuqin didn't win any medals in Tokyo, he now ranks number 4 in the world. Table tennis fans are excited to see him play with fellow Chinese player Ma Long.

Kristóf Milák (Hungary, swimming): In 2019, Kristóf Milák won the world championships when he was only 19 years old. He became the Olympic champion at Tokyo 2020 and won the silver medal in the 100-metre butterfly event. He is known as the undisputed butterfly king.

Armand Duplantis (Sweden, athletics): Duplantis is a pole vaulter. He won the gold medal at the Tokyo Olympics. In 2022, he again ranked first at the World Indoor Championships.

An San (Republic of Korea, archery): An San won three gold medals at the Tokyo Olympics. She also broke a 25-year-old Olympic record.At Tokyo, she became the first archer to win three golds since 1904.

Pauline Ferrand-Prevot (France, mountain bike): At the Tokyo Olympics, Pauline Ferrand-Prevot fell and finished in the tenth place. But at the 2022 Worlds, she won a silver medal. She is a promising star expected to win a medal in Paris 2024.

Who Will Win? Take a Guess

An entertainment and data technology firm has predicted the top 10 medal-winning countries at the Paris games. Nielsen's Gracenote came up with data from major events since the Tokyo 2020 Olympics.

RANK	COUNTRY	MEDALS
1	USA	122
2	CHINA	68
3 and 4	FRANCE and GREAT BRITAIN	62 each
5	JAPAN	54
6	ITALY	45
7	AUSTRALIA	42
8	THE NETHERLANDS	41
9	GERMANY	35
10	REPUBLIC OF KOREA	29

INDIA AT THE OLYMPICS

India first participated in the 1900 Paris Olympics, the second-ever edition of the modern Games. However, there has been some controversy regarding that.

Was the First Medallist Truly an Indian?

In 1900, Kolkata-born Norman Pritchard became the first Indian to take part in the Olympics. He was on a holiday in France and decided to enter his name for the games.

Norman Pritchard ran in five athletics events—the 60-metre, 100-metre and 200-metre races and the 110- and 200-metre hurdles. Although he was eliminated in the heats of the 60- and 100-metre races, Pritchard came second in the 200-metre sprint and India won its first Olympic medal – a silver. He became the first Asian-born athlete to win an Olympic medal. Pritchard then won his second silver medal in the 200-metre hurdles.

Due to Pritchard's British ancestry, there have been debates over Pritchard's nationality. But he travelled to the games with an Indian travel document (a modern-day passport) and had an Indian birth certificate.

According to an Olympic historian, Pritchard had entered the Olympics as an individual and not under the Indian flag. But the International Olympic Committee still considers Norman Pritchard to be an Indian athlete. It attributed both his Olympic medals to India.

Sir Dorabji Tata

First-ever Team India

India first sent its official contingent of athletes at the 1920 Antwerp Olympics. Businessman Dorabji Tata formed an Indian Olympic Association (IOA) to choose and train athletes to participate in the 1920 Olympics. In April 1920, the IOA picked a five-person Indian contingent for Antwerp.

The first-ever Indian Olympic contingent comprised Purma Bannerjee (100-metre and 400-metre), Phadeppa Chaugule (10,000-metre and marathon), Sadashiv Datar (marathon), Kumar Navale and Randhir Shinde (both wrestling).

Purma Bannerjee became the first Indian flag-bearer at the Olympics opening ceremony. Randhir Shinde earned India's first victory at the Olympics. He beat Great Britain's Henry Inman in the men's featherweight (54 kilograms). Because of Shinde's medal, India finished fourth at the 1920 Olympics.

The first official Indian Olympic delegation in 1920

Team India after Independence

After gaining independence from the British in 1947, India participated in the 1948 London Olympics as an independent country for the first time. India sent 86 athletes to participate in nine different sports – athletics, boxing, cycling, hockey, football, swimming, water polo, weightlifting and wrestling.

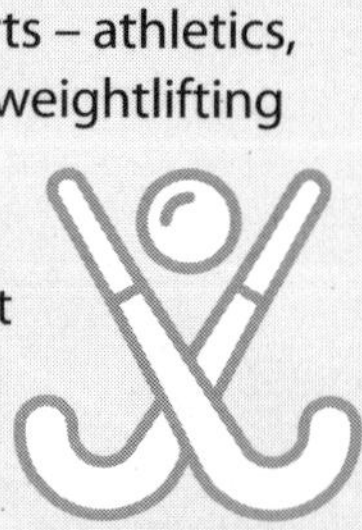

The 1948 London Olympics saw the Indian hockey team win its fourth-consecutive Olympic gold and its first as an independent nation. The previous three hockey gold medals – 1928, 1932 and 1936 – were won under British rule.

Wrestler K.D. Jadhav was the first individual Olympic medallist from independent India. He won the bronze medal at the 1952 Helsinki Olympics.

10 Indian Stars at Paris 2024

The Tokyo games saw India's best performance ever at the Olympics. India won seven medals – a gold, two silver and four bronze medals. It finished 48th on the overall medals tally.

In 2024, India is expected to perform better than 2020. The following sportspersons are expected to win big.

Saurabh Chaudhary (shooting): He competed in two pistol events at Tokyo 2020. In the men's 10-metre air pistol qualification, he topped. His total score was 586 out of 600. He performed well in the 10-metre air pistol mixed event as well. Even though he didn't win any medals in Tokyo, he is a rising star.

Manu Bhaker (shooting): She suffered from an equipment malfunctionand couldn't qualify for the women's 10-metre air pistol final. She also didn't shine in the 25-metre pistol and the 10-metre air pistol mixed events. However, Manu Bhaker is expected to bounce back and present a strong challenge at Paris 2024.

Nikhat Zareen (boxing): Nikhat is a former youth world champion. She has won against the reigning world champion Paltceva Ekaterina of Russia and the two-time world championship gold medallist, Kazakhstan's Nazym Kyzaibay, making her a strong medal contender for Paris 2024.

Elavenil Valarivan (shooting): ElavenilValarivan entered the Tokyo Olympics shooting competition on a high. She was the 10-metre air rifle gold medallist from the ISSF World Cup final. She was also the Asian winner in the mixed 10-metre air rifle event. But in Tokyo she struggled to deal with the Olympic pressure and was ousted in the qualification round. Now, for Paris 2024, Elavenil has former Olympic medallist Gagan Narang as her coach and is expected to do well.

Kamalpreet Kaur (athletics): She gained fame after winning the gold medal in discus throw in the 2019 Federation Cup. She became the first from India to breach the 65-metre mark in the event to qualify for Tokyo 2020. At the games, Kamalpreet finished sixth in a highly competitive field.

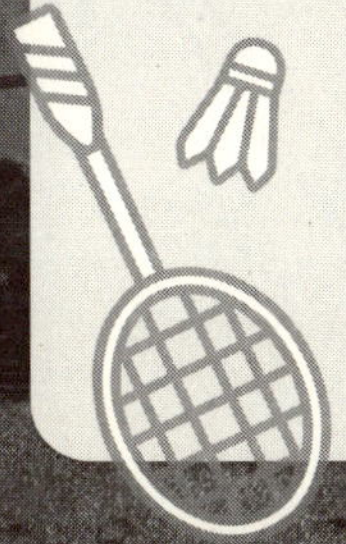

Lakshya Sen (badminton): India has won medals in badminton at the past three Olympics. Lakshya is a former world No. 1 ranker in the juniors with four Badminton

World Federation (BWF) International Series titles in 2019.

Jeremy Lalrinnunga (weightlifting): The weightlifter suffered from lack of proper training and competition due to the COVID-19 pandemic and didn't qualify for Tokyo 2020. However, Jeremy is a former Youth Olympics Games champion. He has performed consistently in the 67-kilogram weight category in the domestic circuit. Jeremy is only 20 years old, so he can go a long way at the Olympics.

Komalika Bari (archery): Komalika Bari is the current youth world champion. She was also a part of the Indian women's team that won the gold medal at the 2021 World Archery World Cup in Paris.

Archana Kamath (table tennis): She is ranked inside 150 in women's singles. Archana is also a former cadet and senior national champion. She was a semi-finalist at the 2018 Youth Olympics and a part of the national team for the ITTF World Team Qualification Tournament in Portugal.

Archana Kamath

Indian hockey women's team: The Indian hockey women's team's performance at Tokyo 2020 surprised many. Despite their hiatus form competitive matches since November 2019, the team reached the semi-finals of the Olympics! Their wins over Ireland, South Africa and Australia earned them praise. Having lost the bronze medal by a whisker, the Indian hockey women's team is expected to dazzle everyone at Paris 2024.

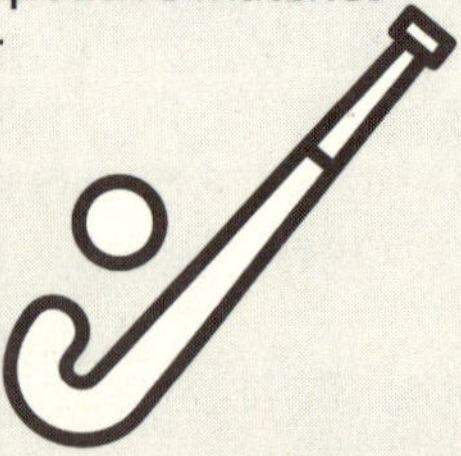

Indian athletes who have qualified for the 2024 Paris Olympics

Number	Athlete	Sport	Event	Status
1	Bhowneesh Mendiratta	Shooting	Men's trap	Quota
2	Rudrankksh Patil	Shooting	Men's 10m air rifle	Quota
3	Swapnil Kusale	Shooting	Men's 50m rifle 3 positions	Quota
4	Akhil Sheoran	Shooting	Men's 50m rifle 3 positions	Quota
5	Mehuli Ghosh	Shooting	Women's 10m air rifle	Quota
6	Sift Kaur Samra	Shooting	Women's 50m rifle 3 positions	Quota
7	Rajeshwari Kumari	Shooting	Women's trap	Quota
8	Akshdeep Singh	Athletics	Men's 20km race walk	Direct (Met qualifying standard)
9	Priyanka Goswami	Athletics	Women's 20km race walk	Direct (Met qualifying standard)
10	Vikash Singh	Athletics	Men's 20km race walk	Direct (Met qualifying standard)
11	Paramjeet Bisht	Athletics	Men's 20km race walk	Direct (Met qualifying standard)
12	Murali Sreeshankar	Athletics	Men's long jump	Direct (Met qualifying standard)
13	Avinash Sable	Athletics	Men's 3000m steeplechase	Direct (Met qualifying standard)

**Updated up till August 2023;*

Source: https://olympics.com/en/news/indian-athletes-qualified-paris-2024-olympics-summer-games

Who Will Miss the Bus?

Even as qualifications have begun for Paris 2024, some Indian players are likely to miss from the tournament.

Deepika Kumari (archery): Deepika Kumari has been a dominant force in Indian archery for over 10 years. She has won medals at the World Championships, World Cups, Asian Championships, Asian Games and Commonwealth Games. She has competed in three Olympics so far, but hasn't won a medal yet. Deepika did not qualify for the Asian Games 2022, a huge setback. She can, however, still qualify for Paris 2024 at the open trials in January 2024.

Deepika Kumari

Rani Rampal: Rani Rampal is one of the finest hockey players of India. The forward has made over 120 goals. But she was recently dropped from Hockey India's 33-member women's core group for the national camp. Rani has also been absent from many national team games. She has been battling injuries since the Tokyo Olympics.

M.C. Mary Kom: Boxer Mary Kom will miss out on the Paris Olympics in 2024. She will turn 40 this year and will be ineligible to compete in Paris. The maximum age to compete at the amateur level in international competitions is 39.

Saina Nehwal: Another player we might not see at the Paris Olympics is Saina Nehwal. Saina's performance has dipped recently. She lost her first game of the BWF World Tour at the Malaysia Open Super 1000. She then made Round 2 exits in the India Open and Indonesia Open.

Run with the Champions

The games organisers have something special in store for the fans. A lucky group of **20,024 people will get the chance to run the Olympic marathon on the same course** – and on the same day – as the world's best run over 42 kilometres. The route starts at Hôtel de Ville and goes to the Palace of Versailles and back. A part of the route goes through the area where the women's march took place in 1789. It was one of the earliest and most significant events of the French Revolution. Traditionally, the men's marathon is the last event of the Olympics. But in Paris 2024, the women's race will bring the games to a close.

Olympic Oddballs

- Along with London, Paris will become the only other city to host the Olympics thrice.
- Paris first staged the Olympic Games in 1900 and then again in 1924.
- So far, there have been 29 Summer Olympic games held in 21 cities.
- India's contingent was 124 players at the Tokyo games. This has been the highest so far at the Olympics.
- The king of Bikaner in Rajasthan, Maharaja Karni Singh, was the first person to represent India at five Olympics. He took part in 1960 Rome, 1964 Tokyo, 1968 Mexico, 1972 Munich and 1980 Moscow Olympics.
- India won its first Olympic gold medal at the 1928 Amsterdam games. It was a medal for the hockey team.
- The German chancellor was very impressed with hockey player Dhyan Chand's skills at the 1936 Berlin games. He had decided to grant German citizenship to Dhyan Chand.
- Tennis player Leander Paes holds the record for most Olympic appearances by an Indian. He has played in seven Olympics, starting from

the 1992 Barcelona games. Leander also won the bronze medal at the 1996 Atlanta Olympics.

- Balbir Singh holds a record of maximum gols in an Olympic hockey final.

  He scored five goals in India's 6-1 win against the Netherlands at the 1952 Helsinki games. The record remains unbeaten.

- P. T. Usha is India's youngest Olympian. She was 16 years and 69 days old when she competed at the 1980 Moscow Olympics.

India's Olympics Tally

SPORT	First and Last medal	Number of Wins
FIELD HOCKEY	Amsterdam **1928**, Tokyo **2020**	**12**
WRESTLING	Helsinki **1952**, Tokyo **2020**	**7**
SHOOTING	Athens **2004**, London **2012**	**4**
ATHLETICS	Paris **1900**, Tokyo **2020**	**3**
BADMINTON	London **2012**, Tokyo **2020**	**3**
BOXING	Beijing **2008**, Tokyo **2020**	**3**
WEIGHTLIFTING	Sydney **2000**, Tokyo **2020**	**2**
TENNIS	Atlanta **1996**	**1**

3 LITERATURE

The word 'literature' means 'acquaintance with letters', from the Latin 'lettera' or letter. Literature is broadly divided into two categories: fiction, which is imaginary, and non-fiction, which is factual. Here are the common types of literature:

Autobiography: A narration of a person's life that they tell themselves.

Biography: A factual narration of a person's life, told by somebody else.

Drama: A piece of writing, with dialogue and action, meant to be performed on stage.

Essay: A written discussion of a topic from an individual's viewpoint.

Fable: A moral story in which the characters are typically animals.

Fairy tale: A fictional story with central themes of fantasy and magic.

Folk tale: Traditional stories, circulated orally among people of a specific community, region or country.

Journal or Diary: The day-to-day recordings of someone's life, usually autobiographical in nature, but often fictional too.

Legend: A story about an important individual or event popularly regarded as historical although not verifiable.

Memoir: An autobiographical account of the writer's memories, emotions and views.

Myth: An ancient religious, spiritual or traditional story describing how the world or humankind came to be.

Novel: A full-length piece of fiction, written in prose. A **novella** is a short novel.

Poetry: A piece written in verse, in which lines may or may not rhyme or stick to a specific meter.

Short story: A narrative in prose, much shorter than a novel, and usually, but not always, about the size of a chapter in a novel.

E-literature: Electronic literature is created in digital environments.It includes conversational characters or 'chatterbots'; interactive fiction, novels in the form of emails, SMS messages or blogs; and poems and stories generated by computers. An e-book is an electronic version of a print book, to be read on a computer or a device such as a tablet, a smartphone or an e-reader.

FEMOIR A MEMOIR WRITTEN BY A WELL-KNOWN FEMALE ACTOR OR COMEDIAN, EMBRACING BODY POSITIVITY, PROFESSIONAL ADVANCEMENT AND A SUPPORTIVE FEMALE COMMUNITY.

TYPES OF FICTION

Fiction includes novels, short stories, fables, folk tales, fairy tales, plays, poetry and comic books. Here are the main types of fiction genres.

Campus novel: A novel in which the main action takes place around the campus of a university, college or school.

Children's: A book written primarily for children is listed in this genre. This includes fiction written in many formats, such as picture books, graphic fiction, short stories and full-length novels. A category higher than children's fiction is young adult (YA) fiction. It broadly includes books for adolescents and young adults in the age group of 14 to 19 years.

Comedy: Fiction that intends to amuse readers and provoke laughter.

Crime: Fiction written about crime and detection. There are several subgenres, such as detective fiction, legal thrillers and courtroom drama.

Fantasy: This genre looks at magic and other forms of the supernatural as its primary inspiration. 'Fantastic' elements may be hidden in a semi-real world setting (like the Harry Potter series); or they may occur in a fantastical world.

MAGICAL REALISM IS A GENRE IN WHICH MAGICAL EVENTS ARE A PART OF ORDINARY LIFE.

Graphic fiction: This genre covers a huge range from picture books and comic books to graphic novels and manga, in which a series of images and word or speech balloons convey a narrative.

Horror: Fiction that primarily aims to scare and incite fear in the reader. Although they largely use supernatural elements, books with gruesome, frightening or suspenseful themes are also part of the genre.

Romance: Novels in this genre are centred on a romantic relationship. This genre extends from classics to Mills & Boon romances.

Spy: Born of the political climate in Europe prior to the First World War, spy fiction began around the time the first modern intelligence services were formed and swiftly became popular through the Second World War.

Thriller: This eventful genre involves suspense and exciting action. It typically follows a hero pitted against a villain who aims to destroy the hero, his country or even the world.

Satire: When an author ridicules or derides a vice or a folly through humour and wit, it is called satire. It is marked by irony, sarcasm, parody and exaggeration.

Wild West Fiction: This genre originated in the American Wild West, cowboy heroism and Native American life.

TYPES OF POETRY

Here are the main forms of poetry:

Acrostic: The first letter, syllable or word of each line or stanza spells out a word/message.

Ballad: A poem that tells a story similar to a folk tale or legend.

Blank/free verse: A poem that does not rhyme, or follow a meter.

Burlesque poetry: In this a serious subject is treated with humour.

Couplet: A poem of two consecutive lines that rhyme.

Elegy: A sad poetic reflection about the death of a person.

Epic: A long serious poem, telling the story of a heroic figure.

Epitaph: A commemorative poem praising the deceased.

Haiku: A Japanese poem of three unrhymed lines of five, seven, and five syllables, usually with a reference to a 'season'.

Limerick: A short, humorous five-line poem.

Lyric: A poem that expresses the thoughts/feelings of the poet.

Narrative: A poem that tells a story.

Ode: A long meditative lyric, with a formal stanzaic structure.

Pastoral: It depicts rural life.

Rhyme: This repeats same or similar sounds in words at the end of lines.

Romantic: Poetry of nature and love.

Shape: A poem written in the shape of an object.

Sonnet: A lyric 14-line poem, with a formal rhyme scheme.

TYPES OF DRAMA

Drama is a work of fiction that is meant to be performed on stage, or acted out.

Epic: A long poem about heroism and events significant for a culture or nation. Oral or primary epics are handed down through the spoken word and written down after centuries. Examples are Greek epics, such as *The Iliad* and Indian epics like the Mahabharata. Literary epics are modern works such as John Milton's *Paradise Lost*.

Romance: Also known as chivalric romance, this deals with the courageous quests and adventures of a heroic individual, often a brave knight.

Tragicomedy: This describes work that blends elements of tragedy and comedy. Black (or serious/dark) comedy is also part of it.

Comedy: This includes parody, satire, burlesque, clowning and romantic comedy, among other types of comedy.

Tragedy: Coming from the poetic and religious traditions of ancient Greece, tragedy takes its inspiration from human suffering. Shakespeare's *Hamlet* and Sophocles's *Antigone* are examples.

CLI-FI OR CLIMATE FICTION IS A SUBGENRE OF SCIENCE FICTION THAT DEALS WITH THE GROWING CONCERN OVER GLOBAL WARMING.

BOOKS TO SCREEN

Coming soon to a screen, all these films are based on books!

- ***Dune (2023):*** Dennis Villeneuve's next instalment in the Dune Saga will hit theatres on 3 November 2023. Timothée Chalamet, returning as Paul Atreides, will deal with the fall of his family and join forces with Chani, played by Zendaya, and the Fremen to save the world.

- ***It Ends with Us (2024):*** Colleen Hoover's NYT bestseller is slated to hit the big screen on 9 February 2024. Stars Blake Lively, Justin Baldoni and Brandon Sklenar present a romance that tackles questions about love and relationships asked by many.

- ***Lessons in Chemistry (2023):*** This Bonnie Garmus book will premiere as an eight episode series on Apple TV+ on 13 October 2023. With Brie Larson in the lead, the series follows chemist Elizabeth Zott's struggle in the 1960s to survive in a male-dominated profession and how a cooking show challenged societal beliefs.

- ***Snow White and the Seven Dwarfs (2024):*** A new musical starring Rachel Zegler as Snow White opposite Gal Gadot as the Evil Queen will hit theatres on 22 March 2024. The film aims to both entertain and change a narrative that has been traditionalized for over two centuries.

- ***The Electric Slate (2024):*** This sci-fi adventure, based on Simon Stålenhag's artbook, follows Michelle and her robot as she hunts for her brother amidst a battle between humans and drones. The film will premiere on Netflix in 2024 with Millie Bobby Brown and Chris Pratt in the lead under the Russo Brothers' direction.

- ***Wicked (2024):*** Following the Broadway musical *Wicked*, the origin story of Gregory Maguire's 1995 character 'Wicked of the West' is set to be adapted into two films, the first of which will be released on 27 November 2024. The films will star Cynthia Erivo as Elphaba and Ariana Grande as Glinda under the direction of Jon M. Chu.

- ***Wonka (2023):*** Fans of Roald Dahl's *Charlie and the Chocolate Factory* can delve into the partnership between Willy Wonka and the Oompa Loompas in this prequel starring Timothée Chalamet as the quirky maker of equally quirky chocolates. The film will be available in Indian theatres on 29 December 2023.

Important International Organizations

- **ACP:** African, Caribbean and Pacific Group of States
- **ADB:** Asian Development Bank
- **AI:** Amnesty International
- **APEC:** Asia-Pacific Economic Cooperation
- **ASEAN:** Association of Southeast Asian Nations
- **EU:** European Union
- **IFAD:** International Fund for Agricultural Development
- **IFRC:** International Federation of Red Cross and Red Crescent Societies
- **IMSO:** International Mobile Satellite Organization
- **INTERPOL:** International Criminal Police Organization
- **IOC:** International Olympic Committee
- **ISO:** International Organization for Standardization
- **ITSO:** International Telecommunications Satellite Organization
- **ITU:** International Telecommunication Union
- **NAM:** Non-Aligned Movement
- **NATO:** North Atlantic Treaty Organization
- **OECD:** Organization for Economic Co-operation and Development
- **OPEC:** Organization of the Petroleum Exporting Countries
- **SAARC:** South Asian Association for Regional Cooperation
- **WMO:** World Meteorological Organization
- **WWF:** World Wide Fund for Nature

UN: The United Nations

UN Specialized Agencies:

- **ESCAP:** Economic and Social Commission for Asia and the Pacific
- **FAO:** Food and Agricultural Organization
- **IBRD:** International Bank for Reconstruction and Development
- **IDA:** International Development Association
- **ILO:** International Labour Organization
- **IMF:** International Monetary Fund
- **UNESCO:** United Nations Educational, Scientific and Cultural Organization
- **UNICEF:** United Nations Children's Fund
- **WHO:** World Health Organization
- **WIPO:** World Intellectual Property

NOTE: Includes sovereign states in the United Nations System. Time zones are calculated from the Greenwich Mean Time (GMT) and are mentioned in hours and minutes; GDP per capita is is approximate, in US dollars and based on the last figures available; Population figures are based on each country's last national census; Life expectancy figures are in years; Internet TLD stands for Internet Top Level Domain; Flags may not match exact proportions. All information updated up to 1 August 2023.

AFGHANISTAN

LOCATION: South-central Asia

CAPITAL: Kabul

AREA: 652,230 sq. km

LANGUAGES: Pashto, Dari

MAIN RELIGION: Islam

CURRENCY: Afghani

LITERACY RATE: 37.3%

LIFE EXPECTANCY: 54.05 years

TIME ZONE: +4.30

TYPE OF GOVERNMENT: Islamic Emirate

HEAD OF STATE AND GOVT: Mullah Haibatullah Akhundzada

GDP PER CAPITA: $1,500

POPULATION: 39,232,003

ISD CODE: 93 **INTERNET TLD:** .af

Since it gained Independence In 1919, Afghanistan's flag has been changed 26 times.

ALBANIA

LOCATION: South-east Europe

CAPITAL: Tirana

AREA: 28,748 sq. km

LANGUAGE: Albanian

MAIN RELIGION: Islam

CURRENCY: Lek

LITERACY RATE: 98.4%

LIFE EXPECTANCY: 79.7 years

TIME ZONE: +1

TYPE OF GOVERNMENT: Parliamentary Republic

HEAD OF STATE: President Bajram Begaj **HEAD OF GOVT:** Prime Minister Edi Rama

GDP PER CAPITA: $14,500

POPULATION: 3,101,621

ISD CODE: 355 **INTERNET TLD:** .al

Albania produces all of its electricity through hydropower or the use of water resources.

ALGERIA

LOCATION: North Africa

CAPITAL: Algiers

AREA: 2,381,741 sq. km

LANGUAGES: Arabic, French, Berber

MAIN RELIGION: Islam

CURRENCY: Algerian Dinar

LITERACY RATE: 81.4%

LIFE EXPECTANCY: 78.27 years

TIME ZONE: +1

TYPE OF GOVERNMENT: Presidential Republic

HEAD OF STATE: President Abdelmadjid Tebboune

HEAD OF GOVT: Prime Minister Ayman Benabderrahmane

GDP PER CAPITA: $11,000

POPULATION: 44,758,398

ISD CODE: 213 **INTERNET TLD:** .dz

In Algeria, petrol is cheaper than water.

Background: Algeria

ANDORRA

LOCATION: West Europe

CAPITAL: Andorra la Vella

AREA: 468 sq. km

LANGUAGES: Catalan, French, Castilian, Portuguese

MAIN RELIGION: Christianity

CURRENCY: Euro

LITERACY RATE: 100%

LIFE EXPECTANCY: 83.61 years

TIME ZONE: +1

TYPE OF GOVERNMENT: Parliamentary Democracy and Co-principality

HEAD OF STATE: Co-prince Emmanuel Macron and Co-prince Archbishop Joan-Enric Vives Sicilia

HEAD OF GOVT: Executive Council President Xavier Espot Zamora

GDP PER CAPITA: $49,900

POPULATION: 85,468

ISD CODE: 376

INTERNET TLD: .ad

Andorra has a small volunteer ceremonial army. Spain and France defend it with their armies.

ANGOLA

LOCATION: South-central Africa

CAPITAL: Luanda

AREA: 1,246,700 sq. km

LANGUAGES: Portuguese, Bantu, other African languages

MAIN RELIGIONS: Indigenous faiths, Christianity

CURRENCY: Kwanza

LITERACY RATE: 71.1%

LIFE EXPECTANCY: 62.51 years

TIME ZONE: +1

TYPE OF GOVERNMENT: Presidential Republic

HEAD OF STATE AND GOVT: President Joao Manuel Goncalves Lourenco

GDP PER CAPITA: $5,900

POPULATION: 35,981,281

ISD CODE: 244

INTERNET TLD: .ao

After its independence from Portugal in 1975, Angola went through a civil war for 27 years.

ANTIGUA AND BARBUDA

LOCATION: Central America

CAPITAL: Saint John's

AREA: 442.6 sq. km

LANGUAGE: English

MAIN RELIGION: Christianity

CURRENCY: East Caribbean Dollar

LITERACY RATE: 99%

LIFE EXPECTANCY: 78.04 years

TIME ZONE: –4

TYPE OF GOVERNMENT: Constitutional Monarchy and Parliamentary Democracy

HEAD OF STATE: King Charles III

HEAD OF GOVT: Prime Minister Gaston Browne

GDP PER CAPITA: $19,100

POPULATION: 101,489

ISD CODE: 1-268 **INTERNET TLD:** .ag

Antigua and Barbuda is often called the land of 365 beaches due to the beautiful and long coastline.

Background: Andorra

ARGENTINA

LOCATION: South America

CAPITAL: Buenos Aires

AREA: 2,780,400 sq. km

LANGUAGE: Spanish

MAIN RELIGION: Christianity

CURRENCY: Argentine Peso

LITERACY RATE: 99%

LIFE EXPECTANCY: 78.55 years

TIME ZONE: –3

TYPE OF GOVERNMENT: Presidential Republic

HEAD OF STATE AND GOVT: President Alberto Fernandez

GDP PER CAPITA: $21,500

POPULATION: 46,621,847

ISD CODE: 54 **INTERNET TLD:** .ar

The country is named after the Latin word *argentum*, which means 'silver' in English.

ARMENIA

LOCATION: South-western Asia, east of Turkey

CAPITAL: Yerevan

AREA: 29,743 sq. km

LANGUAGE: Armenian

MAIN RELIGION: Christianity

CURRENCY: Dram

LITERACY RATE: 99.8%

LIFE EXPECTANCY: 76.4 years

TIME ZONE: +4

TYPE OF GOVERNMENT: Parliamentary Democracy

HEAD OF STATE: President Vahagn Khachaturyan **HEAD OF GOVT:** Prime Minister Nikol Pashinyan

GDP PER CAPITA: $14,200

POPULATION: 2,989,091

ISD CODE: 374 **INTERNET TLD:** .am

One of the oldest centres of civilizations, Armenia was the first country in the world to officially embrace Christianity as its religion (c. 300 BCE).

AUSTRALIA

LOCATION: Between Indian Ocean and South Pacific Ocean

CAPITAL: Canberra

AREA: 7,741,220 sq. km

LANGUAGE: English

MAIN RELIGION: Christianity

CURRENCY: Australian Dollar

LITERACY RATE: 100%

LIFE EXPECTANCY: 83.28 years

TIME ZONE: +8 to +10.30

TYPE OF GOVERNMENT: Constitutional Monarchy and Federal Parliamentary Democracy

HEAD OF STATE: King Charles III
HEAD OF GOVT: Prime Minister Anthony Albanese

GDP PER CAPITA: $49,800

POPULATION: 26,461,166

ISD CODE: 61
INTERNET TLD: .au

Each year, Brisbane, a city in Australia, hosts the world championships of cockroach racing.

Background: Australia

AUSTRIA

LOCATION: Central Europe

CAPITAL: Vienna

AREA: 83,871sq. km

LANGUAGE: German

MAIN RELIGION: Christianity

CURRENCY: Euro

LITERACY RATE: 99%

LIFE EXPECTANCY: 82.48 years

TIME ZONE: +1

TYPE OF GOVERNMENT: Federal Parliamentary Republic

HEAD OF STATE: President Alexander Van der Bellen

HEAD OF GOVT: Chancellor Karl Nehammer

GDP PER CAPITA: $54,100

POPULATION: 8,940,860

ISD CODE: 43 **INTERNET TLD:** .at

The first woman to win the Nobel Peace Prize in 1905, Bertha von Suttner, was from Austria.

AZERBAIJAN

LOCATION: West Asia, bordering Caspian Sea

CAPITAL: Baku

AREA: 86,600 sq. km

LANGUAGE: Azerbaijani

MAIN RELIGION: Islam

CURRENCY: Azerbaijani Manat

LITERACY RATE: 99.8%

LIFE EXPECTANCY: 74.42 years

TIME ZONE: +4

TYPE OF GOVERNMENT: Presidential Republic

HEAD OF STATE: President Ilham Aliyev

HEAD OF GOVT: Prime Minister Ali Hidayat oglu Asadov

GDP PER CAPITA: $14,400

POPULATION: 10,420,515

ISD CODE: 994 **INTERNET TLD:** .az

The 'burning mountain' is a rare natural wonder in the Absheron Peninsula. It 'burns' all year due to natural gas escaping from the ground.

(THE) BAHAMAS

LOCATION: Central America

CAPITAL: Nassau

AREA: 13,880 sq. km

LANGUAGES: English, Creole

MAIN RELIGION: Christianity

CURRENCY: Bahamian Dollar

LITERACY RATE: 99%

LIFE EXPECTANCY: 76.38 years

TIME ZONE: –5

TYPE OF GOVERNMENT: Constitutional Monarchy and Parliamentary Democracy

HEAD OF STATE: King Charles III

HEAD OF GOVT: Prime Minister Philip Davis

GDP PER CAPITA: $30,200

POPULATION: 358,508

ISD CODE: 1-242

INTERNET TLD: .bs

The word 'Bahamas' comes from the Spanish *bajamar*, meaning 'shallow water'. The archipelago has nearly 700 islands, with only about 30 inhabited ones.

BAHRAIN

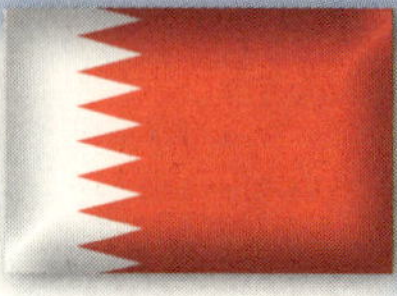

LOCATION: South-central Asia

CAPITAL: Manama

AREA: 760 sq. km

LANGUAGES: Arabic, English, Farsi, Urdu

MAIN RELIGION: Islam

CURRENCY: Bahraini Dinar

LITERACY RATE: 97.5%

LIFE EXPECTANCY: 80.13 years

TIME ZONE: +3

TYPE OF GOVERNMENT: Constitutional Monarchy

HEAD OF STATE: King Hamad bin Isa Al Khalifah **HEAD OF GOVT:** Prime Minister Khalifah bin Salman Al Khalifah

GDP PER CAPITA: $49,400

POPULATION: 1,553,886

ISD CODE: 973 **INTERNET TLD:** .bh

The Bahraini dollar is the world's second highest valued currency after the American dollar.

BANGLADESH

LOCATION: South Asia

CAPITAL: Dhaka

AREA: 148,460 sq. km

LANGUAGE: Bangla (Bengali)

MAIN RELIGION: Islam

CURRENCY: Taka

LITERACY RATE: 74.9%

LIFE EXPECTANCY: 74.96 years

TIME ZONE: +6

TYPE OF GOVERNMENT: Parliamentary Republic

HEAD OF STATE: Mohammed Shahabuddin

HEAD OF GOVT: Prime Minister Sheikh Hasina Wajed

GDP PER CAPITA: $5,900

POPULATION: 167,184,465

ISD CODE: 880 **INTERNET TLD:** .bd

Bangladesh is blessed with deep, rich and fertile soil from the three rivers – the Ganga, the Brahmaputra and the Meghna – that form the deltaic plain upon which it sits.

BARBADOS

LOCATION: Caribbean Sea

CAPITAL: Bridgetown

AREA: 430 sq. km

LANGUAGE: English

MAIN RELIGION: Christianity

CURRENCY: Barbadian Dollar

LITERACY RATE: 99.6%

LIFE EXPECTANCY: 78.79 years

TIME ZONE: –4

TYPE OF GOVERNMENT: Parliamentary Republic

HEAD OF STATE: President Sandra Mason **HEAD OF GOVT:** Prime Minister Mia Mottley

GDP PER CAPITA: $13,800

POPULATION: 303,431

ISD CODE: 1-246 **INTERNET TLD:** .bb

Local people frequently refer to their country as 'Bim' casually. The name comes from the Igbo word *bém*, which means 'my home' in English.

Background: Barbados

BELARUS

LOCATION: Eastern Europe

CAPITAL: Minsk

AREA: 207,600 sq. km

LANGUAGES: Belarusian, Russian

MAIN RELIGION: Christianity (Russian Orthodox Church)

CURRENCY: Belarusian Ruble

LITERACY RATE: 99.9%

LIFE EXPECTANCY: 74.54 years

TIME ZONE: +2

TYPE OF GOVERNMENT: Presidential Republic

HEAD OF STATE: President Alexander Lukashenko **HEAD OF GOVT:** Prime Minister Roman Golovchenko

GDP PER CAPITA: $19,800

POPULATION: 9,383,853

ISD CODE: 375 **INTERNET TLD:** .by

There are more than 20,000 rivers in Belarus.

BELGIUM

LOCATION: North-west Europe

CAPITAL: Brussels

AREA: 30,528 sq. km

LANGUAGES: Dutch, French, German

MAIN RELIGION: Christianity

CURRENCY: Euro

LITERACY RATE: 99%

LIFE EXPECTANCY: 82.06 years

TIME ZONE: +1

TYPE OF GOVERNMENT: Constitutional Monarchy and Parliamentary Democracy

HEAD OF STATE: King Philippe **HEAD OF GOVT:** Prime Minister Alexander De Croo

GDP PER CAPITA: $51,700

POPULATION: 11,913,633

ISD CODE: 32

INTERNET TLD: .be

Belgium produces nearly 220,000 tonnes of chocolate every year. The country is also famous for waffles.

BELIZE

LOCATION: Central America

CAPITAL: Belmopan

AREA: 22,966 sq. km

LANGUAGES: English, Creole, Spanish

MAIN RELIGION: Christianity

CURRENCY: Belize Dollar

LITERACY RATE: 82.7%

LIFE EXPECTANCY: 76.08 years

TIME ZONE: –6

TYPE OF GOVERNMENT: Constitutional Monarchy and Parliamentary Democracy

HEAD OF STATE: King Charles III **HEAD OF GOVT:** Prime Minister Johnny Briceno

GDP PER CAPITA: $8,800

POPULATION: 419,137

ISD CODE: 501 **INTERNET TLD:** .bz

The motto of the country is 'Under the shade, I flourish' due to it being covered with rainforests.

Background: Belgium

BENIN

LOCATION: West Africa

CAPITAL: Porto Novo

AREA: 112,622 sq. km

LANGUAGES: French, Fon, other African languages

MAIN RELIGIONS: Indigenous faiths, Christianity, Islam

CURRENCY: CFA Franc

LITERACY RATE: 45.8%

LIFE EXPECTANCY: 62.6 years

TIME ZONE: +1

TYPE OF GOVERNMENT: Presidential Republic

HEAD OF STATE AND GOVT: President Patrice Talon

GDP PER CAPITA: $3,300

POPULATION: 14,219,908

ISD CODE: 229

INTERNET TLD: .bj

Benin's name comes from a large body of water called 'The Bight of Benin'.

BHUTAN

LOCATION: South Asia

CAPITAL: Thimphu

AREA: 38,394 sq. km

LANGUAGES: Dzongkha, Sharchhopka

MAIN RELIGION: Buddhism

CURRENCY: Ngultrum

LITERACY RATE: 70.9%

LIFE EXPECTANCY: 73.01 years

TIME ZONE: +6

TYPE OF GOVERNMENT: Constitutional Monarchy

HEAD OF STATE: King Jigme Khesar Namgyel Wangchuck **HEAD OF GOVT:** Prime Minister Lotay Tshering

GDP PER CAPITA: $10,900

POPULATION: 876,181

ISD CODE: 975 **INTERNET TLD:** .bt

Bhutan was one of the last countries to introduce television to its people. The government lifted the ban on TV in 1999.

BOLIVIA

LOCATION: Central South America

CAPITAL: La Paz

AREA: 1,098,581 sq. km

LANGUAGES: Spanish, Quechua, Aymara, Guarani

MAIN RELIGION: Christianity

CURRENCY: Boliviano

LITERACY RATE: 92.5%

LIFE EXPECTANCY: 72.5 years

TIME ZONE: –4

TYPE OF GOVERNMENT: Presidential Republic

HEAD OF STATE AND GOVT: President Luis Arce

GDP PER CAPITA: $8,100

POPULATION: 12,186,079

ISD CODE: 591 **INTERNET TLD:** .bo

Lake Titicaca in the Andes is the highest navigable lake in the world, at 3,810 m (12,500 ft) above sea level.

Background: Brazil

BOSNIA AND HERZEGOVINA

LOCATION: South-east Europe

CAPITAL: Sarajevo

AREA: 51,197 sq. km

LANGUAGES: Bosnian, Croatian, Serbian

MAIN RELIGIONS: Christianity, Islam

CURRENCY: Convertible Mark

LITERACY RATE: 98.1%

LIFE EXPECTANCY: 78.22 years

TIME ZONE: +1

TYPE OF GOVERNMENT: Parliamentary Republic

HEAD OF STATE: Chairman of Presidency Zeljko Komsic **HEAD OF GOVT:** Chairman of Council of Ministers Borjana Krišto

GDP PER CAPITA: $15,700

POPULATION: 3,807,764

ISD CODE: 387 **INTERNET TLD:** .ba

The capital city Sarajevo was the first city in Europe with a full-time electric tram.

BOTSWANA

LOCATION: Southern Africa

CAPITAL: Gaborone

AREA: 581,730 sq. km

LANGUAGES: English, Setswana, Kalanga

MAIN RELIGION: Christianity

CURRENCY: Pula

LITERACY RATE: 88.5%

LIFE EXPECTANCY: 66.04 years

TIME ZONE: +2

TYPE OF GOVERNMENT: Parliamentary Republic

HEAD OF STATE AND GOVT: President Mokgweetsi Eric Masisi

GDP PER CAPITA: $14,800

POPULATION: 2,417,596

ISD CODE: 267

INTERNET TLD: .bw

The Okavango Delta was declared as one of the 7 Natural Wonders of Africa in 2013.

BRAZIL

LOCATION: North-east South America

CAPITAL: Brasilia

AREA: 8,515,710 sq. km

LANGUAGES: Portuguese

MAIN RELIGION: Christianity

CURRENCY: Real

LITERACY RATE: 94.3%

LIFE EXPECTANCY: 76.1 years

TIME ZONE: –3

TYPE OF GOVERNMENT: Presidential Federal Republic

HEAD OF STATE AND GOVT: President Luiz Inacio Lula da Silva

GDP PER CAPITA: $14,600

POPULATION: 218,689,757

ISD CODE: 55

INTERNET TLD: .br

Brazil is home to 60 per cent of the Amazon rainforest.

BRUNEI

LOCATION: South-east Asia

CAPITAL: Bandar Seri Begawan

AREA: 5,765 sq. km

LANGUAGE: Malay

MAIN RELIGION: Islam

CURRENCY: Brunei Dollar

LITERACY RATE: 97.6%

LIFE EXPECTANCY: 78.61 years

TIME ZONE: +8

TYPE OF GOVERNMENT: Islamic Absolute Monarchy

HEAD OF STATE AND GOVT: Sultan Hassanal Bolkiah

GDP PER CAPITA: $60,100

POPULATION: 484,991

ISD CODE: 673 **INTERNET TLD:** .bn

The Istana Nurul Iman Palace in Brunei is reportedly the largest residential palace in the world, with 1,788 rooms and 257 bathrooms.

BULGARIA

LOCATION: South-east Europe

CAPITAL: Sofia

AREA: 110,879 sq. km

LANGUAGE: Bulgarian

MAIN RELIGION: Christianity

CURRENCY: Lev

LITERACY RATE: 98.4%

LIFE EXPECTANCY: 75.83 years

TIME ZONE: +2

TYPE OF GOVERNMENT: Parliamentary Republic

HEAD OF STATE: President Rumen Radev **HEAD OF GOVT:** Prime Minister Nikolay Denkov

GDP PER CAPITA: $24,400

POPULATION: 6,827,736

ISD CODE: 359 **INTERNET TLD:** .bg

The first Bulgarian Empire was established in 681 CE, and the name 'Bulgaria' hasn't changed since, making it the only country in Europe to never have changed its name.

BURKINA FASO

LOCATION: West Africa

CAPITAL: Ouagadougou

AREA: 274,200 sq. km

LANGUAGES: French, indigenous African languages

MAIN RELIGION: Islam

CURRENCY: CFA Franc

LITERACY RATE: 46%

LIFE EXPECTANCY: 63.82 years

TIME ZONE: 0

TYPE OF GOVERNMENT: Presidential Republic

HEAD OF STATE: President Capt Ibrahim Traoré **HEAD OF GOVT:** Prime Minister Albert Ouedraogo

GDP PER CAPITA: $2,200

POPULATION: 22,489,126

ISD CODE: 226

INTERNET TLD: .bf

The phrase 'Burkina Faso' means 'Land of the Honest (Incorruptible) Men.'

BURUNDI

LOCATION: Central Africa

CAPITAL: Bujumbura

AREA: 27,830 sq. km

LANGUAGES: Kirundi, French, Swahili

MAIN RELIGION: Christianity

CURRENCY: Burundi Franc

LITERACY RATE: 74.7%

LIFE EXPECTANCY: 67.77 years

TIME ZONE: +2

TYPE OF GOVERNMENT: Presidential Republic

HEAD OF STATE: President Evariste Ndayishimiye **HEAD OF GOVT:** President Evariste Ndayishimiye

GDP PER CAPITA: $700

POPULATION: 13,162,952

ISD CODE: 257 **INTERNET TLD:** .bi

The world's longest freshwater lake, Lake Tanganyika, is in Burundi. It stretches up to 673 km.

CABO VERDE

LOCATION: North Atlantic Ocean, off West Africa

CAPITAL: Praia

AREA: 4,033 sq. km

LANGUAGES: Portuguese, Creole

MAIN RELIGION: Christianity

CURRENCY: Cape Verdean Escudo

LITERACY RATE: 90.8%

LIFE EXPECTANCY: 74.02 years

TIME ZONE: –1

TYPE OF GOVERNMENT: Parliamentary Republic

HEAD OF STATE: President Jose Maria Neves **HEAD OF GOVT:** Prime Minister José Ulisses Correia e Silva

GDP PER CAPITA: $6,100

POPULATION: 603,901

ISD CODE: 238 **INTERNET TLD:** .cv

Only four of Cabo Verde's 10 main islands have agriculture, producing over 90 per cent of the country's food.

CAMBODIA

LOCATION: South-east Asia

CAPITAL: Phnom Penh

AREA: 181,035 sq. km

LANGUAGES: Khmer, French

MAIN RELIGION: Theravada Buddhism

CURRENCY: Riel

LITERACY RATE: 83.9%

LIFE EXPECTANCY: 71.03 years

TIME ZONE: +7

TYPE OF GOVERNMENT: Parliamentary Constitutional Monarchy

HEAD OF STATE: King Norodom Sihamoni **HEAD OF GOVT:** Prime Minister Hun Sen

GDP PER CAPITA: $4,400

POPULATION: 16,891,245

ISD CODE: 855 **INTERNET TLD:** .kh

The Cambodian flag is the only flag in the world to feature a building – the Angkor Wat Temple.

Background: Cabo Verde

CAMEROON

LOCATION: Central Africa

CAPITAL: Yaounde

AREA: 475,440 sq. km

LANGUAGES: French, English, African languages

MAIN RELIGIONS: Indigenous faiths, Christianity, Islam

CURRENCY: CFA Franc

LITERACY RATE: 77.1%

LIFE EXPECTANCY: 63.74 years

TIME ZONE: +1

TYPE OF GOVERNMENT: Presidential Republic

HEAD OF STATE: President Paul Biya

HEAD OF GOVT: Prime Minister Joseph Dion Ngute

GDP PER CAPITA: $3,700

POPULATION: 30,135,732

ISD CODE: 237

INTERNET TLD: .cm

Cameroon is home to the Goliath frog, the world's largest frog, with a length of 33 cm and weighing up to 3.25 kg.

CANADA

LOCATION: North America

CAPITAL: Ottawa

AREA: 9,984,670 sq. km

LANGUAGES: English, French

MAIN RELIGION: Christianity

CURRENCY: Canadian Dollar

LITERACY RATE: 99%

LIFE EXPECTANCY: 83.99 years

TIME ZONE: –3.30 to –8

TYPE OF GOVERNMENT: Constitutional Monarchy and Federal Parliamentary Democracy

HEAD OF STATE: King Charles III

HEAD OF GOVT: Prime Minister Justin Trudeau

GDP PER CAPITA: $47,900

POPULATION: 38,516,736

ISD CODE: 1 **INTERNET TLD:** .ca

More than half of all the lakes in the world are located in Canada, including two of the biggest lakes in the world – Great Bear Lake and Great Slave Lake.

CENTRAL AFRICAN REPUBLIC

LOCATION: Central Africa

CAPITAL: Bangui

AREA: 622,984 sq. km

LANGUAGES: French, Sangho, Arabic, Hansa

MAIN RELIGIONS: Indigenous faiths, Christianity, Islam

CURRENCY: CFA Franc

LITERACY RATE: 37.4%

LIFE EXPECTANCY: 55.96 years

TIME ZONE: +1

TYPE OF GOVERNMENT: Presidential Republic

HEAD OF STATE: President Faustin-Archange Touadera **HEAD OF GOVT:** Prime Minister Felix Moloua

GDP PER CAPITA: $800

POPULATION: 5,552,228

ISD CODE: 236 **INTERNET TLD:** .cf

In the 1880s, when the French colonized this area, they named it Oubangui-Chari as most of it is located in the Oubangui and Chari river basins.

Background: Chile

CHAD

LOCATION: North-central Africa

CAPITAL: N'Djamena

AREA: 1,284,000 sq. km

LANGUAGES: French, Arabic

MAIN RELIGIONS: Islam, Christianity

CURRENCY: CFA Franc

LITERACY RATE: 26.8%

LIFE EXPECTANCY: 59.57 years

TIME ZONE: +1

TYPE OF GOVERNMENT: Presidential Republic

HEAD OF STATE: Interim President Mahamat Idriss Deby Itno (Chairman, Transitional Military Council)

HEAD OF GOVT: Prime Minister Albert Pahimi Padacke

GDP PER CAPITA: $1,400

POPULATION: 18,523,165

ISD CODE: 235 **INTERNET TLD:** .td

Chad is called the 'Dead Heart of Africa' because of its harsh and inhospitable climate.

CHILE

LOCATION: South America

CAPITAL: Santiago

AREA: 756,102 sq. km

LANGUAGE: Spanish

MAIN RELIGION: Christianity

CURRENCY: Chilean Peso

LITERACY RATE: 97%

LIFE EXPECTANCY: 80.02 years

TIME ZONE: –3

TYPE OF GOVERNMENT: Presidential Republic

HEAD OF STATE AND GOVT: President Gabriel Boric

GDP PER CAPITA: $25,400

POPULATION: 18,549,457

ISD CODE: 56 **INTERNET TLD:** .cl

Chile is the longest and narrowest country in the world. It is 4,300 km long and just 175 km wide (on average).

CHINA

LOCATION: East Asia

CAPITAL: Beijing

AREA: 9,596,961 sq. km

LANGUAGES: Mandarin, Cantonese

MAIN RELIGIONS: Atheism (official), Taoism, Buddhism

CURRENCY: Renminbi

LITERACY RATE: 96.8%

LIFE EXPECTANCY: 78.23 years

TIME ZONE: +8

TYPE OF GOVERNMENT: Communist/ Single-party state

HEAD OF STATE: President Xi Jinping

HEAD OF GOVT: Premier Li Qiang

GDP PER CAPITA: $17,600

POPULATION: 1,413,142,846

ISD CODE: 86 **INTERNET TLD:** .cn

The Chinese invented the compass, gunpowder, ice cream and toilet paper. The last invention was used only by emperors.

COLOMBIA

LOCATION: North-west South America

CAPITAL: Bogota

AREA: 1,138,910 sq. km

LANGUAGE: Spanish

MAIN RELIGION: Christianity

CURRENCY: Colombian Peso

LITERACY RATE: 95.6%

LIFE EXPECTANCY: 74.89 years

TIME ZONE: –5

TYPE OF GOVERNMENT: Presidential Republic

HEAD OF STATE AND GOVT: President Gustavo Francisco Petro

GDP PER CAPITA: $14,600

POPULATION: 49,336,454

ISD CODE: 57 **INTERNET TLD:** .co

The river Cano Cristales in La Macarena is known to change colours. It is also called the 'Rainbow River'.

COMOROS

LOCATION: Southern Africa

CAPITAL: Moroni

AREA: 2,235 sq. km

LANGUAGES: Arabic, French, Shikomoro

MAIN RELIGION: Islam

CURRENCY: Comorian Franc

LITERACY RATE: 62%

LIFE EXPECTANCY: 67.5 years

TIME ZONE: +3

TYPE OF GOVERNMENT: Federal Presidential Republic

HEAD OF STATE AND GOVT: President Azali Assoumani

GDP PER CAPITA: $3,200

POPULATION: 888,378

ISD CODE: 269 **INTERNET TLD:** .km

Comoros is called the 'Perfume Isles' because of its fragrant ylang-ylang flower whose oil is a major export traditionally.

(DEMOCRATIC REPUBLIC OF THE) CONGO

LOCATION: Central Africa

CAPITAL: Kinshasa

AREA: 2,344,858 sq. km

LANGUAGE: French

MAIN RELIGION: Christianity

CURRENCY: Congolese Franc

LITERACY RATE: 80%

LIFE EXPECTANCY: 62.23 years

TIME ZONE: +1

TYPE OF GOVERNMENT: Semi-presidential Republic

HEAD OF STATE: President Félix-Antoine Tshisekedi Tshilombo **HEAD OF GOVT:** Prime Minister Jean-Michel Sama Lukonde

GDP PER CAPITA: $1,100

POPULATION: 111,859,928

ISD CODE: 243

INTERNET TLD: .cd

The River Congo and its tributaries provide 12,800 km of waterway for transportation in the country. This is vital for the shipment of goods.

Background: Comoros

(REPUBLIC OF THE) CONGO

LOCATION: Central Africa

CAPITAL: Brazzaville

AREA: 342,000 sq. km

LANGUAGES: French, Lingala, Monokutuba, other African languages

MAIN RELIGION: Christianity

CURRENCY: CFA Franc

LITERACY RATE: 80.6%

LIFE EXPECTANCY: 62.51 years

TIME ZONE: +2

TYPE OF GOVERNMENT: Presidential Republic

HEAD OF STATE: President Denis Sassou-Nguesso **HEAD OF GOVT:** Prime Minister Anatole Collinet Makosso

GDP PER CAPITA: $3,200

POPULATION: 5,677,493

ISD CODE: 242 **INTERNET TLD:** .cg

For its size, the Republic of Congo has a large number of languages, with up to 62 recognized spoken languages, and many more dialects.

COSTA RICA

LOCATION: Central America

CAPITAL: San Jose

AREA: 51,100 sq. km

LANGUAGE: Spanish

MAIN RELIGION: Christianity

CURRENCY: Costa Rican Colon

LITERACY RATE: 98%

LIFE EXPECTANCY: 79.87 years

TIME ZONE: –6

TYPE OF GOVERNMENT: Presidential Republic

HEAD OF STATE AND GOVT: President Rodrigo Chaves Robles

GDP PER CAPITA: $21,200

POPULATION: 5,256,612

ISD CODE: 506

INTERNET TLD: .cr

The 'yiguirro', a clay- coloured thrush, is Costa Rica's national symbol.

COTE D'IVOIRE

LOCATION: Western Africa

CAPITAL: Yamoussoukro

AREA: 322,463 sq. km

LANGUAGES: French, Dioula

MAIN RELIGIONS: Islam, Christianity

CURRENCY: CFA Franc

LITERACY RATE: 89.9%

LIFE EXPECTANCY: 62.71 years

TIME ZONE: 0

TYPE OF GOVERNMENT: Presidential Republic

HEAD OF STATE: President Alassane Ouattara **HEAD OF GOVT:** Prime Minister Patrick Jerome Achi

GDP PER CAPITA: $5,300

POPULATION: 29,344,847

ISD CODE: 225 **INTERNET TLD:** .ci

Elephants are facing extinction in Cote d'Ivoire, once famous for its ivory trade. Its national football team is known as 'Les Elephants', meaning 'The Elephants'.

Background: Costa Rica

CROATIA

LOCATION: South-east Europe

CAPITAL: Zagreb

AREA: 56,594 sq. km

LANGUAGE: Croatian

MAIN RELIGION: Christianity

CURRENCY: Euro

LITERACY RATE: 99.4%

LIFE EXPECTANCY: 77.47 years

TIME ZONE: +1

TYPE OF GOVERNMENT: Parliamentary Republic

HEAD OF STATE: President Zoran Milanovic **HEAD OF GOVT:** Prime Minister Andrej Plenkovic

GDP PER CAPITA: $26,500

POPULATION: 4,169,239

ISD CODE: 385 **INTERNET TLD:** .hr

In 2019, Croatia became the youngest member of the European Parliament.

CUBA

LOCATION: Central America

CAPITAL: Havana

AREA: 110,860 sq. km

LANGUAGE: Spanish

MAIN RELIGION: Christianity

CURRENCY: Cuban Peso

LITERACY RATE: 99.7%

LIFE EXPECTANCY: 79.96 years

TIME ZONE: –5

TYPE OF GOVERNMENT: Communist/ Single-party Republic

HEAD OF STATE: President Miguel Diaz-Canel **HEAD OF GOVT:** Prime Minister Manuel Marrero Cruz

GDP PER CAPITA: $12,300

POPULATION: 10,985,974

ISD CODE: 53 **INTERNET TLD:** .cu

Cubans refer to their island as 'El Cocodrilo' because when viewed from above, it resembles a crocodile.

CYPRUS

LOCATION: Mediterranean

CAPITAL: Nicosia

AREA: 9,251 sq. km

LANGUAGES: Greek, Turkish

MAIN RELIGION: Christianity (Greek Orthodox Church)

CURRENCY: Euro

LITERACY RATE: 99.4%

LIFE EXPECTANCY: 96 years

TIME ZONE: +2

TYPE OF GOVERNMENT: Presidential Republic

HEAD OF STATE AND GOVT: President Nikos Christodoulides

GDP PER CAPITA: $41,700

POPULATION: 1,308,120

ISD CODE: 357 **INTERNET TLD:** .cy

The Cyprus mouflon is a kind of wild sheep that was originally found only in Cyprus.

Background: Croatia

CZECHIA

LOCATION: Central Europe

CAPITAL: Prague

AREA: 78,867 sq. km

LANGUAGE: Czech

MAIN RELIGION: Christianity

CURRENCY: Czech Koruna

LITERACY RATE: 99%

LIFE EXPECTANCY: 79.96 years

TIME ZONE: +1

TYPE OF GOVERNMENT: Parliamentary Republic

HEAD OF STATE: President Petr Pavel **HEAD OF GOVT:** Prime Minister Petr Fiala

GDP PER CAPITA: $40,700

POPULATION: 10,706,242

ISD CODE: 420 **INTERNET TLD:** .cz

Prague is also called 'the city of a hundred spires'.

DENMARK

LOCATION: North Europe

CAPITAL: Copenhagen

AREA: 43,094 sq. km

LANGUAGE: Danish

MAIN RELIGION: Christianity (Evangelical Lutheran church)

CURRENCY: Danish Krone

LITERACY RATE: 99%

LIFE EXPECTANCY: 81.87 years

TIME ZONE: +1

TYPE OF GOVERNMENT: Parliamentary Constitutional Monarchy

HEAD OF STATE: Queen Margrethe II **HEAD OF GOVT:** Prime Minister Mette Frederiksen

GDP PER CAPITA: $58,000

POPULATION: 5,946,984

ISD CODE: 45 **INTERNET TLD:** .dk

There are 443 named islands in the Danish archipelago and only 76 of these are inhabited.

DJIBOUTI

LOCATION: East Africa

CAPITAL: Djibouti City

AREA: 23,200 sq. km

LANGUAGES: French, Arabic

MAIN RELIGION: Islam

CURRENCY: Djiboutian Franc

LITERACY RATE: 70%

LIFE EXPECTANCY: 65.61 years

TIME ZONE: +3

TYPE OF GOVERNMENT: Presidential Republic

HEAD OF STATE: President Ismail Omar Guelleh **HEAD OF GOVT:** Prime Minister Abdoulkader Kamil Mohamed

GDP PER CAPITA: $4,900

POPULATION: 976,143

ISD CODE: 253 **INTERNET TLD:** .dj

Lake Assal in Djibouti lies 156 m (512 ft) below sea level, making it the lowest point in Africa.

Background: Denmark

DOMINICA

LOCATION: Central America

CAPITAL: Roseau

AREA: 751 sq. km

LANGUAGES: English, French

MAIN RELIGION: Christianity

CURRENCY: East Caribbean Dollar

LITERACY RATE: 95.47%

LIFE EXPECTANCY: 78.45 years

TIME ZONE: –4

TYPE OF GOVERNMENT: Parliamentary Republic

HEAD OF STATE: President Charles Savarin **HEAD OF GOVT:** Prime Minister Roosevelt Skerrit

GDP PER CAPITA: $10,900

POPULATION: 74,656

ISD CODE: 1-767 **INTERNET TLD:** .dm

Christopher Columbus came to this island in 1493 on a Sunday. That's why he called it 'Dominica', meaning Sunday in Latin.

DOMINICAN REPUBLIC

LOCATION: Central America

CAPITAL: Santo Domingo

AREA: 48,670 sq. km

LANGUAGE: Spanish

MAIN RELIGION: Christianity

CURRENCY: Dominican Peso

LITERACY RATE: 95.2%

LIFE EXPECTANCY: 72.84 years

TIME ZONE: –4

TYPE OF GOVERNMENT: Presidential Republic

HEAD OF STATE AND GOVT: President Luis Abinader

GDP PER CAPITA: $18,600

POPULATION: 10,790,744

ISD CODE: 809 **INTERNET TLD:** .do

The oldest extant cathedral in the Americas is in Santo Domingo – the Cathedral of Santa Maria la Menor. Its construction began in 1512.

ECUADOR

LOCATION: Western South America

CAPITAL: Quito

AREA: 283,561 sq. km

LANGUAGE: Spanish

MAIN RELIGION: Christianity

CURRENCY: US Dollar

LITERACY RATE: 94.5%

LIFE EXPECTANCY: 78.25 years

TIME ZONE: –5

TYPE OF GOVERNMENT: Presidential Republic

HEAD OF STATE AND GOVT: President Guillermo Lasso

GDP PER CAPITA: $10,700

POPULATION: 17,483,326

ISD CODE: 593 **INTERNET TLD:** .ec

Ecuador is one of 13 countries through which the Equator passes.

EGYPT

LOCATION: North Africa

CAPITAL: Cairo

AREA: 1,001,450 sq. km

LANGUAGES: Arabic, English, French

MAIN RELIGION: Islam

CURRENCY: Egyptian Pound

LITERACY RATE: 73.1%

LIFE EXPECTANCY: 74.72 years

TIME ZONE: +2

TYPE OF GOVERNMENT: Presidential Republic

HEAD OF STATE: President Abdel Fattah el-Sisi **HEAD OF GOVT:** Prime Minister Mostafa Madbouly

GDP PER CAPITA: $11,600

POPULATION: 109,546,720

ISD CODE: 20 **INTERNET TLD:** .eg

The Great Pyramid of Giza in Egypt is the only existing ancient wonder of the world.

EL SALVADOR

LOCATION: Central America

CAPITAL: San Salvador

AREA: 21,041 sq. km

LANGUAGE: Spanish

MAIN RELIGION: Christianity

CURRENCY: US Dollar

LITERACY RATE: 89.1%

LIFE EXPECTANCY: 75.63 years

TIME ZONE: –6

TYPE OF GOVERNMENT: Presidential Republic

HEAD OF STATE AND GOVT: President Nayib Bukele

GDP PER CAPITA: $9,100

POPULATION: 6,602,370

ISD CODE: 503 **INTERNET TLD:** .sv

El Salvador, a country with 21 volcanoes, was in an infamous 100-hour war with neighbouring Honduras, over a soccer game in 1969.

EQUATORIAL GUINEA

LOCATION: Central Africa

CAPITAL: Malabo

AREA: 28,051 sq. km

LANGUAGES: Spanish, French

MAIN RELIGION: Christianity

CURRENCY: CFA Franc

LITERACY RATE: 95.3%

LIFE EXPECTANCY: 63.8 years

TIME ZONE: +1

TYPE OF GOVERNMENT: Presidential Republic

HEAD OF STATE: President Teodoro Obiang Nguema Mbasogo **HEAD OF GOVT:** Prime Minister Manuela Roka Botey

GDP PER CAPITA: $14,600

POPULATION: 1,737,695

ISD CODE: 240 **INTERNET TLD:** .gq

Equatorial Guinea is the smallest African country that is a member of the United Nations.

Background: Egypt

ERITREA

LOCATION: East Africa

CAPITAL: Asmara

AREA: 117,600 sq. km

LANGUAGES: Tigrinya, Arabic, English

MAIN RELIGIONS: Islam, Christianity

CURRENCY: Eritrean Nakfa

LITERACY RATE: 76.6%

LIFE EXPECTANCY: 67.19 years

TIME ZONE: +3

TYPE OF GOVERNMENT: Presidential Republic

HEAD OF STATE AND GOVT: President Isaias Afwerki

GDP PER CAPITA: $1,600

POPULATION: 6,274,796

ISD CODE: 291 **INTERNET TLD:** .er

A one-party nation, the country has not held national or presidential elections since independence in 1993.

ESTONIA

LOCATION: East Europe

CAPITAL: Tallinn

AREA: 45,228 sq. km

LANGUAGE: Estonian, Russian

MAIN RELIGION: Christianity

CURRENCY: Euro

LITERACY RATE: 99.9%

LIFE EXPECTANCY: 78.12 years

TIME ZONE: +2

TYPE OF GOVERNMENT: Parliamentary Republic

HEAD OF STATE: President Alar Keris
HEAD OF GOVT: Prime Minister Kaja Kallas

GDP PER CAPITA: $38,700

POPULATION: 1,202,762

ISD CODE: 372 **INTERNET TLD:** .ee

Estonia has the highest number of meteorite craters per square kilometre in the world.

ESWATINI

LOCATION: Southern Africa

CAPITAL: Mbabane

AREA: 17,364 sq. km

LANGUAGES: English, Swati

MAIN RELIGIONS: Christianity, Islam

CURRENCY: Lilangeni; South African Rand

LITERACY RATE: 88.4%

LIFE EXPECTANCY: 60.22 years

TIME ZONE: +2

TYPE OF GOVERNMENT: Absolute Monarchy

HEAD OF STATE: King Mswati III
HEAD OF GOVT: Prime Minister Cleopas Dlamini

GDP PER CAPITA: $8,900

POPULATION: 1,130,043

ISD CODE: 268 **INTERNET TLD:** .sz

In 2018, King Mswati III renamed Swaziland as 'Kingdom of Eswatini'. It means 'land of the Swazis'.

Background: Estonia

ETHIOPIA

LOCATION: East Africa

CAPITAL: Addis Ababa

AREA: 1,104,300 sq. km

LANGUAGES: Amharic, Oromo

MAIN RELIGIONS: Christianity, Islam

CURRENCY: Ethiopian Birr

LITERACY RATE: 51.8%

LIFE EXPECTANCY: 68.59 years

TIME ZONE: +3

TYPE OF GOVERNMENT: Federal Parliamentary Republic

HEAD OF STATE: President Sahle-Work Zewde **HEAD OF GOVT:** Prime Minister Abiy Ahmed

GDP PER CAPITA: $2,300

POPULATION: 116,462,712

ISD CODE: 251 **INTERNET TLD:** .et

Marathoner Abebe Bikila was the first black African to win an Olympic gold at the 1960 Summer Games in Rome, running barefoot. He won another gold at the 1964 Tokyo Olympics.

FIJI

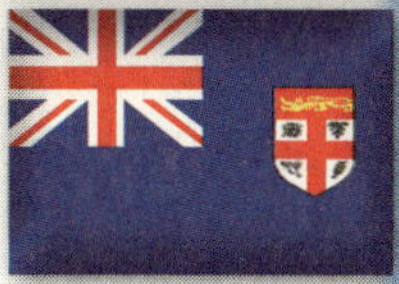

LOCATION: South Pacific Ocean

CAPITAL: Suva

AREA: 18,274 sq. km

LANGUAGES: English, Fijian

MAIN RELIGIONS: Christianity, Hinduism

CURRENCY: Fijian Dollar

LITERACY RATE: 99.1%

LIFE EXPECTANCY: 74.54 years

TIME ZONE: +12

TYPE OF GOVERNMENT: Parliamentary Republic

HEAD OF STATE: President Fiji Ratu Wiliame Katonivere **HEAD OF GOVT:** Prime Minister Josaia Voreqe 'Frank' Bainimarama

GDP PER CAPITA: $10,400

POPULATION: 947,760

ISD CODE: 679 **INTERNET TLD:** .fj

Off the island of Taveuni, there is a place where one can swim from the current day to the day before as the International Date Line runs through it.

FINLAND

LOCATION: North Europe

CAPITAL: Helsinki

AREA: 338,145 sq. km

LANGUAGE: Finnish

MAIN RELIGION: Christianity (Church of Finland)

CURRENCY: Euro

LITERACY RATE: 100%

LIFE EXPECTANCY: 81.96 years

TIME ZONE: +2

TYPE OF GOVERNMENT: Parliamentary Republic

HEAD OF STATE: President Sauli Niinisto

HEAD OF GOVT: Prime Minister Petteri Orpo

GDP PER CAPITA: $48,800

POPULATION: 5,614,571

ISD CODE: 358 **INTERNET TLD:** .fi

The International Failure Day was initiated in Finland where a National Failure Day has been celebrated on 13 October since 2010.

Background: Fiji

FRANCE

LOCATION: West Europe

CAPITAL: Paris

AREA: 643,801 sq. km

LANGUAGE: French

MAIN RELIGION: Christianity

CURRENCY: Euro

LITERACY RATE: 99%

LIFE EXPECTANCY: 82.79 years

TIME ZONE: +1

TYPE OF GOVERNMENT: Semi-presidential Republic

HEAD OF STATE: President Emmanuel Macron **HEAD OF GOVT:** Prime Minister Elisabeth Borne

GDP PER CAPITA: $45,000

POPULATION: 68,521,974

ISD CODE: 33 **INTERNET TLD:** .fr

According to a law passed in 2016, food in French supermarkets cannot be thrown out; it has to be distributed to food banks or other charity organizations.

GABON

LOCATION: West Africa

CAPITAL: Libreville

AREA: 267,667 sq. km

LANGUAGES: French, Fang

MAIN RELIGION: Christianity

CURRENCY: CFA Franc

LITERACY RATE: 85.5%

LIFE EXPECTANCY: 70.03 years

TIME ZONE: +1

TYPE OF GOVERNMENT: Presidential Republic

HEAD OF STATE: President Ali Bongo Ondimba **HEAD OF GOVT:** Prime Minister Alain-Claude Bilie-By-Nze

GDP PER CAPITA: $13,800

POPULATION: 2,397,368

ISD CODE: 241 **INTERNET TLD:** .ga

Gabon's present name comes from 'Gabao', Portuguese for 'cloak', which is the shape of the estuary of the River Komo here.

(THE) GAMBIA

LOCATION: West Africa

CAPITAL: Banjul

AREA: 11,295 sq. km

LANGUAGES: English, Mandinka

MAIN RELIGION: Islam

CURRENCY: Dalasi

LITERACY RATE: 58.1%

LIFE EXPECTANCY: 67.98 years

TIME ZONE: 0

TYPE OF GOVERNMENT: Presidential Republic

HEAD OF STATE AND GOVT: President Adama Barrow

GDP PER CAPITA: $2,100

POPULATION: 2,468,569

ISD CODE: 220 **INTERNET TLD:** .gm

The country is called 'The' Gambia to prevent confusing it with Zambia.

Background: France

GEORGIA

LOCATION: South-west Asia

CAPITAL: Tbilisi

AREA: 69,700 sq. km

LANGUAGES: Georgian, Russian, Armenian, Azerbaijani

MAIN RELIGION: Christianity

CURRENCY: Lari

LITERACY RATE: 99.6

LIFE EXPECTANCY: 77.74 years

TIME ZONE: +4

TYPE OF GOVERNMENT: Semi-presidential Republic

HEAD OF STATE: President Salome Zourabichvili **HEAD OF GOVT:** Prime Minister Irakli Garibashvili

GDP PER CAPITA: $15,500

POPULATION: 4,936,390

ISD CODE: 995 **INTERNET TLD:** .ge

Citizens of around 98 countries can enter Georgia without a visa.

GERMANY

LOCATION: West Europe

CAPITAL: Berlin

AREA: 357,022 sq. km

LANGUAGE: German

MAIN RELIGION: Christianity

CURRENCY: Euro

LITERACY RATE: 99%

LIFE EXPECTANCY: 81.72 years

TIME ZONE: +1

TYPE OF GOVERNMENT: Federal Parliamentary Republic

HEAD OF STATE: President Frank-Walter Steinmeier **HEAD OF GOVT:** Chancellor Olag Scholz

GDP PER CAPITA: $53,200

POPULATION: 84,220,184

ISD CODE: 49 **INTERNET TLD:** .de

German scientists are credited with the discovery of insulin and the invention of the pocket watch, the calculator, the automobile and the jet engine.

GHANA

LOCATION: West Africa

CAPITAL: Accra

AREA: 238,533 sq. km

LANGUAGES: English, indigenous languages

MAIN RELIGION: Christianity

CURRENCY: Cedi

LITERACY RATE: 79%

LIFE EXPECTANCY: 69.72 years

TIME ZONE: 0

TYPE OF GOVERNMENT: Presidential Republic

HEAD OF STATE AND GOVT: President Nana Addo Dankwa Akufo-Addo

GDP PER CAPITA: $5,400

POPULATION: 33,846,114

ISD CODE: 233 **INTERNET TLD:** .gh

During the slave trade days, many European nations built forts and outposts in coastal Ghana. Now most of these have been turned into memorials.

Background: Germany

GREECE

LOCATION: Southern Europe, bordering the Aegean Sea

CAPITAL: Athens

AREA: 131,957 sq. km

LANGUAGE: Greek

MAIN RELIGION: Christianity (Greek Orthodox Church)

CURRENCY: Euro

LITERACY RATE: 97.9%

LIFE EXPECTANCY: 81.71 years

TIME ZONE: +2

TYPE OF GOVERNMENT: Parliamentary Republic

HEAD OF STATE: President Katerina Sakellaropoulou **HEAD OF GOVT:** Prime Minister Kyriakos Mitsotakis

GDP PER CAPITA: $29,500

POPULATION: 10,497,595

ISD CODE: 30 **INTERNET TLD:** .gr

The ancient Greeks are believed to have invented the yo-yo in 500 BCE.

GRENADA

LOCATION: Central America

CAPITAL: St George's

AREA: 344 sq. km

LANGUAGE: English

MAIN RELIGION: Christianity

CURRENCY: East Caribbean Dollar

LITERACY RATE: 98.6%

LIFE EXPECTANCY: 76 years

TIME ZONE: –4

TYPE OF GOVERNMENT: Constitutional Monarchy and Parliamentary Democracy

HEAD OF STATE: King Charles III
HEAD OF GOVT: Prime Minister Dickon Mitchell

GDP PER CAPITA: $13,700

POPULATION: 114,299

ISD CODE: 473 **INTERNET TLD:** .gd

Grenada is home to both black sand and white sand beaches with water so clear that coral formations can be spotted from aircraft above.

GUATEMALA

LOCATION: Central America

CAPITAL: Guatemala City

AREA: 108,889 sq. km

LANGUAGES: Spanish, indigenous languages

MAIN RELIGION: Christianity

CURRENCY: Quetzal

LITERACY RATE: 83.3%

LIFE EXPECTANCY: 73.18 years

TIME ZONE: –6

TYPE OF GOVERNMENT: Presidential Republic

HEAD OF STATE AND GOVT: President Alejandro Giammattei

GDP PER CAPITA: $8,900

POPULATION: 17,980,803

ISD CODE: 502 **INTERNET TLD:** .gt

The name Guatemala means 'land of the trees' in the Maya-Toltec language. More than 21 Mayan languages are spoken here.

Background: Greece

GUINEA

LOCATION: West Africa

CAPITAL: Conakry

AREA: 245,857 sq. km

LANGUAGE: French

MAIN RELIGION: Islam

CURRENCY: Guinean Franc

LITERACY RATE: 45.3%

LIFE EXPECTANCY: 64.27 years

TIME ZONE: 0

TYPE OF GOVERNMENT: Presidential Republic

HEAD OF STATE: President Colonel Mamady Doumbouya **HEAD OF GOVT:** Prime Minister Bernard Goumou

GDP PER CAPITA: $2,600

POPULATION: 13,607,249

ISD CODE: 224 **INTERNET TLD:** .gn

Mount Nimba, located on the border of Guinea and Cote d'Ivoire, is the highest point in both countries.

GUINEA-BISSAU

LOCATION: West Africa

CAPITAL: Bissau

AREA: 36,125 sq. km

LANGUAGE: Portuguese

MAIN RELIGIONS: Islam, Christianity, Animist, indigenous beliefs

CURRENCY: CFA Franc

LITERACY RATE: 52.9%

LIFE EXPECTANCY: 64.1 years

TIME ZONE: 0

TYPE OF GOVERNMENT: Semi-presidential Republic

HEAD OF STATE: President Umaro Sissoco Embalo **HEAD OF GOVT:** Prime Minister Nuno Gomes Nabiam

GDP PER CAPITA: $1,800

POPULATION: 2,078,820

ISD CODE: 245 **INTERNET TLD:** .gw

The capital's name 'Bissau' was added to the country's name in 1974, to prevent mix-ups with the neighbouring Republic of Guinea.

GUYANA

LOCATION: Central America

CAPITAL: Georgetown

AREA: 214,969 sq. km

LANGUAGES: English, indigenous languages

MAIN RELIGIONS: Christianity, Hinduism

CURRENCY: Guyanese Dollar

LITERACY RATE: 88.8%

LIFE EXPECTANCY: 72.15 years

TIME ZONE: –4

TYPE OF GOVERNMENT: Parliamentary Republic

HEAD OF STATE AND GOVT: President Mohamed Irfaan Ali

GDP PER CAPITA: $21,900

POPULATION: 791,739

ISD CODE: 592 **INTERNET TLD:** .gy

At 250.5 m (822 ft), the Kaieteur Falls is about twice the height of Victoria Falls on the border of Zambia and Zimbabwe.

HAITI

LOCATION: Central America

CAPITAL: Port-au-Prince

AREA: 27,750 sq. km

LANGUAGES: French, Creole

MAIN RELIGIONS: Christianity, Haitian Vodou

CURRENCY: Gourde

LITERACY RATE: 61.7%

LIFE EXPECTANCY: 66.3 years

TIME ZONE: –5

TYPE OF GOVERNMENT: Semi-presidential Republic

HEAD OF STATE AND GOVT: Acting President and Prime Minister Ariel Henry

GDP PER CAPITA: $2,900

POPULATION: 11,470,261

ISD CODE: 509 **INTERNET TLD:** .ht

Haiti is the only nation in the world whose independence was gained as part of a successful slave rebellion.

HONDURAS

LOCATION: Central America

CAPITAL: Tegucigalpa

AREA: 112,090 sq. km

LANGUAGE: Spanish

MAIN RELIGION: Christianity

CURRENCY: Lempira

LITERACY RATE: 88.5%

LIFE EXPECTANCY: 75.43 years

TIME ZONE: -6

TYPE OF GOVERNMENT: Presidential Republic

HEAD OF STATE AND GOVT: President Iris Xiomara Castro de Zelaya

GDP PER CAPITA: $5,600

POPULATION: 9,571,352

ISD CODE: 504 **INTERNET TLD:** .hn

The five stars on the flag stand for the five countries of Central America. Honduras is represented by the star in the middle because of its central geographical location.

HUNGARY

LOCATION: Central Europe

CAPITAL: Budapest

AREA: 93,028 sq. km

LANGUAGES: Hungarian, German

MAIN RELIGION: Christianity

CURRENCY: Forint

LITERACY RATE: 99.1%

LIFE EXPECTANCY: 77.4 years

TIME ZONE: +1

TYPE OF GOVERNMENT: Parliamentary Republic

HEAD OF STATE: President Katalin Novak **HEAD OF GOVT:** Prime Minister Viktor Orban

GDP PER CAPITA: $33,600

POPULATION: 9,670,009

ISD CODE: 36 **INTERNET TLD:** .hu

The country has a pre-approved set of names. If the desired name is not on the list, the parents must apply for it.

Background: Hungary

ICELAND

LOCATION: North Europe

CAPITAL: Reykjavik

AREA: 103,000 sq. km

LANGUAGES: Icelandic, English, German

MAIN RELIGION: Christianity

CURRENCY: Icelandic Krona

LITERACY RATE: 99%

LIFE EXPECTANCY: 83.83 years

TIME ZONE: 0

TYPE OF GOVERNMENT: Unitary Parliamentary Republic

HEAD OF STATE: President Gudni Thorlacius Johannesson

HEAD OF GOVT: Prime Minister Katrín Jakobsdottir

GDP PER CAPITA: $53,600

POPULATION: 360,872

ISD CODE: 354 **INTERNET TLD:** .is

Only one per cent of the land in Iceland is considered arable.

INDIA

LOCATION: South Asia

CAPITAL: New Delhi

AREA: 3,287,263 sq. km

LANGUAGES: Hindi, English and 21 other official languages

MAIN RELIGIONS: Hinduism, Islam, Sikhism, Christianity, Jainism, Buddhism

CURRENCY: Indian Rupee

LITERACY RATE: 74.4%

LIFE EXPECTANCY: 67.69 years

TIME ZONE: +5.30

TYPE OF GOVERNMENT: Federal Parliamentary Republic

HEAD OF STATE: President Droupadi Murmu **HEAD OF GOVT:** Prime Minister Narendra Modi

GDP PER CAPITA: $6,600

POPULATION: 1,399,179,585

ISD CODE: 91 **INTERNET TLD:** .in

India has the third highest number of billionaires in the world, after USA and China.

INDONESIA

LOCATION: South-East Asia

CAPITAL: Jakarta

AREA: 1,904,569 sq. km

LANGUAGE: Bahasa

MAIN RELIGION: Islam

CURRENCY: Indonesian Rupiah

LITERACY RATE: 96%

LIFE EXPECTANCY: 73.33 years

TIME ZONE: +7

TYPE OF GOVERNMENT: Presidential Republic

HEAD OF STATE AND GOVT: President Joko Widodo

GDP PER CAPITA: $11,900

POPULATION: 279,476,346

ISD CODE: 62 **INTERNET TLD:** .id

Indonesia comprises more than 17,000 islands, of which around 6,000 are inhabited.

Background: India

IRAN

LOCATION: Middle East

CAPITAL: Tehran

AREA: 1,648,195 sq. km

LANGUAGES: Persian, Azerbaijani, Turkish

MAIN RELIGION: Islam

CURRENCY: Iranian Rial

LITERACY RATE: 88.7%

LIFE EXPECTANCY: 75.44 years

TIME ZONE: +3.30

TYPE OF GOVERNMENT: Theocratic Republic

HEAD OF STATE: Supreme Leader Ali Hosseini-Khamenei **HEAD OF GOVT:** President Ebrahim Raisi

GDP PER CAPITA: $15,000

POPULATION: 87,590,873

ISD CODE: 98 **INTERNET TLD:** .ir

Iran's proven oil reserves are the fourth largest in the world, after Venezuela, Saudi Arabia and Canada.

IRAQ

LOCATION: Middle East

CAPITAL: Baghdad

AREA: 438,317 sq. km

LANGUAGES: Arabic, Kurdish

MAIN RELIGION: Islam

CURRENCY: New Iraqi Dinar

LITERACY RATE: 85.6%

LIFE EXPECTANCY: 73.45 years

TIME ZONE: +3

TYPE OF GOVERNMENT: Federal Parliamentary Republic

HEAD OF STATE: President Latif Rashid **HEAD OF GOVT:** Prime Minister Mohammed Shia' Al Sudani

GDP PER CAPITA: $9,000

POPULATION: 41,266,109

ISD CODE: 964 **INTERNET TLD:** .iq

Oil exports account for about 95 per cent of Iraq's foreign exchange earnings.

IRELAND

LOCATION: West Europe

CAPITAL: Dublin

AREA: 70,273 sq. km

LANGUAGES: Gaelic, English

MAIN RELIGION: Christianity

CURRENCY: Euro

LITERACY RATE: 99%

LIFE EXPECTANCY: 81.87 years

TIME ZONE: 0

TYPE OF GOVERNMENT: Parliamentary Republic

HEAD OF STATE: President Michael D. Higgins **HEAD OF GOVT:** Prime Minister Leo Varadkar

GDP PER CAPITA: $102,500

POPULATION: 5,323,991

ISD CODE: 353 **INTERNET TLD:** .ie

Irish surnames are well-known for beginning with Mac/Mc or 'O'. 'Mac' means 'son of' and 'O' means 'grandson of' in Gaelic.

 Background: Ireland

ISRAEL

LOCATION: Middle East

CAPITAL: Jerusalem

AREA: 20,770 sq. km

LANGUAGES: Hebrew, English, Arabic

MAIN RELIGIONS: Judaism, Islam

CURRENCY: Israeli (New) Shekel

LITERACY RATE: 97.8%

LIFE EXPECTANCY: 83.54 years

TIME ZONE: +2

TYPE OF GOVERNMENT: Parliamentary Democracy

HEAD OF STATE: President Isaac Herzog **HEAD OF GOVT:** Prime Minister Benyamin Netanyahu

GDP PER CAPITA: $42,100

POPULATION: 9,043,387

ISD CODE: 972 **INTERNET TLD:** .il

Israeli banknotes have Braille on them to help visually challenged people identify them easily.

ITALY

LOCATION: Southern Europe

CAPITAL: Rome

AREA: 301,340 sq. km

LANGUAGE: Italian

MAIN RELIGION: Christianity

CURRENCY: Euro

LITERACY RATE: 99.2%

LIFE EXPECTANCY: 82.79 years

TIME ZONE: +1

TYPE OF GOVERNMENT: Parliamentary Republic

HEAD OF STATE: President Sergio Mattarella **HEAD OF GOVT:** Prime Minister Giorgia Meloni

GDP PER CAPITA: $41,900

POPULATION: 61,021,855

ISD CODE: 39 **INTERNET TLD:** .it

Most of the world's top sports cars – Ferrari, Lamborghini, Bugatti, Maserati and Alfa Romeo – are manufactured in Italy.

JAMAICA

LOCATION: Central America

CAPITAL: Kingston

AREA: 10,991 sq. km

LANGUAGE: English

MAIN RELIGION: Christianity

CURRENCY: Jamaican Dollar

LITERACY RATE: 88.7%

LIFE EXPECTANCY: 76.01 years

TIME ZONE: –5

TYPE OF GOVERNMENT: Constitutional Monarchy and Parliamentary Democracy

HEAD OF STATE: King Charles III

HEAD OF GOVT: Prime Minister Andrew Holness

GDP PER CAPITA: $9,600

POPULATION: 2,820,982

ISD CODE: 1-876 **INTERNET TLD:** .jm

Ian Fleming designed and built his home called 'Goldeneye' in Jamaica and wrote 10 James Bond novels there.

Background: Italy

JAPAN

LOCATION: East Asia

CAPITAL: Tokyo

AREA: 377,915 sq. km

LANGUAGE: Japanese

MAIN RELIGIONS: Shintoism, Buddhism

CURRENCY: Yen

LITERACY RATE: 99%

LIFE EXPECTANCY: 85 years

TIME ZONE: +9

TYPE OF GOVERNMENT: Parliamentary Constitutional Monarchy

HEAD OF STATE: Emperor Naruhito
HEAD OF GOVT: Prime Minister Fumio Kishida

GDP PER CAPITA: $40,800

POPULATION: 123,719,238

ISD CODE: 81 **INTERNET TLD:** .jp

Mt Fuji (3,776.2 m/12,389.2 ft), the tallest mountain in the country, is an active volcano.

JORDAN

LOCATION: Middle East

CAPITAL: Amman

AREA: 89,342 sq. km

LANGUAGES: Arabic, English

MAIN RELIGION: Islam

CURRENCY: Jordanian Dinar

LITERACY RATE: 98.4%

LIFE EXPECTANCY: 76.26 years

TIME ZONE: +2

TYPE OF GOVERNMENT: Parliamentary Constitutional Monarchy

HEAD OF STATE: King Abdullah II
HEAD OF GOVT: Prime Minister Bisher al-Khasawneh

GDP PER CAPITA: $9,200

POPULATION: 11,086,716

ISD CODE: 962 **INTERNET TLD:** .jo

The world's lowest point on dry land is the Dead Sea shore, shared by Israel and Jordan. It is 418 m/1,371 ft below sea level.

KAZAKHSTAN

LOCATION: Central Asia

CAPITAL: Astana

AREA: 2,724,900

LANGUAGES: Kazakh, Russian

MAIN RELIGIONS: Islam, Christianity

CURRENCY: Tenge

LITERACY RATE: 99.8%

LIFE EXPECTANCY: 72.8 years

TIME ZONE: +6

TYPE OF GOVERNMENT: Presidential Republic

HEAD OF STATE: President Kassym-Zhomart Tokayev **HEAD OF GOVT:** Prime Minister Alikhan Smailov

GDP PER CAPITA: $26,100

POPULATION: 19,543,464

ISD CODE: 7 **INTERNET TLD:** .kz

The Baikonur Cosmodrome is the world's oldest and largest (by area) space launch facility.

Background: Jordan

KENYA

LOCATION: East Africa

CAPITAL: Nairobi

AREA: 580,367 sq. km

LANGUAGES: English, Kiswahili

MAIN RELIGIONS: Christianity, Islam

CURRENCY: Kenyan Shilling

LITERACY RATE: 82.6%

LIFE EXPECTANCY: 70.04 years

TIME ZONE: +3

TYPE OF GOVERNMENT: Presidential Republic

HEAD OF STATE & GOVT: President William Rutto

GDP PER CAPITA: $4,700

POPULATION: 57,052,004

ISD CODE: 254 **INTERNET TLD:** .ke

Wangari Maathai, a social, environmental and political activist, and the first African woman to win a Nobel Peace prize, was Kenyan.

KIRIBATI

LOCATION: Oceania

CAPITAL: Tarawa

AREA: 811 sq. km

LANGUAGES: Kiribati, English

MAIN RELIGION: Christianity

CURRENCY: Australian Dollar

LITERACY RATE: 97.7%

LIFE EXPECTANCY: 68.22 years

TIME ZONE: +12

TYPE OF GOVERNMENT: Presidential Republic

HEAD OF STATE AND GOVT: President Taneti Maamau

GDP PER CAPITA: $1,900

POPULATION: 115,372

ISD CODE: 686 **INTERNET TLD:** .ki

It is the first country to celebrate new year since it is 14 hours ahead of GMT.

KUWAIT

LOCATION: Middle East

CAPITAL: Kuwait City

AREA: 17,818 sq. km

LANGUAGES: Arabic

MAIN RELIGION: Islam

CURRENCY: Kuwaiti Dinar

LITERACY RATE: 96.5%

LIFE EXPECTANCY: 79.35 years

TIME ZONE: +3

TYPE OF GOVERNMENT: Constitutional Monarchy (Emirate)

HEAD OF STATE: Sheikh Nawaf Al-Ahmad Al-Jaber Al-Sabah **HEAD OF GOVT:** Prime Minister Sheikh Ahmed Nawaf Al-Ahmed Al-Sabah

GDP PER CAPITA: $43,900

POPULATION: 3,103,580

ISD CODE: 965 **INTERNET TLD:** .kw

More than two-thirds of the people who reside in Kuwait do not hold Kuwaiti citizenship and cannot vote in parliamentary elections.

KYRGYZSTAN

LOCATION: Central Asia

CAPITAL: Bishkek

AREA: 199,951 sq. km

LANGUAGES: Kyrgyz, Uzbek, Russian

MAIN RELIGION: Islam

CURRENCY: Som

LITERACY RATE: 99.6%

LIFE EXPECTANCY: 72.63 years

TIME ZONE: +6

TYPE OF GOVERNMENT: Parliamentary Republic

HEAD OF STATE AND GOVT: President Sadyr Japarov

GDP PER CAPITA: $4,800

POPULATION: 6,122,781

ISD CODE: 996 **INTERNET TLD:** .kg

There are more than 88 major mountain ranges in Kyrgyzstan, which make up more than 70 per cent of the country's territory.

LAOS

LOCATION: South-East Asia

CAPITAL: Vientiane

AREA: 236,800 sq. km

LANGUAGES: Lao, French, English

MAIN RELIGION: Buddhism

CURRENCY: Kip

LITERACY RATE: 87.1%

LIFE EXPECTANCY: 68.59 years

TIME ZONE: +7

TYPE OF GOVERNMENT: Communist state

HEAD OF STATE: President Thongloun Sisoulith **HEAD OF GOVT:** Prime Minister Sonexay Siphandone

GDP PER CAPITA: $7,800

POPULATION: 7,852,377

ISD CODE: 856 **INTERNET TLD:** .la

In Laos, the country is known as Sathalanalat Paxathipatai Paxaxon Lao.

LATVIA

LOCATION: Eastern Europe

CAPITAL: Riga

AREA: 64,589 sq. km

LANGUAGES: Latvian, Russian

MAIN RELIGION: Christianity

CURRENCY: Euro

LITERACY RATE: 99.9%

LIFE EXPECTANCY: 76.16 years

TIME ZONE: +2

TYPE OF GOVERNMENT: Parliamentary Republic

HEAD OF STATE: President Egils Levits **HEAD OF GOVT:** Prime Minister Krisjanis Karins

GDP PER CAPITA: $32,100

POPULATION: 1,821,750

ISD CODE: 371 **INTERNET TLD:** .lv

Tourists can visit the Karosta Prison Hotel in Liepaja, which is a former military jail, for a prison experience, including interrogation and a night stay in a cold cell.

Background: Latvia

LEBANON

LOCATION: Middle East

CAPITAL: Beirut

AREA: 10,400 sq. km

LANGUAGES: Arabic, French, English

MAIN RELIGIONS: Islam, Christianity

CURRENCY: Lebanese Pound

LITERACY RATE: 95.1%

LIFE EXPECTANCY: 79 years

TIME ZONE: +2

TYPE OF GOVERNMENT: Parliamentary Republic

HEAD OF STATE: Vacant **HEAD OF GOVT:** Prime Minister Najib Miqati

GDP PER CAPITA: $13,000

POPULATION: 5,331,203

ISD CODE: 961 **INTERNET TLD:** .lb

Lebanon is the only country in the Middle East that does not have even a patch of desert.

LESOTHO

LOCATION: Southern Africa

CAPITAL: Maseru

AREA: 30,355 sq. km

LANGUAGES: Sesotho, English

MAIN RELIGION: Christianity

CURRENCY: Loti

LITERACY RATE: 81%

LIFE EXPECTANCY: 59.87 years

TIME ZONE: +2

TYPE OF GOVERNMENT: Parliamentary Constitutional Monarchy

HEAD OF STATE: King Letsie III
HEAD OF GOVT: Prime Minister Sam Matekane

GDP PER CAPITA: $2,300

POPULATION: 2,210,646

ISD CODE: 266 **INTERNET TLD:** .ls

Lesotho is the only country that lies entirely 1,500 m (4,920 ft) above sea level. Villages can only be reached by riding horses, trekking, or by a light aircraft.

LIBERIA

LOCATION: West Africa

CAPITAL: Monrovia

AREA: 111,369 sq. km

LANGUAGES: English, ethnic languages

MAIN RELIGIONS: Indigenous faiths, Christianity, Islam

CURRENCY: Liberian Dollar

LITERACY RATE: 48.3%

LIFE EXPECTANCY: 65.8 years

TIME ZONE: 0

TYPE OF GOVERNMENT: Presidential Republic

HEAD OF STATE AND GOVT: President George Weah

GDP PER CAPITA: $1,400

POPULATION: 5,506,280

ISD CODE: 231 **INTERNET TLD:** .lr

Liberia was founded by freed people of colour from the USA.

LIBYA

LOCATION: North Africa

CAPITAL: Tripoli

AREA: 1,759,540

LANGUAGES: Arabic, Italian, English

MAIN RELIGION: Islam

CURRENCY: Libyan Dinar

LITERACY RATE: 91%

LIFE EXPECTANCY: 77.42 years

TIME ZONE: +2

TYPE OF GOVERNMENT: Transitional

HEAD OF STATE: Chairman, Presidential Council: Mohammed Al Menfi **HEAD OF GOVT:** Interim Prime Minister Abdul Hamid Dubaybah

GDP PER CAPITA: $22,000

POPULATION: 7,252,573

ISD CODE: 218 **INTERNET TLD:** .ly

95 per cent of Libya is covered by the Sahara desert. It is very arid, and in some places it rains only once in 10 or more years.

LIECHTENSTEIN

LOCATION: Central Europe

CAPITAL: Vaduz

AREA: 160 sq. km

LANGUAGE: German

MAIN RELIGION: Christianity

CURRENCY: Swiss Franc

LITERACY RATE: 99%

LIFE EXPECTANCY: 82.76 years

TIME ZONE: +1

TYPE OF GOVERNMENT: Constitutional Monarchy

HEAD OF STATE: Prince Hans Adam II
HEAD OF GOVT: Prime Minister Daniel Risch

GDP PER CAPITA: $171,254

POPULATION: 39,993

ISD CODE: 423 **INTERNET TLD:** .li

Liechtenstein has no airport. The closest airport is in Zurich in Switzerland.

LITHUANIA

LOCATION: East Europe

CAPITAL: Vilnius

AREA: 65,300 sq. km

LANGUAGES: Lithuanian, Russian

MAIN RELIGION: Christianity

CURRENCY: Euro

LITERACY RATE: 99.8%

LIFE EXPECTANCY: 75.95 years

TIME ZONE: +2

TYPE OF GOVERNMENT: Semi-presidential Republic

HEAD OF STATE: President Gitanas Nauseda **HEAD OF GOVT:** Prime Minister Ingrida Simonyte

GDP PER CAPITA: $39,300

POPULATION: 2,655,755

ISD CODE: 370 **INTERNET TLD:** .lt

Lithuania was the first Soviet Republic to declare independence from the USSR.

Background: Liechtenstein

LUXEMBOURG

LOCATION: West Europe

CAPITAL: Luxembourg City

AREA: 2,586 sq. km

LANGUAGES: Luxembourgish, French, German, Portuguese

MAIN RELIGION: Christianity

CURRENCY: Euro

LITERACY RATE: 100%

LIFE EXPECTANCY: 83.17 years

TIME ZONE: +1

TYPE OF GOVERNMENT: Constitutional Monarchy

HEAD OF STATE: Grand Duke Henri **HEAD OF GOVT:** Prime Minister Xavier Bettel

GDP PER CAPITA: $115,700

POPULATION: 660,924

ISD CODE: 352 **INTERNET TLD:** .lu

Luxembourg is one of the founding members of the European Union, NATO and the United Nations.

MADAGASCAR

LOCATION: Southern African coast

CAPITAL: Antananarivo

AREA: 587,041 sq. km

LANGUAGES: Malagasy, English, French

MAIN RELIGIONS: Indigenous faiths, Christianity, Islam

CURRENCY: Malagasy Ariary

LITERACY RATE: 77.3%

LIFE EXPECTANCY: 68.47 years

TIME ZONE: +3

TYPE OF GOVERNMENT: Semi-presidential Republic

HEAD OF STATE: President Andry Nirina Rajoelina **HEAD OF GOVT:** Prime Minister Christian Ntsay

GDP PER CAPITA: $1,500

POPULATION: 28,812,195

ISD CODE: 261 **INTERNET TLD:** .mg

Madagascar is also known as the Red Island because in many areas the soil has a distinct reddish tint.

MALAWI

LOCATION: Southern Africa

CAPITAL: Lilongwe

AREA: 118,484 sq. km

LANGUAGES: Chichewa, Chinyanja

MAIN RELIGIONS: Christianity, Islam

Lake Malawi, from which the country gets its name, is also called the 'Calendar Lake' since it is about 365 miles (number of days in a year) (587.4 km) long and 52 miles (number of weeks in a year) (83.7 km) wide.

CURRENCY: Malawian Kwacha

LITERACY RATE: 67.3%

LIFE EXPECTANCY: 72.71 years

TIME ZONE: +2

TYPE OF GOVERNMENT: Presidential Republic

HEAD OF STATE AND GOVT: President Lazarus Chakwera

GDP PER CAPITA: $1,500

POPULATION: 21,279,597

ISD CODE: 265 **INTERNET TLD:** .mw

MALAYSIA

LOCATION: South-East Asia

CAPITAL: Kuala Lumpur

AREA: 329,847 sq. km

LANGUAGES: Bahasa Malaysia (Malay), English, Chinese

MAIN RELIGIONS: Islam, Buddhism

CURRENCY: Ringgit

LITERACY RATE: 95%

LIFE EXPECTANCY: 76.38 years

TIME ZONE: +8

TYPE OF GOVERNMENT: Federal Parliamentary Constitutional Monarchy

HEAD OF STATE: King Abdullah Sultan Ahmad Shah **HEAD OF GOVT:** Prime Minister Anwar Ibrahim

GDP PER CAPITA: $26,300

POPULATION: 34,219,975

ISD CODE: 60 **INTERNET TLD:** .my

The world's largest flower, the Rafflesia (1 m/3.3 ft in diameter), is found here.

(THE) MALDIVES

LOCATION: South-East Asia

CAPITAL: Male

AREA: 298 sq. km

LANGUAGES: Dhivehi, English

MAIN RELIGION: Islam

CURRENCY: Rufiyaa

LITERACY RATE: 97.9%

LIFE EXPECTANCY: 77.19 years

TIME ZONE: +5

TYPE OF GOVERNMENT: Presidential Republic

HEAD OF STATE AND GOVT: President Ibrahim Mohamed Solih

GDP PER CAPITA: $18,800

POPULATION: 389,568

ISD CODE: 960 **INTERNET TLD:** .mv

In 2009, Maldives became the world's first country to hold an official presidential cabinet meeting underwater.

MALI

LOCATION: West Africa

CAPITAL: Bamako

AREA: 1,240,192 sq. km

LANGUAGES: Bambara, French

MAIN RELIGION: Islam

CURRENCY: CFA Franc

LITERACY RATE: 35.5%

LIFE EXPECTANCY: 62.81 years

TIME ZONE: 0

TYPE OF GOVERNMENT: Semi-presidential Republic

HEAD OF STATE: Transitional President Colonel Assimi Goita **HEAD OF GOVT:** Transitional Prime Minister Choguel Maiga

GDP PER CAPITA: $2,100

POPULATION: 21,359,722

ISD CODE: 223 **INTERNET TLD:** .ml

Gao in Mali is where the equator divides the world into eastern and western hemispheres.

MALTA

LOCATION: Southern Europe

CAPITAL: Valletta

AREA: 316 sq. km

LANGUAGES: Maltese, English

MAIN RELIGION: Christianity

CURRENCY: Euro

LITERACY RATE: 94.9%

LIFE EXPECTANCY: 83.39 years

TIME ZONE: +1

TYPE OF GOVERNMENT: Parliamentary Republic

HEAD OF STATE: President George Vella

HEAD OF GOVT: Prime Minister Robert Abela

GDP PER CAPITA: $44,700

POPULATION: 467,138

ISD CODE: 356 **INTERNET TLD:** .mt

Malta was known as 'Melita', meaning 'the island of honey', by ancient Greeks and Romans.

MARSHALL ISLANDS

LOCATION: Northern Pacific Ocean

CAPITAL: Majuro

AREA: 181 sq. km

LANGUAGES: Marshallese, English

MAIN RELIGION: Christianity

CURRENCY: US Dollar

LITERACY RATE: 98.3%

LIFE EXPECTANCY: 74.92 years

TIME ZONE: +12

TYPE OF GOVERNMENT: Mixed Presidential Parliamentary Republic

HEAD OF STATE AND GOVT: President Hilda David Kabua

GDP PER CAPITA: $6,000

POPULATION: 80,966

ISD CODE: 692 **INTERNET TLD:** .mh

Almost 2,000,000 sq. km of ocean was declared a shark sanctuary here in 2011. It is the largest shark sanctuary in the world.

MAURITANIA

LOCATION: Western Africa

CAPITAL: Nouakchott

AREA: 1,030,700 sq. km

LANGUAGES: Arabic, Pulaar

MAIN RELIGION: Islam

CURRENCY: Ouguiya

LITERACY RATE: 67%

LIFE EXPECTANCY: 65.57 years

TIME ZONE: 0

TYPE OF GOVERNMENT: Presidential Republic

HEAD OF STATE: President Mohamed Ould Ghazouani **HEAD OF GOVT:** Prime Minister Mohamed Ould Bilal

GDP PER CAPITA: $5,300

POPULATION: 4,244,878

ISD CODE: 222 **INTERNET TLD:** .mr

If you look at Mauritania from space, you can see a clear bull's eye-like geological feature, which is 50 km across, called 'The Eye of Africa.'

MAURITIUS

LOCATION: Indian Ocean

CAPITAL: Port Louis

AREA: 2,040 sq. km

LANGUAGES: Creole, French, Bhojpuri, English

MAIN RELIGIONS: Hinduism, Christianity, Islam

CURRENCY: Mauritian Rupee

LITERACY RATE: 92.2%

LIFE EXPECTANCY: 75.13 years

TIME ZONE: +4

TYPE OF GOVERNMENT: Parliamentary Republic

HEAD OF STATE: President Prithvirajsing Roopun **HEAD OF GOVT:** Prime Minister Pravind Kumar Jugnauth

GDP PER CAPITA: $21,000

POPULATION: 1,309,448

ISD CODE: 230 **INTERNET TLD:** .mu

Inspired by the dodo, an extinct bird once endemic to Mauritius, Lewis Carroll wrote the book *Alice's Adventures in Wonderland* in 1865.

MEXICO

LOCATION: North America

CAPITAL: Mexico City

AREA: 1,964,375 sq. km

LANGUAGE: Spanish

MAIN RELIGION: Christianity

CURRENCY: Mexican Peso

LITERACY RATE: 95.2%

LIFE EXPECTANCY: 73.46 years

TIME ZONE: –6

TYPE OF GOVERNMENT: Federal Presidential Republic

HEAD OF STATE AND GOVT: President Andres Manuel Lopez Obrador

GDP PER CAPITA: $19,100

POPULATION: 129,875,529

ISD CODE: 52 **INTERNET TLD:** .mx

Mexico City is sinking at the rate of 15–20 cm a year because it is built on an aquifer.

MICRONESIA

LOCATION: Island group in the North Pacific Ocean

CAPITAL: Palikir

AREA: 702 sq. km

LANGUAGE: English

MAIN RELIGION: Christianity

CURRENCY: US Dollar

LITERACY RATE: 98.8%

LIFE EXPECTANCY: 74.71 years

TIME ZONE: +11

TYPE OF GOVERNMENT: Federal Presidential Republic

HEAD OF STATE AND GOVT: President Wesley W. Simina

GDP PER CAPITA: $3,300

POPULATION: 100,319

ISD CODE: 691 **INTERNET TLD:** .fm

Micronesia houses the ruins of Nan Madol, an artificial group of islands connected by canals built in the eighth or ninth century CE. This gives it the name 'Venice of the Pacific'.

MOLDOVA

LOCATION: East Europe

CAPITAL: Chisinau

AREA: 33,851 sq. km

LANGUAGES: Moldovan, Russian

MAIN RELIGION: Christianity

CURRENCY: Moldovan Leu

LITERACY RATE: 99.6%

LIFE EXPECTANCY: 72.72 years

TIME ZONE: +2

TYPE OF GOVERNMENT: Parliamentary Republic

HEAD OF STATE: President Maia Sandu **HEAD OF GOVT:** Prime Minister Dorin Recean

GDP PER CAPITA: $14,000

POPULATION: 3,250,532

ISD CODE: 372 **INTERNET TLD:** .md

Emil Racovita, a cave in Criva, Moldova, is among the largest caves in the world. There are 20 underground lakes inside the cave.

MONACO

LOCATION: West Europe

CAPITAL: Monaco

AREA: 2 sq. km

LANGUAGES: French, English, Italian

MAIN RELIGION: Christianity

CURRENCY: Euro

LITERACY RATE: 99%

LIFE EXPECTANCY: 89.64 years

TIME ZONE: +1

TYPE OF GOVERNMENT: Constitutional Monarchy

HEAD OF STATE: Prince Albert II **HEAD OF GOVT:** Minister of State Pierre Dartout

GDP PER CAPITA: $115,400

POPULATION: 31,597

ISD CODE: 377 **INTERNET TLD:** .mc

It takes an hour for an average person to walk the width of the entire country.

MONGOLIA

LOCATION: North Asia

CAPITAL: Ulaanbaatar

AREA: 1,564,116 sq. km

LANGUAGE: Mongol

MAIN RELIGIONS: Buddhism, Christianity, Islam

CURRENCY: Togrog/Tugrik

LITERACY RATE: 99.2%

LIFE EXPECTANCY: 71.65 years

TIME ZONE: +8

TYPE OF GOVERNMENT: Semi-presidential Republic

HEAD OF STATE: President Ukhnaagiin Khurelsukh **HEAD OF GOVT:** Prime Minister Luvsannamsrai Oyun-Erdene

GDP PER CAPITA: $11,700

POPULATION: 3,255,468

ISD CODE: 976 **INTERNET TLD:** .mn

Fossilized dinosaur remains and the first dinosaur eggs were found in the Gobi Desert in Mongolia in the 1920s.

Background: Mexico

MONTENEGRO

LOCATION: South-eastern Europe

CAPITAL: Podgorica

AREA: 13,812 sq. km

LANGUAGES: Montenegrin, Serbian

MAIN RELIGIONS: Islam, Christianity

CURRENCY: Euro

LITERACY RATE: 99%

LIFE EXPECTANCY: 77.99 years

TIME ZONE: +1

TYPE OF GOVERNMENT: Parliamentary Republic

HEAD OF STATE: President Jakov Milatovic **HEAD OF GOVT:** Prime Minister Dritan Abazovic

GDP PER CAPITA: $20,600

POPULATION: 602,445

ISD CODE: 382 **INTERNET TLD:** .me

The name Montenegro, meaning 'Black Mountain', was probably derived from the thick 'black' forests that covered Mount Lovcen, the highest point in Montenegro in medieval times.

MOROCCO

LOCATION: North Africa

CAPITAL: Rabat

AREA: 446,550 sq. km

LANGUAGE: Arabic

MAIN RELIGION: Islam

CURRENCY: Moroccan Dirham

LITERACY RATE: 75.9%

LIFE EXPECTANCY: 73.95 years

TIME ZONE: 0

TYPE OF GOVERNMENT: Parliamentary Constitutional Monarchy

HEAD OF STATE: King Mohammed VI
HEAD OF GOVT: Prime Minister Aziz Akhannouch

GDP PER CAPITA: $8,100

POPULATION: 37,067,420

ISD CODE: 212 **INTERNET TLD:** .ma

Morocco is often called the 'Oasis of the Senses'. From the Sahara Desert to the snow-capped Atlas Mountains, the country's landscape is very diverse.

MOZAMBIQUE

LOCATION: South-eastern Africa

CAPITAL: Maputo

AREA: 799,380 sq. km

LANGUAGES: Makhuwa, Portuguese

MAIN RELIGIONS: Christianity, Islam

CURRENCY: Metical

LITERACY RATE: 63.4%

LIFE EXPECTANCY: 57.7 years

TIME ZONE: +2

TYPE OF GOVERNMENT: Presidential Republic

HEAD OF STATE AND GOVT: President Filipe Nyusi

GDP PER CAPITA: $1,200

POPULATION: 32,513,805

ISD CODE: 258 **INTERNET TLD:** .mz

Mozambique has won two Olympic medals, both won by Maria de Lurdes Mutola (nicknamed 'Maputo Express') in the women's 800 m – a bronze in 1996 and a gold in 2000.

MYANMAR (BURMA)

LOCATION: South-East Asia

CAPITAL: Naypyidaw

AREA: 676,578 sq. km

LANGUAGE: Burmese

MAIN RELIGION: Buddhism

CURRENCY: Kyat

LITERACY RATE: 89.1%

LIFE EXPECTANCY: 70.21 years

TIME ZONE: +6.5

TYPE OF GOVERNMENT: Parliamentary Republic

HEAD OF STATE AND GOVT: Prime Minister Senior General Min Aung Hlaing

GDP PER CAPITA: $4,000

POPULATION: 57,970,293

ISD CODE: 95 **INTERNET TLD:** .mm

In 2005, the capital of Myanmar was shifted from Yangon to Naypyidaw.

NAMIBIA

LOCATION: Southern Africa

CAPITAL: Windhoek

AREA: 824,292 sq. km

LANGUAGES: English, Afrikaans

MAIN RELIGION: Christianity

CURRENCY: Namibian Dollar

LITERACY RATE: 92.3%

LIFE EXPECTANCY: 67.04 years

TIME ZONE: +1

TYPE OF GOVERNMENT: Presidential Republic

HEAD OF STATE AND GOVT: President Hage Geingob

GDP PER CAPITA: $9,100

POPULATION: 2,777,232

ISD CODE: 264 **INTERNET TLD:** .na

One in four households in Namibia lives in poverty. The wealthiest 10 per cent of people command more than half the country's income.

NAURU

LOCATION: South Pacific Ocean

CAPITAL: No officially designated capital; Yaren is the largest city

AREA: 21 sq. km

LANGUAGES: Nauruan, English

MAIN RELIGION: Christianity

CURRENCY: Australian Dollar

LITERACY RATE: 98%

LIFE EXPECTANCY: 68.25 years

TIME ZONE: +12

TYPE OF GOVERNMENT: Parliamentary Republic

HEAD OF STATE AND GOVT: President Russ Kun

GDP PER CAPITA: $11,900

POPULATION: 9,852

ISD CODE: 674 **INTERNET TLD:** .nr

Nauru is the world's smallest island nation. It is the only republican state in the world without an official capital.

Background: Namibia

NEPAL

LOCATION: South Asia

CAPITAL: Kathmandu

AREA: 147,181 sq. km

LANGUAGE: Nepali

MAIN RELIGION: Hinduism

CURRENCY: Nepalese Rupee

LITERACY RATE: 71.2%

LIFE EXPECTANCY: 72.67 years

TIME ZONE: +5.45

TYPE OF GOVERNMENT: Federal Parliamentary Republic

HEAD OF STATE: President Ram Chandra Poudel **HEAD OF GOVT:** Prime Minister Pushpa Kamal Dahal

GDP PER CAPITA: $3,800

POPULATION: 30,899,443

ISD CODE: 977 **INTERNET TLD:** .np

Nepal's flag is the only national flag in the world that is neither a rectangle nor a square.

(THE) NETHERLANDS

LOCATION: North-western Europe

CAPITAL: Amsterdam

AREA: 41,543 sq. km

LANGUAGES: Dutch, Frisian

MAIN RELIGION: Christianity

CURRENCY: Euro

LITERACY RATE: 99%

LIFE EXPECTANCY: 82.36 years

TIME ZONE: +1

TYPE OF GOVERNMENT: Parliamentary Constitutional Monarchy

HEAD OF STATE: King Willem-Alexander **HEAD OF GOVT:** Prime Minister Mark Rutte

GDP PER CAPITA: $56,600

POPULATION: 17,463,930

ISD CODE: 31 **INTERNET TLD:** .nl

The country's landscape is dotted with windmills, a famous hallmark. There are as many as 300 castles open to the general public.

NEW ZEALAND

LOCATION: South-western Pacific Ocean

CAPITAL: Wellington

AREA: 267,710 sq. km

LANGUAGE: English

MAIN RELIGION: Christianity

CURRENCY: New Zealand Dollar

LITEACY RATE: 99%

LIFE EXPECTANCY: 82.74 years

TIME ZONE: +12

TYPE OF GOVERNMENT: Constitutional Monarchy and Parliamentary Democracy

HEAD OF STATE: King Charles III **HEAD OF GOVT:** Prime Minister Chris Hipkins

GDP PER CAPITA: $42,900

POPULATION: 5,109,702

ISD CODE: 64 **INTERNET TLD:** .nz

With 2.5 million cars for four million people (including children), the car ownership percentage in New Zealand is one of the world's highest.

NICARAGUA

LOCATION: Central America

CAPITAL: Managua

AREA: 130,370 sq. km

LANGUAGE: Spanish

MAIN RELIGION: Christianity

CURRENCY: Cordoba

LITERACY RATE: 82.6%

LIFE EXPECTANCY: 75.05 years

TIME ZONE: –6

TYPE OF GOVERNMENT: Presidential Republic

HEAD OF STATE AND GOVT: President Jose Daniel Ortega Saavedra

GDP PER CAPITA: $5,600

POPULATION: 6,359,689

ISD CODE: 505 **INTERNET TLD:** .ni

Nicaragua is famous for its dance form known as 'Palo de Mayo'. The country's most popular sport is baseball.

NIGER

LOCATION: West Africa

CAPITAL: Niamey

AREA: 1,267,000 sq. km

LANGUAGES: French, Hausa, Djerma

MAIN RELIGION: Islam

CURRENCY: CFA Franc

LITERACY RATE: 37.3%

LIFE EXPECTANCY: 60.48 years

TIME ZONE: +1

TYPE OF GOVERNMENT: Semi-presidential Republic

HEAD OF STATE: President Mohamed Bazoum **HEAD OF GOVT:** Prime Minister Ouhoumoudou Mahamadou

GDP PER CAPITA: $1,200

POPULATION: 25,396,840

ISD CODE: 227 **INTERNET TLD:** .ne

The remains of the dinosaur *Nigersaurus*, known for its long neck and hammerhead skull, were discovered in Niger in the 1950s.

NIGERIA

LOCATION: West Africa

CAPITAL: Abuja

AREA: 923,769 sq. km

LANGUAGES: English, Hausa

MAIN RELIGIONS: Islam, Christianity

CURRENCY: Naira

LITERACY RATE: 62%

LIFE EXPECTANCY: 61.79 years

TIME ZONE: +1

TYPE OF GOVERNMENT: Presidential Federal Republic

HEAD OF STATE AND GOVT: President Bola Tinubu

GDP PER CAPITA: $4,900

POPULATION: 230,842,743

ISD CODE: 234 **INTERNET TLD:** .ng

Football is the national sport of Nigeria. The national team is called the 'Super Eagles'. They have made it to the World Cup Finals five times.

Background: Netherlands

NORTH KOREA

LOCATION: East Asia

CAPITAL: Pyongyang

AREA: 120,540 sq. km

LANGUAGE: Korean

MAIN RELIGIONS: Officially atheist; Buddhism, Chondogyo, Christianity

CURRENCY: Won

LITERACY RATE: 100%

LIFE EXPECTANCY: 71.88 years

TIME ZONE: +9

TYPE OF GOVERNMENT: Communist Dictatorship

HEAD OF STATE: Chairman Kim Jong-un **HEAD OF GOVT:** Supreme People's Assembly President Choe Ryong-hae

GDP PER CAPITA: $1,700

POPULATION: 26,072,217

ISD CODE: 850 **INTERNET TLD:** .kp

The old name for North Korea is Joseon or Choson (Land of Morning Calm).

NORTH MACEDONIA

LOCATION: South-eastern Europe

CAPITAL: Skopje

AREA: 25,713 sq. km

LANGUAGES: Macedonian, Albanian

MAIN RELIGIONS: Christianity (Macedonian Orthodox Church), Islam

CURRENCY: Macedonian Dinar

LITERACY RATE: 98.4%

LIFE EXPECTANCY: 77.09 years

TIME ZONE: +1

TYPE OF GOVERNMENT: Parliamentary Republic

HEAD OF STATE: President Stevo Pendarovski **HEAD OF GOVT:** Prime Minister Dimitar Kovacevski

GDP PER CAPITA: $16,500

POPULATION: 2,133,410

ISD CODE: 389 **INTERNET TLD:** .mk

Macedonia was formerly a part of Yugoslavia and gained independence in 1991.

NORWAY

LOCATION: Northern Europe

CAPITAL: Oslo

AREA: 385,207 sq. km

LANGUAGE: Norwegian

MAIN RELIGION: Christianity

CURRENCY: Norwegian Kroner

LITERACY RATE: 100%

LIFE EXPECTANCY: 82.75 years

TIME ZONE: +1

TYPE OF GOVERNMENT: Parliamentary Constitutional Monarchy

HEAD OF STATE: King Harald V

HEAD OF GOVT: Prime Minister Jonas Gahr Store

GDP PER CAPITA: $65,700

POPULATION: 5,597,924

ISD CODE: 47 **INTERNET TLD:** .no

The Nobel Peace Prize is awarded in Oslo. The Norwegian king is present at the award ceremony.

Background: Norway

OMAN

LOCATION: Middle East

CAPITAL: Muscat

AREA: 309,500 sq. km

LANGUAGES: Arabic, English, Urdu

MAIN RELIGION: Islam

CURRENCY: Omani Rial

LITERACY RATE: 95.7%

LIFE EXPECTANCY: 77.16 years

TIME ZONE: +4

TYPE OF GOVERNMENT: Absolute Monarchy

HEAD OF STATE AND GOVT: Sultan Haitham bin Tariq Al Said

GDP PER CAPITA: $34,300

POPULATION: 3,833,465

ISD CODE: 968 **INTERNET TLD:** .om

The leaves of the *Myrtus communis* or the 'Yas' shrub found in Oman are used for making perfume.

PAKISTAN

LOCATION: South Asia

CAPITAL: Islamabad

AREA: 881,913 sq. km

LANGUAGES: Urdu, Punjabi, Sindhi

MAIN RELIGION: Islam

CURRENCY: Pakistani Rupee

LITERACY RATE: 58%

LIFE EXPECTANCY: 69.96 years

TIME ZONE: +5

TYPE OF GOVERNMENT: Federal Parliamentary Republic

HEAD OF STATE: President Arif Alvi

HEAD OF GOVT: Prime Minister Shehbaz Sharif

GDP PER CAPITA: $5,200

POPULATION: 247,653,551

ISD CODE: 92 **INTERNET TLD:** .pk

Pakistan is home to the largest earth-filled dam in the world, Tarbela dam.

PALAU

LOCATION: Group of islands in the North Pacific Ocean

CAPITAL: Melekeok

AREA: 459 sq. km

LANGUAGES: Palauan, Filipino, English

MAIN RELIGION: Christianity

CURRENCY: US Dollar

LITERACY RATE: 96.6%

LIFE EXPECTANCY: 74.91 years

TIME ZONE: +9

TYPE OF GOVERNMENT: Presidential Republic

HEAD OF STATE AND GOVT: President Surangel Whipps, Jr

GDP PER CAPITA: $13,800

POPULATION: 21,779

ISD CODE: 680 **INTERNET TLD:** .pw

In 1783, Palau was accidentally discovered by the shipwrecked crew of Captain Henry Wilson when he reached the shores of an island called Ulong.

Background: Oman

PANAMA

LOCATION: Central America

CAPITAL: Panama City

AREA: 75,417 sq. km

LANGUAGE: Spanish

MAIN RELIGION: Christianity

CURRENCY: Balboa, US Dollar

LITERACY RATE: 95.7%

LIFE EXPECTANCY: 78.44 years

TIME ZONE: –5

TYPE OF GOVERNMENT: Presidential Republic

HEAD OF STATE AND GOVT: President Laurentino Cortizo Cohen

GDP PER CAPITA: $29,000

POPULATION: 4,404,108

ISD CODE: 507 **INTERNET TLD:** .pa

The currency of Panama is named after Vasco Nunez de Balboa, the Spanish explorer who was the first to cross the Isthmus of Panama to the Pacific Ocean in 1513.

PAPUA NEW GUINEA

LOCATION: Between the Coral Sea and the South Pacific Ocean

CAPITAL: Port Moresby

AREA: 462,840 sq. km

LANGUAGES: Tok Pisin, English, Hiri Motu

MAIN RELIGION: Christianity

CURRENCY: Kina

LITERACY RATE: 64.2%

LIFE EXPECTANCY: 69.74 years

TIME ZONE: +11

TYPE OF GOVERNMENT: Constitutional Monarchy and Parliamentary Democracy

HEAD OF STATE: King Charles III
HEAD OF GOVT: Prime Minister James Marape

GDP PER CAPITA: $3,700

POPULATION: 9,819,350

ISD CODE: 675 **INTERNET TLD:** .pg

Seashells were the national currency of Papua New Guinea until 1933.

PARAGUAY

LOCATION: Central South America

CAPITAL: Asuncion

AREA: 406,757 sq. km

LANGUAGES: Spanish, Guarani

MAIN RELIGION: Christianity

CURRENCY: Guarani

LITERACY RATE: 94.5%

LIFE EXPECTANCY: 78.61 years

TIME ZONE: –4

TYPE OF GOVERNMENT: Presidential Republic

HEAD OF STATE AND GOVT: President Mario Abdo Benitez

GDP PER CAPITA: $13,700

POPULATION: 7,439,863

ISD CODE: 595 **INTERNET TLD:** .py

Due to its central location in South America, Paraguay is sometimes referred to as 'Corazon de America', or the Heart of America.

PERU

LOCATION: Western South America

CAPITAL: Lima

AREA: 1,285,216 sq. km

LANGUAGES: Spanish, Quechua

MAIN RELIGION: Christianity

CURRENCY: Nuevo Sol

LITERACY RATE: 94.5%

LIFE EXPECTANCY: 68.94 years

TIME ZONE: –5

TYPE OF GOVERNMENT: Presidential Republic

HEAD OF STATE AND GOVT: President Dina Ercilia Boluarte

GDP PER CAPITA: $12,500

POPULATION: 32,440,172

ISD CODE: 51 **INTERNET TLD:** .pe

There are as many as 3,000-4,000 varieties of potato grown in Peru.

(THE) PHILIPPINES

LOCATION: South-east Asia

CAPITAL: Manila

AREA: 300,000 sq. km

LANGUAGES: Filipino, English

MAIN RELIGION: Christianity

CURRENCY: Philippine Peso

LITERACY RATE: 96.3%

LIFE EXPECTANCY: 70.48 years

TIME ZONE: +8

TYPE OF GOVERNMENT: Presidential Republic

HEAD OF STATE AND GOVT: President Bongbong Marcos

GDP PER CAPITA: $8,100

POPULATION: 116,434,200

ISD CODE: 63 **INTERNET TLD:** .ph

There are more than 200 volcanoes on the islands of the Philippines, though only a few are active.

POLAND

LOCATION: Central Europe

CAPITAL: Warsaw

AREA: 312,696 sq. km

LANGUAGE: Polish

MAIN RELIGION: Christianity

CURRENCY: Zloty

LITERACY RATE: 99.8%

LIFE EXPECTANCY: 79 years

TIME ZONE: +1

TYPE OF GOVERNMENT: Parliamentary Republic

HEAD OF STATE: President Andrzej Duda **HEAD OF GOVT:** Prime Minister Mateusz Morawiecki

GDP PER CAPITA: $34,900

POPULATION: 37,991,766

ISD CODE: 48 **INTERNET TLD:** .pl

The Poles consider their name-days more important than their birthdays. Name-days are days of the year on which certain Christian saints are honoured. All those who share the name of the saint celebrate the day.

Background: Peru

PORTUGAL

LOCATION: South-western Europe

CAPITAL: Lisbon

AREA: 92,212 sq. km

LANGUAGES: Portuguese

MAIN RELIGION: Christianity

CURRENCY: Euro

LITERACY RATE: 95.9%

LIFE EXPECTANCY: 81.71 years

TIME ZONE: 0

TYPE OF GOVERNMENT: Semi-presidential Republic

HEAD OF STATE: President Marcelo Rebelo de Sousa **HEAD OF GOVT:** Prime Minister Antonio Luis Santosa da Costa

GDP PER CAPITA: $33,700

POPULATION: 10,223,150

ISD CODE: 351 **INTERNET TLD:** .pt

Ferdinand Magellan, a Portuguese explorer, was the first to complete a circumnavigation of the earth, in 1522.

QATAR

LOCATION: Middle East

CAPITAL: Doha

AREA: 11,581 sq. km

LANGUAGES: Arabic, English

MAIN RELIGION: Islam

CURRENCY: Qatari Riyal

LITERACY RATE: 93.5%

LIFE EXPECTANCY: 80.03 years

TIME ZONE: +3

TYPE OF GOVERNMENT: Absolute Monarchy

HEAD OF STATE: Amir Tamim bin Hamad Al Thani **HEAD OF GOVT:** Prime Minister Sheikh Mohammed bin Abdulrahman Al Thani

GDP PER CAPITA: $92,900

POPULATION: 2,532,104

ISD CODE: 974 **INTERNET TLD:** .qa

Qatar was the first Middle Eastern nation to host the FIFA World Cup, in November–December 2022.

ROMANIA

LOCATION: South-east Europe

CAPITAL: Bucharest

AREA: 238,397 sq. km

LANGUAGES: Romanian, Hungarian

MAIN RELIGION: Christianity

CURRENCY: Romanian Leu

LITERACY RATE: 98.9%

LIFE EXPECTANCY: 76.31 years

TIME ZONE: +2

TYPE OF GOVERNMENT: Semi-presidential Republic

HEAD OF STATE: President Klaus Iohannis **HEAD OF GOVT:** Prime Minister Catalin Predoiu

GDP PER CAPITA: $30,800

POPULATION: 18,326,327

ISD CODE: 40 **INTERNET TLD:** .ro

The earliest reliably dated European modern human fossils were discovered in 2002 at Pestera cu Oase ('Cave with Bones'). They were 37,800 to 42,000 years old.

RUSSIA

LOCATION: North Asia/east Europe

CAPITAL: Moscow

AREA: 17,098,246 sq. km

LANGUAGE: Russian

MAIN RELIGION: Christianity

CURRENCY: Ruble

LITERACY RATE: 99.7%

LIFE EXPECTANCY: 72.72 years

TIME ZONE: +3 to +12

TYPE OF GOVERNMENT: Semi-presidential Federation

HEAD OF STATE: President Vladimir Putin **HEAD OF GOVT:** Prime Minister Mikhail Mishustin

GDP PER CAPITA: $28,000

POPULATION: 141,698,923

ISD CODE: 7 **INTERNET TLD:** .ru

Two major physical landmarks in Russia are the Urals, the oldest mountains in the world, and Lake Baikal, the world's deepest lake and the largest reservoir of freshwater on Earth.

RWANDA

LOCATION: Central Africa

CAPITAL: Kigali

AREA: 26,338 sq. km

LANGUAGES: Kinyarwanda, French, English

MAIN RELIGION: Christianity

CURRENCY: Rwandan Franc

LITERACY RATE: 75.9%

LIFE EXPECTANCY: 66.21 years

TIME ZONE: +2

TYPE OF GOVERNMENT: Presidential Republic

HEAD OF STATE: President Paul Kagame **HEAD OF GOVT:** Prime Minister Edouard Ngirente

GDP PER CAPITA: $2,200

POPULATION: 13,400,541

ISD CODE: 250 **INTERNET TLD:** .rw

Sixty per cent of Rwandan parliamentarians are women.

SAINT KITTS AND NEVIS

LOCATION: Islands in the Caribbean Sea

CAPITAL: Basseterre

AREA: 261 sq. km

LANGUAGE: English

MAIN RELIGION: Christianity

CURRENCY: East Caribbean Dollar

LITERACY RATE: 97.8%

LIFE EXPECTANCY: 77.33 years

TIME ZONE: –4

TYPE OF GOVERNMENT: Constitutional Monarchy and Federal Parliamentary Democracy

HEAD OF STATE: King Charles III **HEAD OF GOVT:** Prime Minister Terrance Drew

GDP PER CAPITA: $26,500

POPULATION: 54,817

ISD CODE: 1-869 **INTERNET TLD:** .kn

Christopher Columbus discovered the island and named it after his patron saint, St Christopher. It was later shortened to Saint Kitts.

Background: Russia

SAINT LUCIA

LOCATION: Caribbean

CAPITAL: Castries

AREA: 617 sq. km

LANGUAGE: English

MAIN RELIGION: Christianity

CURRENCY: East Caribbean Dollar

LITERACY RATE: 90.1%

LIFE EXPECTANCY: 79.18 years

TIME ZONE: –4

TYPE OF GOVERNMENT: Constitutional Monarchy and Parliamentary Democracy

HEAD OF STATE: King Charles III
HEAD OF GOVT: Prime Minister Philip J. Pierre

GDP PER CAPITA: $13,000

POPULATION: 167,591

ISD CODE: 1-758 **INTERNET TLD:** .lc

La Soufriere volcano in Malgretoute, Saint Lucia, is the world's only drive-in volcano! You can drive right into its crater.

SAINT VINCENT AND THE GRENADINES

LOCATION: Central America/Caribbean Sea

CAPITAL: Kingstown

AREA: 389 sq. km

LANGUAGE: English

MAIN RELIGION: Christianity

CURRENCY: East Caribbean Dollar

LITERACY RATE: 96%

LIFE EXPECTANCY: 76.93 years

TIME ZONE: –4

TYPE OF GOVERNMENT: Constitutional Monarchy and Parliamentary Democracy

HEAD OF STATE: King Charles III
HEAD OF GOVT: Prime Minister Ralph Gonsalves

GDP PER CAPITA: $13,700

POPULATION: 100,804

ISD CODE: 1-784 **INTERNET TLD:** .vc

The first few scenes of *The Pirates of the Caribbean: The Curse of the Black Pearl* were shot here.

SAMOA

LOCATION: Group of islands in the South Pacific

CAPITAL: Apia

AREA: 2,842 sq. km

LANGUAGES: Samoan, English

MAIN RELIGION: Christianity

CURRENCY: Tala

LITERACY RATE: 99.1%

LIFE EXPECTANCY: 75.46 years

TIME ZONE: +13

TYPE OF GOVERNMENT: Parliamentary Republic

HEAD OF STATE: President Va'aletoa Sualauvi II **HEAD OF GOVT:** Prime Minister Fiame Naomi Mata'afa

GDP PER CAPITA: $5,500

POPULATION: 207,501

ISD CODE: 685 **INTERNET TLD:** .ws

Tattooing is a great tradition in Samoa, and both men and women have been getting intricate tattoos for at least 2,000 years.

Background: Saint Lucia

SAN MARINO

LOCATION: Southern Europe

CAPITAL: San Marino

AREA: 61.2 sq. km

LANGUAGE: Italian

MAIN RELIGION: Christianity

CURRENCY: Euro

LITERACY RATE: 99.9%

LIFE EXPECTANCY: 84.05 years

TIME ZONE: +1

TYPE OF GOVERNMENT: Parliamentary Republic

HEAD OF STATE: Captains Alessandro Scarano and Adele Tonnini **HEAD OF GOVT:** Secretary of State for Foreign Affairs Luca Beccari

GDP PER CAPITA: $56,400

POPULATION: 34,892

ISD CODE: 378 **INTERNET TLD:** .sm

The constitution of San Marino, enacted in 1600, is the world's oldest constitution still in effect.

SAO TOME AND PRINCIPE

LOCATION: West Central Africa; islands in the Sea of Guinea

CAPITAL: Sao Tome

AREA: 1,001 sq. km

LANGUAGE: Portuguese

MAIN RELIGION: Christianity

CURRENCY: Dobra

LITERACY RATE: 94.8%

LIFE EXPECTANCY: 67.39 years

TIME ZONE: +0

TYPE OF GOVERNMENT: Semi-presidential Republic

HEAD OF STATE: President Carlos Manuel Vila Nova **HEAD OF GOVT:** Prime Minister Patrice Trovoada

GDP PER CAPITA: $4,100

POPULATION: 220,372

ISD CODE: 239 **INTERNET TLD:** .st

Sao Tome and Principe, comprising two islands, is the smallest nation in Africa. Sao Tome houses 90 per cent of the population.

SAUDI ARABIA

LOCATION: Middle East

CAPITAL: Riyadh

AREA: 2,149,690 sq. km

LANGUAGE: Arabic

MAIN RELIGION: Islam

CURRENCY: Saudi Riyal

LITERACY RATE: 97.6%

LIFE EXPECTANCY: 76.91 years

TIME ZONE: +3

TYPE OF GOVERNMENT: Absolute Monarchy

HEAD OF STATE AND GOVT: King Salman bin Abd al-Aziz Al Saud

GDP PER CAPITA: $44,300

POPULATION: 35,939,806

ISD CODE: 966 **INTERNET TLD:** .sa

Saudi Arabia is the world's largest producer of desalinated water.

Background: San Marino

SENEGAL

LOCATION: West Africa

CAPITAL: Dakar

AREA: 196,712 sq. km

LANGUAGES: French, Wolof

MAIN RELIGION: Islam

CURRENCY: CFA Franc

LITERACY RATE: 56.3%

LIFE EXPECTANCY: 70.25 years

TIME ZONE: 0

TYPE OF GOVERNMENT: Presidential Republic

HEAD OF STATE: President Macky Sall **HEAD OF GOVT:** Prime Minister Amadou BA

GDP PER CAPITA: $3,500

POPULATION: 18,384,660

ISD CODE: 221 **INTERNET TLD:** .sn

Senegal is known for its tradition of storytelling, performed by storytellers called 'griots'. They have kept West African history alive through stories and music.

SERBIA

LOCATION: East Europe

CAPITAL: Belgrade

AREA: 88,361 sq. km

LANGUAGES: Serbian, Hungarian

MAIN RELIGION: Christianity

CURRENCY: Serbian Dinar

LITERACY RATE: 99.5%

LIFE EXPECTANCY: 75.08 years

TIME ZONE: +1

TYPE OF GOVERNMENT: Parliamentary Republic

HEAD OF STATE: President Aleksandar Vucic **HEAD OF GOVT:** Prime Minister Ana Brnabic

GDP PER CAPITA: $19,800

POPULATION: 6,693,375

ISD CODE: 381 **INTERNET TLD:** .rs

Serbia is one of the biggest producers and exporters of raspberries in the world. In the harvest season, more than 200,000 people are employed in this industry.

SEYCHELLES

LOCATION: Indian Ocean

CAPITAL: Victoria

AREA: 455 sq. km

LANGUAGES: Creole, English, French

MAIN RELIGION: Christianity

CURRENCY: Seychelles Rupee

LITERACY RATE: 95.9%

LIFE EXPECTANCY: 76.36 years

TIME ZONE: +4

TYPE OF GOVERNMENT: Presidential Republic

HEAD OF STATE AND GOVT: President Wavel Ramkalawan

GDP PER CAPITA: $28,800

POPULATION: 97,617

ISD CODE: 248 **INTERNET TLD:** .sc

***Medusagyne oppositifolia* or the jellyfish tree (named so after the shape of its fruit), which is endemic to Seychelles, was thought extinct until a few plants were discovered in the 1970s.**

Background: Senegal

SIERRA LEONE

LOCATION: West Africa

CAPITAL: Freetown

AREA: 71,740 sq. km

LANGUAGES: English, Krio, Temne

MAIN RELIGIONS: Islam, Christianity

CURRENCY: Leone

LITERACY RATE: 47.7%

LIFE EXPECTANCY: 59.07 years

TIME ZONE: +0

TYPE OF GOVERNMENT: Presidential Republic

HEAD OF STATE AND GOVT: President Julius Maada Bio

GDP PER CAPITA: $1,600

POPULATION: 8,908,040

ISD CODE: 232 **INTERNET TLD:** .sl

Sierra Leone gets its name from Portuguese 'Serra Leao', meaning 'lion mountain range'.

SINGAPORE

LOCATION: South-East Asia

CAPITAL: Singapore City

AREA: 725.7 sq. km

LANGUAGES: English, Mandarin, Malay

MAIN RELIGION: Buddhism, Islam

CURRENCY: Singapore Dollar

LITERACY RATE: 97.5%

LIFE EXPECTANCY: 86.51 years

TIME ZONE: +8

TYPE OF GOVERNMENT: Parliamentary Republic

HEAD OF STATE: President Halimah Yacob **HEAD OF GOVT:** Prime Minister Lee Hsien Loong

GDP PER CAPITA: $106,000

POPULATION: 5,975,383

ISD CODE: 65 **INTERNET TLD:** .sg

A city, a capital and a state all at once, Singapore is one of only three city states in the world. The other two are Monaco and Vatican City.

SLOVAKIA

LOCATION: Central Europe

CAPITAL: Bratislava

AREA: 49,035 sq. km

LANGUAGES: Slovak, Hungarian

MAIN RELIGION: Christianity

CURRENCY: Euro

LITERACY RATE: 99.6%

LIFE EXPECTANCY: 78.55 years

TIME ZONE: +1

TYPE OF GOVERNMENT: Parliamentary Republic

HEAD OF STATE: President Zuzana Caputova **HEAD OF GOVT:** Prime Minister Eduard Heger

GDP PER CAPITA: $31,900

POPULATION: 5,425,319

ISD CODE: 421 **INTERNET TLD:** .sk

Stefan Banic, a Slovak, invented the first actively used parachute, patenting it in 1913.

Background: Singapore

SLOVENIA

LOCATION: Central Europe

CAPITAL: Ljubljana

AREA: 20,271 sq. km

LANGUAGE: Slovene

MAIN RELIGIONS: Christianity, Islam

CURRENCY: Euro

LITERACY RATE: 99.7%

LIFE EXPECTANCY: 82.02 years

TIME ZONE: +1

TYPE OF GOVERNMENT: Parliamentary Republic

HEAD OF STATE: President Natasa Pirc Musar **HEAD OF GOVT:** Prime Minister Robert Golob

GDP PER CAPITA: $40,000

POPULATION: 2,099,790

ISD CODE: 386 **INTERNET TLD:** .si

A grapevine that grows in the city of Maribor here is believed to be the world's oldest extant vine. It's over 450 years old.

SOLOMON ISLANDS

LOCATION: South Pacific Ocean

CAPITAL: Honiara

AREA: 28,400 sq. km

LANGUAGES: Pijin (Solomonese Pidgin), English

MAIN RELIGION: Christianity

CURRENCY: Solomon Island Dollar

LITERACY RATE: 84.1%

LIFE EXPECTANCY: 76.96 years

TIME ZONE: +11

TYPE OF GOVERNMENT: Constitutional Monarchy and Parliamentary Democracy

HEAD OF STATE: King Charles III **HEAD OF GOVT:** Prime Minister Manasseh Sogavare

GDP PER CAPITA: $2,400

POPULATION: 714,766

ISD CODE: 677 **INTERNET TLD:** .sb

Marovo Lagoon, the largest saltwater lagoon in the world, is located in New Georgia in the Solomon Islands.

SOMALIA

LOCATION: East Africa

CAPITAL: Mogadishu

AREA: 637,657 sq. km

LANGUAGES: Somali, Arabic

MAIN RELIGION: Islam

CURRENCY: Somali Shilling

LITERACY RATE: 37.8%

LIFE EXPECTANCY: 56.12 years

TIME ZONE: +3

TYPE OF GOVERNMENT: Federal Parliamentary Republic

HEAD OF STATE: President Hassan Sheikh Mohamud **HEAD OF GOVT:** Prime Minister Hamza Abdi Barre

GDP PER CAPITA: $1,100

POPULATION: 12,693,796

ISD CODE: 252 **INTERNET TLD:** .so

Somalia is located on a peninsula in East Africa, which juts out into the Arabian Sea. It is called the 'Horn of Africa' for its horn-like shape.

Background: South Africa

SOUTH AFRICA

LOCATION: Southern Africa

CAPITAL: Pretoria (executive), Cape Town (judicial), Bloemfontein (legislative)

AREA: 1,221,037 sq. km

LANGUAGES: IsiZulu, IsiXhosa, Afrikaans, and seven other official languages

MAIN RELIGIONS: Christianity, Islam, Hinduism, traditional African religions

CURRENCY: South African Rand

LITERACY RATE: 95%

LIFE EXPECTANCY: 65.6 years

TIME ZONE: +2

TYPE OF GOVERNMENT: Parliamentary Republic

HEAD OF STATE AND GOVT: President Cyril Ramaphosa

GDP PER CAPITA: $13,300

POPULATION: 58,048,332

ISD CODE: 27 **INTERNET TLD:** .za

The Vredefort Dome is the world's largest meteor scar (originally 300 km wide!).

SOUTH KOREA

LOCATION: East Asia

CAPITAL: Seoul

AREA: 100,363 sq. km

LANGUAGE: Korean

MAIN RELIGIONS: Christianity, Buddhism

CURRENCY: South Korean Won

LITERACY RATE: 97.97%

LIFE EXPECTANCY: 83.17 years

TIME ZONE: +9

TYPE OF GOVERNMENT: Presidential Republic

HEAD OF STATE: President Yoon Suk-yeol **HEAD OF GOVT:** Prime Minister Yoon Suk Yeol

GDP PER CAPITA: $44,200

POPULATION: 51,966,948

ISD CODE: 82 **INTERNET TLD:** .kr

South Korean men above 18 years have to serve in the army for two years.

SOUTH SUDAN

LOCATION: East-central Africa

CAPITAL: Juba

AREA: 619,745 sq. km

LANGUAGES: English, indigenous languages, including Dinka, Nuer, Bari and Zande

MAIN RELIGIONS: Animist, Christianity, Islam

CURRENCY: South Sudanese Pound

LITERACY RATE: 34.5%

LIFE EXPECTANCY: 59.71 years

TIME ZONE: +3

TYPE OF GOVERNMENT: Presidential Republic

HEAD OF STATE AND GOVT: President Salva Kiir Mayardit

GDP PER CAPITA: $1,600

POPULATION: 12,118,379

ISD CODE: 211 **INTERNET TLD:** .ss

South Sudan is the world's youngest country, having gained independence from Sudan in 2011 after a two-decade-long civil war.

SPAIN

LOCATION: South-western Europe

CAPITAL: Madrid

AREA: 505,990 sq. km

LANGUAGE: Spanish

MAIN RELIGION: Christianity

CURRENCY: Euro

LITERACY RATE: 98.6%

LIFE EXPECTANCY: 82.78 years

TIME ZONE: +1

TYPE OF GOVERNMENT: Parliamentary Constitutional Monarchy

HEAD OF STATE: King Felipe VI

HEAD OF GOVT: President and Prime Minister Pedro Sanchez

GDP PER CAPITA: $37,900

POPULATION: 47,222,613

ISD CODE: 34 **INTERNET TLD:** .es

Sobrino de Botín, a restaurant in Madrid, is said to be continuously operating since 1725!

SRI LANKA

LOCATION: South Asia

CAPITAL: Sri Jayawardenepura Kotte; Colombo (commercial capital)

AREA: 65,610 sq. km

LANGUAGES: Sinhala, Tamil

MAIN RELIGIONS: Buddhism, Hinduism

CURRENCY: Sri Lankan Rupee

LITERACY RATE: 92.3%

LIFE EXPECTANCY: 78.24 years

TIME ZONE: +5.30

TYPE OF GOVERNMENT: Presidential Republic

HEAD OF STATE AND GOVT: President Ranil Wickremesinghe

GDP PER CAPITA: $13,400

POPULATION: 23,326,272

ISD CODE: 94 **INTERNET TLD:** .lk

Sri Lanka was known as Ceylon before 1972. In 1960, Sirimavo Bandaranaike of Sri Lanka (then Ceylon) became the first woman prime minister in history.

SUDAN

LOCATION: North-eastern Africa

CAPITAL: Khartoum

AREA: 1,886,068 sq. km

LANGUAGES: Arabic, English

MAIN RELIGIONS: Islam, Christianity

CURRENCY: Sudanese Pound

LITERACY RATE: 60.7%

LIFE EXPECTANCY: 67.45 years

TIME ZONE: +2

TYPE OF GOVERNMENT: Federal Presidential Democratic Republic

HEAD OF STATE AND GOVT: Sovereign Council Chairman and Commander-in-Chief of Sudanese Armed Forces General Abdel Fattah Al-Burhan

GDP PER CAPITA: $3,700

POPULATION: 49,197,555

ISD CODE: 249 **INTERNET TLD:** .sd

Sudan is home to more pyramids than Egypt.

SURINAME

LOCATION: North-eastern South America

CAPITAL: Paramaribo

AREA: 163,821 sq. km

LANGUAGES: Dutch, English

MAIN RELIGIONS: Christianity, Hinduism

CURRENCY: Surinamese Dollar

LITERACY RATE: 95%

LIFE EXPECTANCY: 72.57 years

TIME ZONE: –3

TYPE OF GOVERNMENT: Presidential Republic

HEAD OF STATE AND GOVT: President Chan Santokhi

GDP PER CAPITA: $14,800

POPULATION: 639,759

ISD CODE: 597 **INTERNET TLD:** .sr

Tropical rainforests cover about 80 per cent of the land area in Suriname.

SWEDEN

LOCATION: Northern Europe

CAPITAL: Stockholm

AREA: 450,295 sq. km

LANGUAGE: Swedish

MAIN RELIGION: Christianity

CURRENCY: Swedish Krona

LITERACY RATE: 99%

LIFE EXPECTANCY: 82.8 years

TIME ZONE: +1

TYPE OF GOVERNMENT: Parliamentary Constitutional Monarchy

HEAD OF STATE: King Carl XVI Gustaf

HEAD OF GOVT: Prime Minister Ulf Kristersson

GDP PER CAPITA: $53,600

POPULATION: 10,536,338

ISD CODE: 46 **INTERNET TLD:** .se

A popular Swedish souvenir is the road sign for 'moose crossing'. Every year, many of these signs are stolen from the roads.

SWITZERLAND

LOCATION: Central Europe

CAPITAL: Bern (de facto); no official capital

AREA: 41,285 sq. km

LANGUAGES: German, French, Italian

MAIN RELIGION: Christianity

CURRENCY: Swiss Franc

LITERACY RATE: 99%

LIFE EXPECTANCY: 83.42 years

TIME ZONE: +1

TYPE OF GOVERNMENT: Federal Republic

HEAD OF STATE AND GOVT: President of the Swiss Confederation Alain Berset

GDP PER CAPITA: $71,000

POPULATION: 8,563,760

ISD CODE: 41 **INTERNET TLD:** .ch

Seventy percent of the country is covered with mountains and it has over 1,500 lakes.

Background: Sweden

SYRIA

LOCATION: Middle East

CAPITAL: Damascus

AREA: 185,180 sq. km

LANGUAGE: Arabic

MAIN RELIGION: Islam

CURRENCY: Syrian Pound

LITERACY RATE: 86.4%

LIFE EXPECTANCY: 74.55 years

TIME ZONE: +2

TYPE OF GOVERNMENT: Presidential Republic

HEAD OF STATE: President Bashar al-Assad **HEAD OF GOVT:** Prime Minister Hussein Arnous

GDP PER CAPITA: $2,900

POPULATION: 22,933,531

ISD CODE: 963 **INTERNET TLD:** .sy

Damascus has been inhabited for more than 4,000 years, making it one of the oldest continuously inhabited settlements in the world.

TAJIKISTAN

LOCATION: Central Asia

CAPITAL: Dushanbe

AREA: 143,100 sq. km

LANGUAGES: Tajik, Russian

MAIN RELIGION: Islam

CURRENCY: Somoni

LITERACY RATE: 99.8%

LIFE EXPECTANCY: 69.66 years

TIME ZONE: +5

TYPE OF GOVERNMENT: Presidential Republic

HEAD OF STATE: President Emomali Rahmon **HEAD OF GOVT:** Prime Minister Qokhir Rasulzoda

GDP PER CAPITA: $3,900

POPULATION: 9,245,937

ISD CODE: 992 **INTERNET TLD:** .tj

The Iskanderkul Lake of Tajikistan has been named after Alexander the Great. The country was an integral part of the ancient Silk Route.

TANZANIA

LOCATION: East Africa

CAPITAL: Dodoma

AREA: 947,303 sq. km

LANGUAGES: Swahili, English

MAIN RELIGIONS: Islam, Christianity, indigenous faiths

CURRENCY: Tanzanian Shilling

LITERACY RATE: 81.8%

LIFE EXPECTANCY: 70.48 years

TIME ZONE: +3

TYPE OF GOVERNMENT: Presidential Republic

HEAD OF STATE AND GOVT: President Samia Suluhu Hassan

GDP PER CAPITA: $2,600

POPULATION: 65,642,682

ISD CODE: 255 **INTERNET TLD:** .tz

At 264 sq. km, the Ngorongoro Crater, in the Crater Highlands area of Tanzania, is the largest inactive, intact and unfilled crater in the world. It is home to many wild animals.

Background: Thailand

THAILAND

LOCATION: South-East Asia

CAPITAL: Bangkok

AREA: 513,120 sq. km

LANGUAGE: Thai

MAIN RELIGION: Buddhism

CURRENCY: Baht

LITERACY RATE: 94.1%

LIFE EXPECTANCY: 77.91 years

TIME ZONE: +7

TYPE OF GOVERNMENT: Constitutional Monarchy

HEAD OF STATE: King Vajiralongkorn **HEAD OF GOVT:** Prime Minister Prayut Chan-o-cha

GDP PER CAPITA: $17,100

POPULATION: 69,794,997

ISD CODE: 66 **INTERNET TLD:** .th

Thailand is the only South-East Asian country to have never been dominated by a Western power and hence retains most of its original culture.

TIMOR-LESTE

LOCATION: South-east Asia

CAPITAL: Dili

AREA: 14,874 sq. km

LANGUAGES: Tetum, Portuguese

MAIN RELIGION: Christianity

CURRENCY: US Dollar

LITERACY RATE: 68.1%

LIFE EXPECTANCY: 70.21 years

TIME ZONE: +9

TYPE OF GOVERNMENT: Semi-presidential Republic

HEAD OF STATE: President Jose Ramos-Horta **HEAD OF GOVT:** Prime Minister Xanana Gusmao

GDP PER CAPITA: $5,000

POPULATION: 1,476,042

ISD CODE: 670 **INTERNET TLD:** .tl

Nine days after East Timor gained independence from Portugal in 1975, it was occupied by Indonesia. It became independent of Indonesian rule in 2002.

TOGO

LOCATION: West Africa

CAPITAL: Lome

AREA: 56,785 sq. km

LANGUAGES: French, Ewe, Mina, Kabye, Dagomba, other indigenous languages

MAIN RELIGIONS: Indigenous beliefs, Christianity, Islam

CURRENCY: CFA Franc

LITERACY RATE: 66.5%

LIFE EXPECTANCY: 71.71 years

TIME ZONE: +0

TYPE OF GOVERNMENT: Presidential Republic

HEAD OF STATE: President Faure Gnassingbe **HEAD OF GOVT:** Prime Minister Victoire Tomegah Dogbe

GDP PER CAPITA: $2,100

POPULATION: 8,703,961

ISD CODE: 228 **INTERNET TLD:** .tg

Togo is the world's fourth largest producer of phosphate, a mineral used for fertilizers.

TONGA

LOCATION: South Pacific Ocean

CAPITAL: Nuku'alofa

AREA: 748 sq. km

LANGUAGES: Tongan, English

MAIN RELIGION: Christianity

CURRENCY: Pa'anga

LITERACY RATE: 99.4%

LIFE EXPECTANCY: 77.78

TIME ZONE: +13

TYPE OF GOVERNMENT: Constitutional Monarchy

HEAD OF STATE: King Tupou VI
HEAD OF GOVT: Prime Minister Siaosi Sovaleni

GDP PER CAPITA: $6,100

POPULATION: 105,221

ISD CODE: 676 **INTERNET TLD:** .to

Captain James Cook, the famous British navigator, named Tonga the 'Friendly Islands'.

TRINIDAD AND TOBAGO

LOCATION: Caribbean Sea

CAPITAL: Port of Spain

AREA: 5,131 sq. km

LANGUAGE: English

MAIN RELIGIONS: Christianity, Hinduism

CURRENCY: Trinidad and Tobago Dollar

LITERACY RATE: 99%

LIFE EXPECTANCY: 76.19 years

TIME ZONE: –4

TYPE OF GOVERNMENT: Parliamentary Republic

HEAD OF STATE: President Christine Kangaloo **HEAD OF GOVT:** Prime Minister Keith Rowley

GDP PER CAPITA: $23,000

POPULATION: 1,407,460

ISD CODE: 1-868 **INTERNET TLD:** .tt

It is believed that Daniel Defoe and Robert Louis Stevenson based their respective novels, *Robinson Crusoe* and *Treasure Island*, on the islands of Trinidad and Tobago.

TUNISIA

LOCATION: Northern Africa

CAPITAL: Tunis

AREA: 163,610 sq. km

LANGUAGES: Arabic, French

MAIN RELIGION: Islam

CURRENCY: Tunisian Dinar

LITERACY RATE: 82.7%

LIFE EXPECTANCY: 77.07 years

TIME ZONE: +1

TYPE OF GOVERNMENT: Parliamentary Republic

HEAD OF STATE: President Kais Saied
HEAD OF GOVT: Prime Minister Najla Bouden

GDP PER CAPITA: $10,400

POPULATION: 11,976,182

ISD CODE: 216 **INTERNET TLD:** .tn

The city of Kairouan in Tunisia is considered one of the most important cities for Islam after Mecca, Medina and Jerusalem.

Background: Turkey

TURKEY (TURKIYE)

LOCATION: West Asia/East Europe

CAPITAL: Ankara

AREA: 783,356 sq. km

LANGUAGE: Turkish

MAIN RELIGION: Islam

CURRENCY: Turkish Lira

LITERACY RATE: 96.7%

LIFE EXPECTANCY: 76.47 years

TIME ZONE: +3

TYPE OF GOVERNMENT: Presidential Republic

HEAD OF STATE AND GOVT: President Recep Tayyip Erdogan

GDP PER CAPITA: $31,500

POPULATION: 83,593,483

ISD CODE: 90 **INTERNET TLD:** .tr

Istanbul, the largest city in Turkey by population, is the only city in the world built on two continents (Asia and Europe).

TURKMENISTAN

LOCATION: Central Asia

CAPITAL: Ashgabat

AREA: 491,210 sq. km

LANGUAGES: Turkmen, Russian

MAIN RELIGION: Islam

CURRENCY: Turkmenistani Manat

LITERACY RATE: 99.7%

LIFE EXPECTANCY: 72.11 years

TIME ZONE: +5

TYPE OF GOVERNMENT: Presidential Republic ;authoritarian

HEAD OF STATE AND GOVT: President Serdar Berdimuhamedow

GDP PER CAPITA: $15,500

POPULATION: 5,690,818

ISD CODE: 993 **INTERNET TLD:** .tm

In Turkmenistan's Karakum Desert, the Darvaza Gas Crater ('The Burning Gates') gives off a glow that can be seen from miles away.

TUVALU

LOCATION: South Pacific Ocean

CAPITAL: Funafuti

AREA: 26 sq. km

LANGUAGES: Tuvaluan, English

MAIN RELIGION: Christianity (Church of Tuvalu)

CURRENCY: Tuvaluan Dollar, Australian Dollar

LITERACY RATE: Not available

LIFE EXPECTANCY: 68.69 years

TIME ZONE: +12

TYPE OF GOVERNMENT: Constitutional Monarchy and Parliamentary Democracy

HEAD OF STATE: King Charles III **HEAD OF GOVT:** Prime Minister Kausea Natano

GDP PER CAPITA: $4,900

POPULATION: 11,639

ISD CODE: 688; **INTERNET TLD:** .tv

Eight of the nine islands of Tuvalu are inhabited; the name 'Tuvalu' means 'eight standing together'.

UGANDA

LOCATION: East-central Africa

CAPITAL: Kampala

AREA: 241,038 sq. km

LANGUAGES: English, Swahili

MAIN RELIGIONS: Christianity, Islam

CURRENCY: Ugandan Shilling

LITERACY RATE: 79%

LIFE EXPECTANCY: 69.32 years

TIME ZONE: +3

TYPE OF GOVERNMENT: Presidential Republic

HEAD OF STATE AND GOVT: President Yoweri Museveni

GDP PER CAPITA: $2,200

POPULATION: 47,729,952

ISD CODE: 256 **INTERNET TLD:** .ug

There are large reserves of crude oil and natural gas in Uganda that are still largely untapped. The largest export is coffee.

UKRAINE

LOCATION: Eastern Europe

CAPITAL: Kiev

AREA: 603,628 sq. km

LANGUAGES: Ukrainian, Russian

MAIN RELIGION: Christianity (Ukrainian Orthodox Church)

CURRENCY: Hryvnia

LITERACY RATE: 100%

LIFE EXPECTANCY: 73.72 years

TIME ZONE: +2

TYPE OF GOVERNMENT: Semi-presidential Republic

HEAD OF STATE: President Volodymyr Zelenskyy **HEAD OF GOVT:** Prime Minister Denys Shmyhal

GDP PER CAPITA: $12,900

POPULATION: 43,306,477

ISD CODE: 380 **INTERNET TLD:** .ua

The town called Rakhiv and the village of Dilove near Rakhiv are two of the contenders for the geographical centre of Europe.

UNITED ARAB EMIRATES

LOCATION: Middle East

CAPITAL: Abu Dhabi

AREA: 83,600 sq. km

LANGUAGE: Arabic

MAIN RELIGION: Islam

CURRENCY: UAE Dirham

LITERACY RATE: 98.1%

LIFE EXPECTANCY: 79.75 years

TIME ZONE: +4

TYPE OF GOVERNMENT: Federation of Monarchies

HEAD OF STATE: President Muhammad Bin Zayid Al-Nuhayyan **HEAD OF GOVT:** Prime Minister Mohammed bin Rashid Al Maktoum

GDP PER CAPITA: $69,700

POPULATION: 9,973,449

ISD CODE: 971 **INTERNET TLD:** .ae

The United Arab Emirates is divided into seven emirates. Over two-thirds of its population lives in either Abu Dhabi or Dubai.

UNITED KINGDOM

LOCATION: West Europe

CAPITAL: London

AREA: 242,495 sq. km

LANGUAGE: English

MAIN RELIGION: Christianity

CURRENCY: Pound Sterling

LITERACY RATE: 99%

LIFE EXPECTANCY: 82.05 years

TIME ZONE: +0

TYPE OF GOVERNMENT: Parliamentary Constitutional Monarchy

HEAD OF STATE: King Charles III **HEAD OF GOVT:** Prime Minister Rishi Sunak

GDP PER CAPITA: $45,000

POPULATION: 68,138,484

ISD CODE: 44 **INTERNET TLD:** .uk

The United Kingdom was the first country in the world to use postage stamps.

UNITED STATES OF AMERICA

LOCATION: North America

CAPITAL: Washington DC

AREA: 9,833,520 sq. km

LANGUAGES: English, Spanish

MAIN RELIGION: Christianity

CURRENCY: US Dollar

LITERACY RATE: 99%

LIFE EXPECTANCY: 80.75 years

TIME ZONE: –3 to –10

TYPE OF GOVERNMENT: Constitutional Federal Republic

HEAD OF STATE AND GOVT: President Joseph R. Biden, Jr (Joe Biden)

GDP PER CAPITA: $63,700

POPULATION: 339,665,118

ISD CODE: 1 **INTERNET TLD:** .us

The USA is the only country to have ever used nuclear weapons.

URUGUAY

LOCATION: Southern South America

CAPITAL: Montevideo

AREA: 176,215 sq. km

LANGUAGES: Spanish, Portunol

MAIN RELIGION: Christianity

CURRENCY: Uruguayan Peso

LITERACY RATE: 98.8%

LIFE EXPECTANCY: 78.66 years

TIME ZONE: –3

TYPE OF GOVERNMENT: Presidential Republic

HEAD OF STATE AND GOVT: President Luis Lacalle Pou

GDP PER CAPITA: $22,800

POPULATION: 3,416,264

ISD CODE: 598 **INTERNET TLD:** .uy

Uruguay has the world's longest national anthem (six minutes). Greece actually has the longest one, but generally uses a shorter version.

Background: United Kingdom

UZBEKISTAN

LOCATION: Central Asia

CAPITAL: Tashkent

AREA: 448,978 sq. km

LANGUAGES: Uzbek, Russian

MAIN RELIGION: Islam

CURRENCY: Uzbekistani Som

LITERACY RATE: 100%

LIFE EXPECTANCY: 75.55 years

TIME ZONE: +5

TYPE OF GOVERNMENT: Presidential Republic; highly authoritarian

HEAD OF STATE: President Shavkat Miromonovich Mirziyoyev **HEAD OF GOVT:** Prime Minister Abdulla Aripov

GDP PER CAPITA: $7,700

POPULATION: 31,360,836

ISD CODE: 998 **INTERNET TLD:** .uz

Uzbekistan has the fourth largest gold deposits in the world. The country mines 80 tonnes of gold every year.

VANUATU

LOCATION: South Pacific Ocean

CAPITAL: Port Vila

AREA: 12,189 sq. km

LANGUAGES: Bislama, English

MAIN RELIGION: Christianity

CURRENCY: Vanuatu Vatu

LITERACY RATE: 89.1%

LIFE EXPECTANCY: 75.4 years

TIME ZONE: +11

TYPE OF GOVERNMENT: Parliamentary Republic

HEAD OF STATE: President Nikenike Vurobaravu **HEAD OF GOVT:** Prime Minister Ishmael Kalsakau

GDP PER CAPITA: $2,800

POPULATION: 313,046

ISD CODE: 678 **INTERNET TLD:** .vu

Vanuatu is an archipelago consisting of approximately 82 islands of volcanic origin.

VATICAN CITY

LOCATION: Southern Europe (a city state in Rome, Italy)

CAPITAL: Vatican City

AREA: 0.44 sq. km

LANGUAGES: Italian, Latin, French

MAIN RELIGION: Christianity

CURRENCY: Euro

LITERACY RATE: 100%

LIFE EXPECTANCY: Not available

TIME ZONE: +1

TYPE OF GOVERNMENT: Ecclesiastical Elective Monarchy

HEAD OF STATE: Pope Francis

HEAD OF GOVT: Fernando Vergez Alzaga

GDP PER CAPITA: Not applicable

POPULATION: 1,000

ISD CODE: 379 **INTERNET TLD:** .va

Vatican City is the smallest country in the world by both area and population. St Peter's Basilica in Vatican City is the largest church in the world.

Background: Vatican City

VENEZUELA

LOCATION: Northern South America

CAPITAL: Caracas

AREA: 916,445 sq. km

LANGUAGE: Spanish

MAIN RELIGION: Christianity

CURRENCY: Bolivar Soberano

LITERACY RATE: 97.5%

LIFE EXPECTANCY: 74.25 years

TIME ZONE: –4

TYPE OF GOVERNMENT: Federal Presidential Republic

HEAD OF STATE AND GOVT: President Nicolas Maduro Moros and President Juan Gerardo Guaido Marquez – each accepted as legitimate by certain countries

GDP PER CAPITA: $7,700

POPULATION: 30,518,260

ISD CODE: 58 **INTERNET TLD:** .ve

The world's highest uninterrupted waterfall, Angel Falls, is in Venezuela. Its height is 979 m (3,212 ft).

VIETNAM

LOCATION: South-East Asia

CAPITAL: Hanoi

AREA: 331,212 sq. km

LANGUAGES: Vietnamese, English

MAIN RELIGIONS: Buddhism, Christianity

CURRENCY: Vietnamese Dong

LITERACY RATE: 95.8%

LIFE EXPECTANCY: 75.79 years

TIME ZONE: +7

TYPE OF GOVERNMENT: Communist state

HEAD OF STATE: President Vo Van Thuong **HEAD OF GOVT:** Prime Minister Pham Minh Chinh

GDP PER CAPITA: $10,600

POPULATION: 104,799,174

ISD CODE: 84

INTERNET TLD: .vn

Vietnam is the world's largest producer of cashew nuts and black pepper.

YEMEN

LOCATION: Southern West Asia

CAPITAL: Ataq city (interim capital)

AREA: 527,968 sq. km

LANGUAGE: Arabic

MAIN RELIGION: Islam

CURRENCY: Yemeni Rial

LITERACY RATE: 70.1%

LIFE EXPECTANCY: 67.83 years

TIME ZONE: +3

TYPE OF GOVERNMENT: Transitional

HEAD OF STATE: Chairman of the Presidential Leadership Council Rashad al-Alimi **HEAD OF GOVT:** Chairperson, Presidential Council Rashad Muhammad al-Alimi

GDP PER CAPITA: $2,500

POPULATION: 31,565,602

ISD CODE: 967 **INTERNET TLD:** .ye

The *Dracaena cinnabari* or the dragon blood tree, a uniquely umbrella shaped tree, grows in the Yemeni island of Socotra. It gets its name from its dark red resin.

Background: Zambia

COUNTRIES

ZAMBIA

LOCATION: Southern Africa

CAPITAL: Lusaka

AREA: 752,618 sq. km

LANGUAGES: English, Bemba, Nyanja

MAIN RELIGIONS: Christianity, Islam

CURRENCY: Zambian Kwacha

LITERACY RATE: 86.7%

LIFE EXPECTANCY: 66.6 years

TIME ZONE: +2

TYPE OF GOVERNMENT: Presidential Republic

HEAD OF STATE AND GOVT: President Hakainde Hichilema

GDP PER CAPITA: $3,200

POPULATION: 20,216,029

ISD CODE: 260

INTERNET TLD: .zm

***Termitomyces titanicus*, the largest edible mushroom in the world, is found in Zambia. Its cap is about 1 m (3.3 ft) in diameter.**

ZIMBABWE

LOCATION: Southern Africa

CAPITAL: Harare

AREA: 390,757 sq. km

LANGUAGES: English, Shona, Ndebele

MAIN RELIGIONS: Christianity, indigenous faiths

CURRENCY: Zimbabwe Dollar

LITERACY RATE: 89.7%

LIFE EXPECTANCY: 63.79 years

TIME ZONE: +2

TYPE OF GOVERNMENT: Presidential Republic

HEAD OF STATE AND GOVT: President Emmerson Mnangagwa

GDP PER CAPITA: $2,100

POPULATION: 15,418,674

ISD CODE: 263 **INTERNET TLD:** .zw

Background: Zimbabwe

Lake Kariba in Zimbabwe, constructed on the River Zambezi, is one of the largest man-made lakes in the world.

CHANGING Shapes of Nations

THE country that was called Yugoslavia was divided into seven countries in the 1990s.

1. Bosnia and Herzegovina
2. Croatia
3. Kosovo*
4. Macedonia
5. Montenegro
6. Serbia
7. Slovenia

When the Soviet Union broke up in 1991, these were the independent countries it was divided into:

1. Armenia 2. Azerbaijan 3. Belarus 4. Estonia 5. Georgia 6. Kazakhstan 7. Kyrgyzstan 8. Latvia 9. Lithuania 10. Moldova 11. Russia 12. Tajikistan 13. Turkmenistan 14. Ukraine 15. Uzbekistan

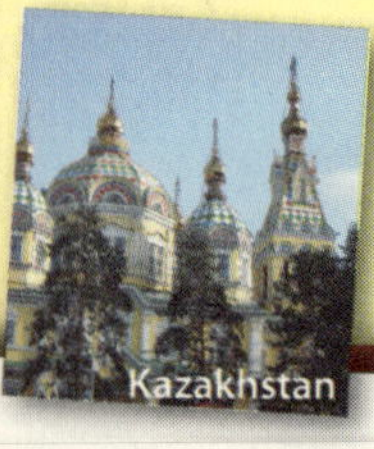

Kazakhstan

Lithuania

Turkmenistan

*The Republic of Kosovo declared its independence in 2008, and is partially recognized. Serbia still claims it as part of its territory. It is administered by the UN.

SUPERLATIVES

Fastest Animal (land) Cheetah (speed: 80–120 km/h)

Largest Animal (land) African elephant (length: 2.5–4 m/ 8.2–13 ft; weight: 2.5–7 tonnes)

Largest Animal (sea) Blue whale (length: 25–32 m/ 82–105 ft; weight: 170 tonnes)

Slowest Animal Sloth (speed: 1.8–2.4 m/6–8 ft per minute)

Largest Archipelago Malay Archipelago >25,000 s (Indonesia and Malaysia)

Tallest Animal (land) Giraffe (height: 4.2–5.7 m/ 14–19 ft; weight 794–1,900 kg)

Largest Bay Hudson Bay, Canada (shoreline: 12,268 km)

Fastest Bird Swift (length: 9–23 cm/3.5–9 in.; speed: 110 km/h)

Largest Bird Ostrich (length: 2.1–2.7 m/7–9 ft; weight: 90–130 kg)

Smallest Bird Hummingbird (length: 7.5–13 cm/3–5 in)

Longest Bridge Danyang–Kunshan Grand Bridge, China (length: 165 km/541,338 ft)

Tallest Building (office) Burj Khalifa, Dubai, UAE (height: 829.8 m/ 2,722 ft)

Busiest Canal (ship) Kiel Canal (linking North Sea at Brunsbuttel to Baltic Sea at Kiel–Holtenau) (length: 98.26 km)

Highest Capital City La Paz, Bolivia (altitude: 3,640 m/ 11,942 ft)

Longest Canal (ship) Suez Canal (linking Red Sea and the Mediterranean) (length: 193.3 km)

Largest Cinema Kinepolis-Madrid Ciudad de la Imagen megaplex, Spain (seating capacity: 9,200; screens: 25)

Smallest Country Vatican City (0.44 sq. km)

Highest City La Rinconada, Peru; (altitude: 5,100 m/16,728 ft)

Most Populated City Tokyo, Japan (est. population: 37,194,000)

Busiest Container Port Shanghai, China (throughput in million TEUs,* 2019: 43.3)

* *Twenty-foot Equivalent Unit*

Smallest Continent Australia (area: 7.69 million sq. km)

Largest Continent Asia (area: 44.58 million sq. km)

Largest Coral Formation The Great Barrier Reef, Australia (stretching over 2,300 km)

Largest Country Russia (area: 17,098,242 sq. km)

Longest Corridor Ramanathaswamy Temple, Rameswaram, Tamil Nadu, India (length: 1,220 m/4,002 ft)

Most Populated Country India (est. population, 2023: 1,425,775,850)

Largest Dam Three Gorges Dam, China (over River Yangtze; length: 2,309 m/7,575.46 ft; height: 185 m/606.96 ft)

Largest Desert Antarctic Desert, Antarctica (area: 14,244,935 sq. km)

Biggest Dome Singapore National Stadium, Singapore (diameter: 312 m/1023 ft)

Largest Delta Ganga–Brahmaputra Delta, Bay of Bengal (area: 105,641 sq. km)

Longest Epic The Mahabharata (over 200,000 verse lines)

Largest Flower Rafflesia arnoldii (diameter: 1m/3.3 ft)

Tallest Geyser (active) Steamboat Geyser, Yellowstone National Park, USA (height: 2,316 m/7,598 ft)

Largest Gorge Grand Canyon, USA (average depth: 1,584 m/5,200 ft)

Largest Gulf Gulf of Mexico (shoreline: 5,000 km)

Deepest Lake Lake Baikal, Siberia, Russia (max. depth: 1,642 m/5,387 ft)

Largest Island Greenland, Kingdom of Denmark (area: 2,166,086 sq. km)

Highest Lake Lake Tilicho, Nepal (altitude: 4,919 m/16,138 ft)

Largest Lake (inland waterbody) Caspian Sea (surface area: 371,000 sq. km)

Largest Lake (freshwater)
Lake Superior, USA and Canada (surface area: 82,000 sq. km)

Biggest Library
The British Library, UK (catalogued items: 170–200 million)

Longest Lifespan of an Animal
Giant tortoise (life expectancy: 190–200 years)

Highest Melting Point
Tungsten (3,422˚C)

Tallest Minaret
Djamaa el Djazair, Algeria (height: 265 m/870 ft)

Tallest Minaret (freestanding)
Qutub Minar, Delhi, India (height: 72.5 m/238 ft)

Longest Mountain Range (above water)
Andes, South America (length: 7,242 km)

Highest Mountain Peak
Mt Everest, Himalayan mountain range (height: 8,848 m/29,029 ft)

Biggest Museum
The Louvre, Paris, France (area: 72,735 sq. m/782,910 sq. ft)

Deepest Ocean Point
Challenger Deep (Mariana Trench, Pacific Ocean) (depth: 11,033.76 m/36,200 ft)

Largest Ocean
The Pacific (surface area: 361,132,000 sq. km)

Largest Palace
Forbidden City, Beijing, China (area: 720,000 sq. m/7,750,015 sq. ft)

Largest Peninsula
Arabian Peninsula (3,250,000 sq. km)

Driest Place*
Arica, Chile (average annual rainfall: 0.76 mm/0.03 in.)

Coldest Place (region)
Antarctica (lowest recorded temperature: –89.2°C; average annual temperature: –50°C.)

Highest Plateau
Tibetan Plateau (altitude: 4,500 m/ 14,800 ft)

Longest Mountain Range (underwater)
Mid-Atlantic Ridge (length: around 16,000 km) in the Atlantic Ocean

Railway Station with Most Platforms
Grand Central Terminal, New York, USA; (platforms: 44; area: 190,000 sq. m/2,045,143 sq. ft)

Longest Platform (railway)
Gorakhpur station, Uttar Pradesh, India (length:1,366.33 m/4,482.7 ft)

** Outside of polar regions*

WORLD

Longest Railway Route
Trans-Siberian Railway (length: 9,289 km)

Longest River
Nile, Egypt (length: 6,650 km)

Largest River (volume)
The Amazon, South America (average discharge: 219,000 cubic m/sec)

Longest Earthen Dam
Hirakud Dam, Odisha, India (length: 25.79 km)

Largest River Basin
Amazon Basin, South America (area: 7,000,000 sq. km)

Largest Seabird
Wandering albatross (wingspan: 3.3–3.6 m/ 10.83–11.81 ft)

Rainiest Spot
Mawsynram, Meghalaya, India (average annual rainfall: 11,873 mm/467 in.)

Largest Stadium
Narendra Modi Stadium, India (seating capacity: 132,000)

Tallest Statue
Statue of Unity, Gujarat, India (height: 182 m/597 ft)

Tallest Dam
Jinping–I Dam, Sichuan, China (height: 305 m/1,000 ft)

Broadest Strait
Davis Strait, Greenland and Canada (length: 950 km)

Longest Strait
Strait of Malacca (Andaman Sea–South China Sea) (length: 800 km)

Narrowest Strait
Euripus Channel–Chalcis, between mainland Greece and the Gulf of Euboea in the Aegean Sea (width: 41.15 m/135 ft)

Longest Tunnel (canal)
Delaware Aqueduct, New York, USA (length: 137 km)

Longest Tunnel (railway)
Gotthard Base Tunnel, Switzerland (length: 57 km)

Longest Tunnel (road)
Laerdal Tunnel, Norway (length: 24.5 km)

Highest Volcano
Nevados Ojos del Salado, Andes, Argentina–Chile (height: 6,893 m/22,615 ft)

Longest Wall
Great Wall of China, Beijing, China (length: 21,196 km)

Largest Volcano
Puhahonu, Hawaii, USA (volume: 150,000 cubic km)

Highest Waterfall
Angel Falls, Venezuela (height: 979 m/3,212 ft)

5 EARTH

Earth is 4.54 billion years old. From outer space, it looks like a huge blue marble ball with white swirls and areas of brown, yellow, green and white. It is the only planet with liquid water on the surface.

EARTH NUMBERS

Diameter from North to South Pole
12,714 km (7,900 miles)

Diameter from equator
12,756 km (7,926 miles)

Earth's rotation per hour
15 degrees

Equatorial circumference
40,030.2 km

Surface Area
510,064,472 km^2

Density
5.513g/cm^3

Volume
1,083,206,916,846 km^3

DAYS ON EARTH ARE BECOMING LONGER: Around 4.5 billion years ago, when Earth was formed, the average day is speculated to be approximately six hours long. By 260 million years ago, this had increased to 21.9 hours. Today, as we know, a day is 24 hours long. However, it is constantly increasing by 1.7 milliseconds per day.

EARTH IS RECYCLABLE: The tectonic forces present within the Earth moves the land upward and downward, altering the layers of crust, pushing it further to the magma-filled layer of the Earth. Eventually, the crust melts due to the heat and emerges back as crust through the volcanic eruptions of lava.

EARTH'S ROTATION IS SLOWING DOWN: Earth's spinning is known to be slowing down by 17 milliseconds per hundred hours. Due to this, our days will lengthen eventually. However, since the rate of rotation is so slow, it is said that our days would increase to 25 hours only in around 140 million years.

LAND: Earth comprises 32.1 per cent iron, 30.1 per cent oxygen, 15.1 per cent silicon and 13.9 per cent magnesium. Iron is the dominant element in the Earth's core. A sample from there would have 88 per cent of iron. Additionally, Earth's crust is made of 47 per cent oxygen.

AIR: Earth's atmosphere is made of 78 per cent nitrogen, 21 per cent oxygen and 1 per cent other elements, making it conducive to sustaining life.

WATER: The larger part of Earth is covered by water. It exists in three forms: solid, liquid and gas. As a solid, it is found on mountaintops in the form of snow or glaciers. It is present in rivers, oceans, streams as a liquid and as water vapour (or a gaseous form) in the atmosphere.

KNOW YOUR PLANET

Unlike gas planets like Jupiter, Earth is one of the four solar terrestrial planets (planets with a rocky body, as opposed to gas).

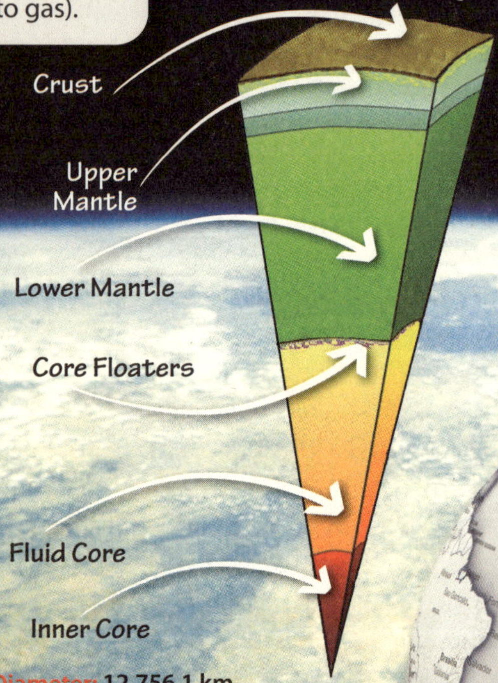

CHEMICAL COMPOSITION

The mass of Earth is approximately 5.9722×10^{24} kg. Earth is made up of nearly a hundred elements, of which oxygen, silicon, aluminium, iron, calcium, sodium, potassium and nickel are the main ones.

Diameter: 12,756.1 km
Distance from the Sun: 152 million km (at aphelion); average: 149.6 million km
Temperature: Maximum: 57.7°C; minimum: –89.1°C

SHAPE

If you take an orange and squish it at the top and bottom, it will bulge out towards the centre. In a similar way, Earth is a sphere slightly squished at the poles and bulging at the equator. So, if you were to draw a line across the equator and a line through the poles, the line across the equator would actually be 43 km longer than the one through the poles. Therefore, Earth is not a perfect sphere, and is instead what is termed an 'oblate spheroid'. This shape is caused by the rotation of Earth.

INTERNAL STRUCTURE

PLATE TECTONICS

The outer layer of Earth, called the **lithosphere**, is separated into vast pieces known as the tectonic plates, from 80 km to 400 km thick, which drift atop the soft, underlying mantle. They move both sideways, and up and down, at an estimated speed of 1 cm to 10 cm per year. Most of Earth's seismic activity (volcanoes and earthquakes) occurs at the boundaries where the plates interact.

SURFACE

About 70.8 per cent of Earth's surface is covered in water. There are many physical features submerged under it, such as the longest mountain ranges (the Mid-Atlantic Ridge), volcanoes, trenches, canyons, oceanic plateaus and plains. This is known as the **hydrosphere**. The remaining 29.2 per cent of Earth is covered with mountains, deserts, plains, plateaus and other features. This surface undergoes constant changes due to the effects of the movement of the tectonic plates and erosion.

> "Seventy-five per cent of Earth's atmosphere is found within the first 11 km above the planet's surface. The outermost layer (the exosphere) is the largest, extending from the top of the thermosphere (about 700 km above sea level) to about 10,000 km. It merges with outer space, where there is no atmosphere."

GEOLOGIC TIMELINE

PHANEROZOIC EON

540 mya–today

'Visible Life': organisms with skeletons or hard shells

MESOZOIC ERA

'The Age of Reptiles'

248–65 mya

Cretaceous Period
146–65 mya

Lower
First flowering plants, primates, crocodilians

Upper
Extinction of dinosaurs

CENOZOIC ERA

'The Age of Mammals'

65 mya–now

Quaternary Period
'The Age of Man'
(1.8 mya–now)

Holocene Epoch
(11,000 years ago –now): Human civilization

Pleistocene Epoch
(1.8–0.011 mya): (Last Ice Age) First human (*Homo sapiens*); mammoths, mastodons, giant ground sloths; mass extinction

Tertiary Period
65–1.8 mya

Neogene Period
24-1.8 mya

Pliocene Epoch
(5–1.8 mya): First hominids (Australopithecines); megalodons; modern whales

Miocene Epoch
(24–5 mya): More mammals (horses, dogs, bears); modern birds; apes and monkeys

Palaeogene Period
(65–24 mya)

Oligocene Epoch
(38–24 mya): Small extinction; new mammals (pigs, deer, cats, rhinos, tapirs); grasses common

Eocene Epoch
(54–38 mya): Mammals abound; rodents, primitive whales appear

Palaeocene Epoch
(65–54 mya): First large mammals; primitive primates

Jurassic Period
(208–146 mya): Dinosaurs diversify; first birds, ferns, gingkos, conifers

Triassic Period
(248–208 mya): First dinosaurs, first mammals; many molluscs, reptiles; small-scale extinction

Permian Period
(280–248 mya): Reptiles and amphibians dominate; first bugs and beetles; major extinctions

Pennsylvanian Period
(325–280 mya): First reptiles; many ferns; cockroaches and mayflies

Carboniferous Period
(360–280 mya): Coal swamps, corals, seed ferns, other plants; amphibians common

Mississippian Period
(360–325 mya): Seed ferns; first winged insects

Devonian Period
(408–360 mya): First amphibians; many coral reefs

Silurian Period
438–408 mya: First vascular land plants; jawed fishes

PALAEOZOIC ERA
540–248 mya

Ordovician Period
(505–438 mya): Primitive plants; first corals, fishes, seaweed, fungi, bivalves

Cambrian Period
(540–500 mya): First fishes, marine invertebrates, like shellfish

EARTH IS FORMED 4.54 BILLION YEARS AGO

PROTEROZOIC EON

2.5 bya–540 mya: First multicelled animals, including sponges

Vendian/ Ediacaran Period
(600–540 mya)

ARCHEOZOIC EON

3.9–2.5 bya: First life forms: one-celled organisms; algae; bacteria appear in sea

HADEAN EON

4.6–3.9 mya: The solidifying of Earth's continental and oceanic crusts

Note: mya: million years ago; bya: billion years ago

THE BIG SEVEN

Earth's land surface is divided broadly into continents and there are many theories defining them. The most accepted definition for a 'continent' would be 'a large, continuous, discrete mass of land, separated from others by expanses of water'. Conventionally, there are seven continents: Asia, Africa, Europe, North America, South America, Australia/Oceania (Australia, New Zealand and islands of South-East Asia) and Antarctica.

NORTH AMERICA

Area: 21,330,000 sq. km; **Percentage of Earth's landmass:** 16.5%; **Population:** 592,072,212; **Percentage of world population*:** 7.6%; **Density of population per sq. km:** 28

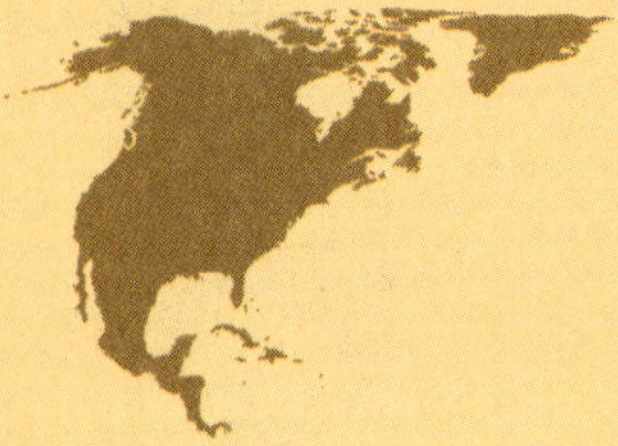

EUROPE

Area: 22,134,900 sq. km; **Percentage of Earth's landmass:** 6.8%; **Population:** 747,636,026; **Percentage of world population:** 9.59%; **Density of population per sq. km:** 34

ASIA

Area: 44,579,000 sq. km; **Percentage of Earth's landmass:** 29.5%; **Population:** 3,261,050,390; **Percentage of world population:** 41.84%; **Density of population per sq. km:** 105

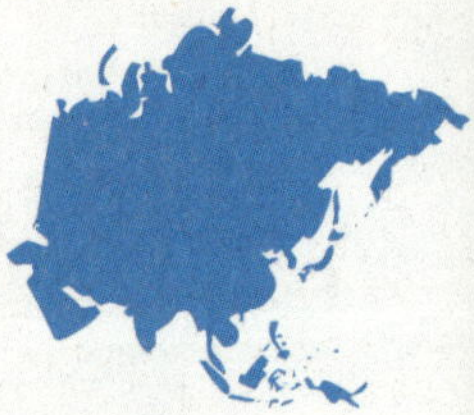

SOUTH AMERICA

Area: 17,461,112 sq. km; **Percentage of Earth's landmass:** 12%; **Population:** 430,759,766; **Percentage of world population:** 5.53%; **Density of population per sq. km:** 25

AUSTRALIA/ OCEANIA

Area: 8,486,460 sq. km; **Percentage of Earth's landmass:** 5.9%; **Population:** 43,111,704; **Percentage of world population:** 0.55%; **Density of population per sq. km:** 5

AFRICA

Area: 29,648,481 sq. km; **Percentage of Earth's landmass:** 20.4%; **Population:** 1,340,598,147; **Percentage of world population:** 17.2%; **Density of population per sq. km:** 45

ANTARCTICA

Area: 13,720,000 sq. km; **Percentage of Earth's landmass:** 9.2%; **Population:** (scientists/ sailors) 4,490; **Percentage of world population:** 0.00002%; **Density of population per sq. km:** 0.00003

*Note: *Population figures are from 2020; percentages may not add up to 100 due to rounding off of numbers.*

Wildlife trade may lead to ecosystems collapsing

A new research from the University of Sheffield focused on how distinct animal species are being exploited shamelessly for trade purposes in many parts of the world. This exploitation has the potential to alter key ecological processes. Researchers are calling for financial and political conservation resources to be directed towards major hotspots of wildlife trade.

Professor David Edwards from the University of Sheffield's School of Biosciences and senior author of the aforementioned research said, 'Thousands of species are traded globally and many of these are done so unsustainably. We urgently need to focus conservation resources towards trade hotspots, such as those in the tropics, to prevent extinctions. At present, we're in grave danger of losing some of the world's most evolutionarily and functionally distinct animals, and this could have major consequences for our planet's ecosystems...'

The research also found that larger species, like the African Forest Elephant, are disproportionately exploited in trade which causes a severe imbalance in the ecosystems where they play a unique role. Dr Oscar Morton from the University of Sheffield's School of Biosciences and a co-author of the research stated, 'When we remove or deplete certain species for trade, we risk changing the myriad of interconnected services that the ecosystem provides. This is similar to removing bricks from a building – if we remove too many we risk the whole building crumbling down. But at present we understand frighteningly little of the scale of the issue or its wider implications for ecosystems.' It has clearly become an urgent need to control the heartless wildlife trade that is hurting the efficient working of nature.

Human greed makes Earth's axis wobble

Human beings' greed has once again let down Mother Nature. Unrestricted withdrawal of groundwater has caused a measurable change in the tilt of the Earth's axis of rotation. Earth spins around an imaginary axis which passes through the North Pole, its centre of mass and the South Pole, just like a top spins around its spindle. Generally, the axis of rotation of any celestial body tends to be stable, but a significant shifting of mass within or on the surface of a planet can result in small, but quantifiable changes. Ki-Weon Seo, a geophysicist at Seoul National University, stated, 'Every mass moving around on the surface of the Earth can change the rotation axis.'

The unrestrained extraction of groundwater has led to the tilt of Earth's axis changing by approximately 80 cm, a phenomenon that has been talked about in the *Journal of Geophysical Research Letters*. Over a period of 17 years, between 1993 and 2010, a startling 2,150 gigatonnes of groundwater were extracted globally.

Until recently, researchers thought that these water-driven effects would be caused mainly by the melting of glaciers and ice caps, but when that data stopped making sense, they had to give heed to the possibility that groundwater was playing a major role in this phenomenon. Gravitational surveys have measured the depletion of underground reservoirs, which is caused in large part by irrigation, especially in northwestern India and western North America.

Our thoughtless avarice has, quite literally, shaken up our planet!

Climate change is burning down our forests

Currently, the average global temperature is 1.2° C hotter than it was in pre-industrial times. This is causing extreme heatwaves all over the world. These severe rises in temperature will only be controlled if human beings curb the emission of greenhouse gases in the atmosphere that are taking place because of excessive industrial radiation and several other sources that can be controlled on a personal level by people.

Although, climate change is not the sole root of forest fires, it definitely plays a key role in the same. Wildfire risk depends on a number of factors, including temperature, soil moisture and the

presence of trees, shrubs, and other potential fuel. All these factors have strong direct or indirect ties to climate variability and climate change. Climate change results in an increase in hot and dry conditions that help wildfires in burning faster, spreading farther and raging even more intensely.

Wildfires have impacted many countries across the globe in 2023. Climate change has contributed heavily to the worst wildfires that Canada has ever witnessed. An estimate of 7,774 square kilometres burned as of August. Thirteen provinces and territories have been affected, with large fires in Alberta, British Columbia, the Northwest Territories, Nova Scotia, Ontario, and Quebec. Wildfires also caused havoc in Greece with the authorities being forced to evacuate 20,000 tourists. Residents of Alexandroupolis in Greece were also suggested to keep their windows closed due to the heavy smoke from the wildfires. The island of Hawaii also suffered because of widespread wildfires that killed at least 114 people, with an approximate of 13,000 missing persons. The island suffered a loss of around $6 billion.

It is estimated that there will be a rise in global wildfires by 14 per cent by 2030, 30 per cent by 2050 and 50 per cent by the end of this century. Comprehensive strategies and integrated approaches for wildfire management need to be implemented in order to keep the rising wildfires under check. Another step that can be taken is working towards climate control to restrict severe climate change. There are many precautions that can be taken on a personal level so that each individual can contribute towards controlling climate change – including travelling by sustainable means of transport, use of renewable energy and responsible garbage disposal.

Microplastics contaminate rainwater in Patna

The capital of Bihar has had plastic raining down on it! Scientists recently detected nine different types of microplastics in Patna's rainwater – the most common ones being polyethylene, terephthalate and polypropylene. Researchers from IIT Patna collected rainwater samples from urban and peri-urban localities in Patna over a period of 63 days to understand the extent of contaminants in the water. Such research has been conducted before in the United Kingdom, Canada and Ireland, but India had never been subject to such a study before this. Urban areas may very well be suffering with this issue because of vehicle movement, building work and plastic waste mismanagement. 'These are plastics found in clothing, packaging, and even vehicular emissions from tyres,' said Subrata Hait, an associate professor at the department of civil and environmental engineering at IIT Patna.

Such microplastics in the atmosphere are likely to cause health issues such as lung inflammation and increase the possibility of reproductive issues, cancer and genetic mutations. The study also revealed that microplastics have the potential to attach themselves to other suspended particles in the air, leading to an increase in their toxicity. A more efficient plastic management system can help in bringing this situation under control.

Earth's lakes are drying up

A recent study found that more than half of the Earth's lakes and reservoirs have reduced in volume since the 1990s because of several reasons. 'Lakes are in trouble globally, and it has implications far and wide,' said Balaji Rajagopalan, a professor at the University of Colorado Boulder. He continued by saying, 'It really caught our attention that 25 percent of the world's population is living in a lake basin that is on a declining trend. meaning some two billion people are impacted by the findings.'

About 56 per cent of dwindling in natural lakes is believed to have been caused by climate warming and human consumption. A team of international researchers reported that some of the world's most important freshwater sources, from the Caspian Sea between Europe and Asia to South America's Lake Titicaca, faced a loss of water at an approximate rate of around 22 gigatonnes per year for nearly 30 years.

The loss of lake water will result in a big shock for people who depend heavily upon that water for irrigation and drinking. Natural lakes and dams store about 87 per cent of the Earth's freshwater, although they cover just 3 per cent of the planet's surface. 'A thorough understanding of water supply drivers is critical to effectively managing reservoirs and river systems. The better we understand anthropogenic effects on our water supply, the better prepared we as water managers will be,' said Bart Leeflang, the Colorado River programme manager for the Central Utah Water Conservancy District. All scientists and researchers agree that the planet will face severe consequences if global warming is not controlled to curb the drying up of these important sources of water.

Circular economy: The answer to sustainability

Focusing on the world's goal of achieving zero emissions by 2050, the UNDP has introduced a 'Plastic Waste Management Program' in India. In conjunction with the government's Swachch Bharat mission, plastic waste is collected, segregated and recycled to form raw materials used in constructing roads, planks, kiosks, benches and other usable products under this regime. So far, up to 83,900 metric tonnes of plastic waste has been repurposed, breaking the cycle of create-use-discard to form a closed loop that keeps waste products out of the natural environment for as long as possible. Campaigns for people to return their used plastic bottles and bags for recycling have also been launched in partnership with retail chains. Another important aspect is the placement of plastic gulaks in schools for students to contribute to these efforts. Such reuse of waste not only reduces environmental pollution (about 44 per cent reduction in greenhouse gas emissions) caused by single-use plastics but also benefits the economy and increases employment opportunities. The projected revenue upon the successful execution of this program is ₹14 lakh crore by 2030! Currently, it is implemented in 35 cities across 19 states in India, with the country's informal workforce such as waste pickers (for example Safai Saathis) playing the key role.

6 SPACE

Space has always been called the final frontier, but its exploration by humans has revealed many of its secrets. Here are just a few, while several more are still clouded in mystery!

The highest mountain known to us yet is on an asteroid called Vesta. Measuring a tremendous **22 km** in height, it is three times as tall as Mount Everest!

99 per cent of the mass of the solar system is the Sun.

Consider yourself lucky that you have ground beneath your feet on Earth! You wouldn't be able to walk on Jupiter, Saturn, Uranus or Neptune because they have no solid surface!

Humans have sent spacecraft to all of the planets in our solar system – Mercury, Venus, Earth, Mars, Jupiter, Saturn, Uranus and Neptune – as well as two dwarf planets, Pluto and Ceres.

The huge canyon system on Mars, known as Valles Marineris, is **4,000** km long, more than **10 times** as long as the Grand Canyon on Earth. Early spacecraft to Mars did not spot it because they flew over other parts of the planet. It was finally noticed by the global mapping mission Mariner 9 in 1971.

Currently, the biggest star known to us is called UY Scuti. This red supergiant star s located **9,500** light years away in the Scutum constellation. It is more than **1,708** times the size of the Sun. The star with the highest mass is RMC 136a1, whose mass equals **315** Suns.

It has been estimated that the Milky Way will collide with the Andromeda galaxy, our closest neighbour in the galaxy, in around 4.5 billion years. This is likely to result in a vast elliptical galaxy.

The planet Neptune was discovered in 1846, but since then it has not yet completed one full orbit around the Sun. It takes **165** years to complete one such orbit!

OUR UNIVERSE

Our Earth revolves around the Sun. The Sun is the centre of our galaxy, the Milky Way, which is part of the Local Group of galaxies. This group is being gravitationally pulled towards a larger system of galaxies, known as the Virgo Cluster. Our galaxy is part of a vast system of dust, gas, stars and millions of galaxies. The most commonly accepted theory that explains the origin of the universe as we know it is the Big Bang theory. According to this theory, the universe had its origins in a massive explosion 12–14 billion years ago, creating huge lumps of gas and matter that slowly cooled. As the universe grows older, the matter thins out and the galaxies expand outwards. Stars are still forming with the original hydrogen from the Big Bang. There is a finite amount of hydrogen that exists, and once it is gone, all the stars will stop shining.

GALAXIES

A galaxy is a huge congregation of stars held together by the force of gravity. Galaxies are dotted around the universe like islands. Our solar system is part of the Milky Way, which belongs to the Local Group of galaxies. The neighbouring Andromeda Galaxy is the largest galaxy in this system, followed by the Milky Way. The Local Group has about three dozen galaxies.

Although Indian mathematician-astronomer Aryabhata and Greek philosopher Aristarchus of Samos had speculated on our universe being Sun-centric or *heliocentric*, it was Polish astronomer Nicolaus Copernicus (1473–1543) who predicted it mathematically.

SOLAR SYSTEM

There is no single theory that explains how and why the solar system formed, but the currently accepted theory says that it happened about five billion years ago. Many scientists believe that the solar system evolved from a giant cloud of dust and gas (the solar nebula), which then began to collapse under the weight of its own gravity. As it did so, the matter in this cloud began moving or spinning in a giant circle, much like the water in a drain moves around its centre in a whirlpool. At the centre of this spinning cloud, due to intense pressure and heat, a small star or 'protostar' began to form. This protostar grew larger

THE SUN

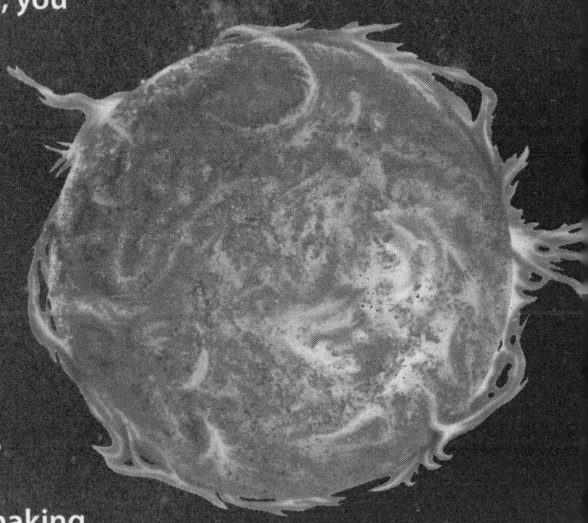

If you thought the Sun is a fireball, you are wrong. It is not really on fire, but glows because in its core – where the temperature reaches 15,000,000°C – there is a huge nuclear reaction constantly going on, converting hydrogen into helium, and releasing masses of energy as light and heat. Other than hydrogen and helium, the Sun contains nitrogen, carbon and small traces of other gases. In fact, it contains about 98 per cent of the matter making up our solar system. The middle layer of the Sun churns up and down in a circular motion, deeper into it and back out again. This creates many phenomena, such as making the Sun a giant magnet, as well as causing dark, cooler areas on its surface, known as 'sunspots'. This churning also causes sudden bright explosions, called solar flares, which release a huge amount of energy and light.

> **The Sun has a diameter of roughly 1.4 million km. This is almost 110 times the diameter of Earth – that means one million Earths could fit inside the Sun.**

and larger, as it collected more and more of the dust and gas that collapsed into it. Further away from this central star were smaller clumps of dust and gas that were also collapsing. The central star eventually became our Sun, while the smaller clumps became the main planets, minor or dwarf planets, moons, comets, asteroids, gas and dust. As the universe continued to cool and expand, each object tried to break away. However, the Sun, being so large, exerted an immense force of gravity on these planets. Caught between flying off into space and colliding into the Sun, the planets kept to elliptical orbits, revolving around the Sun, each at its own speed.

THE PLANETS

MERCURY: In Roman mythology, Mercury was the messenger of the gods, and the protector of travellers and merchants. Its atmosphere has been blown away by solar winds; there is almost no air in it. It can be seen from Earth after an hour or so of the rising Sun (eastern horizon) or setting Sun (western horizon). It is the fastest orbiting planet, with long days due to its slow rotation. It has no moons or rings. As its iron core cooled, it shrank and acquired wrinkles, called lobate scarps.
Diameter: 4,880 km
Distance from the Sun: 58 million km
Duration of one orbit: 87.969 days
Rotation: 59 days
Average temperature: Maximum: 430°C during the day; –180°C at night

---

VENUS: It's named after the Roman goddess of beauty and love. Venus and Earth are about the same size, and early astronomers believed that Venus was Earth's sister planet and had life on it. However, its temperatures were found to be too harsh for life to survive. Heat is trapped on the planet's surface by its thick layer of atmospheric clouds. It is the hottest of the planets, with the longest days. Venus has no moons or rings, and it is the only planet that rotates clockwise.
Diameter: 12,100 km
Distance from the Sun: 108 million km
Duration of one orbit: 225 days
Rotation: 243 days
Average temperature: 471°C

MARS: Named after the Roman god of war, this planet Mars is known as the Red Planet because of its red soil. It is prone to extreme dust storms, leading to a fascinating topography with huge sand dunes that shift constantly. Mars excites scientists because its seasons are more like Earth's than those of any other planet, and as many as 50 Mars missions have been recorded so far. Evidence suggests that Mars once had rivers, streams, lakes and even an ocean. As its atmosphere depleted into outer space, its surface water began to evaporate and eventually dried up. Now the only water on Mars is either frozen in the polar caps, or underground. It has higher mountains and deeper canyons than any other planet. It also has the solar system's biggest volcano, Olympus Mons. The planet has two moons: Deimos and Phobos.
Diameter: 6,778 km
Distance from the Sun: 228 million km
Duration of one orbit: 687 days
Rotation: 25 hours
Average temperature: –28°C

JUPITER: In Roman

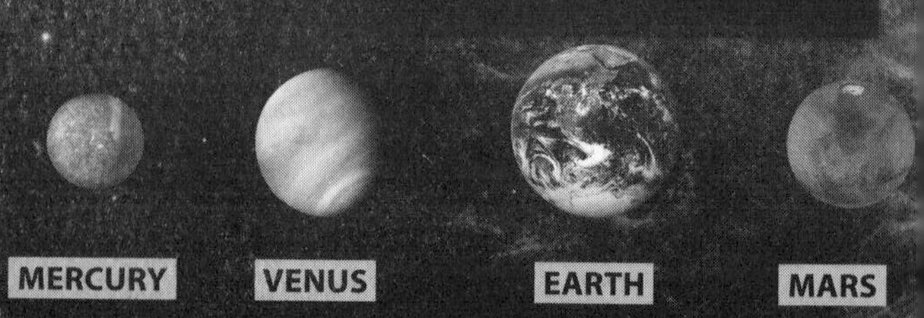

mythology, Jupiter overthrew his father Saturn, the king of gods. It is the largest of the solar system's planets and four of its 63 moons are planet-sized themselves. Jupiter's Great Red Spot is where a giant storm has been raging for at least 400 years across an area larger than Earth. This giant planet has no solid surface. Under its atmosphere is a large liquid ocean made of mostly hydrogen and some helium. There's no in-between layer; the atmosphere cools and thickens and becomes the ocean! You can see four of Jupiter's moons with a pair of binoculars at night. Jupiter spins really fast, taking only 10 hours to go from night to day. For that reason its middle has been stretched out.
Diameter: 142,984 km (11 times Earth's diameter)
Distance from the Sun: 778 million km
Duration of one orbit: 4,332 days
Rotation: 10 hours
Average temperature: –108°C

SATURN: Saturn was the Roman god of agriculture, the son of Uranus, the king of gods, whom he dethroned before being overthrown himself by his son Jupiter. Saturn has hundreds of beautiful rings made of ice and rock. In October 2009, NASA's Spitzer Space Telescope discovered a never-seen-before glowing ring around Saturn. Under the clouds of methane and helium, the planet's sky turns slowly into liquid until it becomes a giant ocean of chemicals. Saturn has 47 moons.
Diameter: 120,500 km
Distance from the Sun: 1.43 billion km
Duration of one orbit: 10,756 days
Rotation: 10 hours
Average temperature: –138°C

URANUS: Uranus was the Roman god of the skies, husband of Earth and the king of the gods. Unlike the other planets and most moons in our solar system, Uranus spins on its side, on a

"NASA administrator Jim Bridenstine believes Pluto is a planet. But, despite new observations by the New Horizons spacecraft, Pluto still does not meet all the three conditions defining a planet laid down by the International Astronomical Union in 2006, which classified Pluto as a dwarf planet."

* Planet illustrations not to scale

horizontal rather than a vertical axis. It is believed that long ago a very large object smashed into it and changed the direction of its spin. Uranus may have an ocean of water beneath its clouds, a large rocky core and trillions of large diamonds. It has 13 narrow rings and 27 moons.
Diameter: 51,118 km (four times the size of Earth)
Distance from the Sun: 2.87 billion km
Duration of one orbit: 30,687 days
Rotation: 17.2 hours
Average temperature: −195°C

NEPTUNE: Neptune was the Roman god of water and oceans. For many centuries, nobody knew of this planet. It was discovered relatively late by Johann Galle and Heinrich D'Arrest in 1846. It was the first planet to be discovered by mathematical predictions. On Neptune rages a giant storm, the Great Dark Spot, much like the storm on Jupiter. It is not known how long this storm has been active because it was studied only recently with the help of robotic exploratory probes. Neptune has 13 moons and six rings that circle it.
Diameter: 49,528 km (four times the size of Earth)
Distance from the Sun: 4.5 billion km
Duration of one orbit: 60,190 days
Rotation: 16 hours
Average temperature: −201°C

For Earth, see the *Earth* section

NASA's Historic Lunar Mission Takes Off

On 16 November 2022, history was made as NASA's highly anticipated Artemis I mission took off from the Kennedy Space Center in Cape Canaveral, Florida. Artemis I is one of NASA's three ambitious missions to restart human lunar exploration. Its design includes the Space Launch System – one of the most powerful rockets ever built, as per NASA. This is combined with the cutting-edge Orion Module, aptly known as the Capsule, a new spacecraft with advanced habitat for astronauts. The Orion spacecraft proved its mettle during an uncrewed flight test, covering a staggering distance 432,210 km from Earth – the farthest any spacecraft has travelled into space. Its 25.5-day journey came to an end with a successful splash into the Pacific Ocean on 11 December 2022. NASA is now gearing up for Artemis 2 and Artemis 3 missions.

A portion of the far side of the Moon looms large just beyond the Orion spacecraft. The darkest spot visible near the middle of the image is Mare Orientale.

Mission dearMoon to Rewrite History

Nearly five decades after NASA's Apollo 17 mission which was launched in 1972, history is about to be rekindled by Elon Musk's SpaceX vision. With mission dearMoon, it aims to send humans back to the moon. A fully reusable transportation system, the 'Starship' Rocket plans to carry both people and cargo to Earth, Moon, Mars and beyond. It is designed with a self-sufficient and cost-effective refuelling system which uses methane and oxygen. Among the select few who will be part of this endeavour is businessman Yusaku Maezawam, who is also sponsoring the trip for eight others.

The Mystery of the Venusian Clouds

Venus, the hottest planet in the solar system, has a thick, toxic atmosphere filled with carbon dioxide and yellow sulphuric acid clouds that cause a runaway greenhouse effect. Although life on Venus seems impossible, the region about 60 km from the hot ground, that is, the Venusian clouds' chemical composition is mind-boggling to scientists. The hypothesis that microbial life could reside here has been posited, but of course any such life would be drastically different from that on Earth. Scientists have discovered that there is an unknown UV absorber chemical compound that absorbs more than half of the

PSYCHE: Secrets of the Heart of a Planet

In the depths of the asteroid belt, orbiting the Sun between Mars and Jupiter lies the metal-rich asteroid called Psyche. Scientists believe Asteroid Psyche might be the leftover deposit of a long-lost planet, its outer layers stripped away over eons of relentless collisions during the solar system's formation. If this is true, Asteroid Psyche will provide an extensive and profound glimpse into our planet's past. Mission Psyche is a 450,616,320 km journey that will transmit groundbreaking data back to Earth using photons or light particles instead of usual radio waves. The mission is set to go on 10 October 2023, and scheduled to arrive at 16 Psyche in August 2029. Whereafter, it would orbit for 21 months and study the asteroid's properties.

radiation from the Sun that hits Venus. This chemical in theory could be a photosynthetic pigment that supports any possible life. Adding to the intrigue, the detection of phosphine in the Venus's atmosphere has been confounding. On Earth, phosphine is a biological signature and is indicative of life. In May 2023, a Massachusetts Institute of Technology based mission sent a single-instrument probe to the Venusian Clouds. The Venus life finder mission is definitely a game-changer.

JUICE: Unlocking the Mysteries of Jupiter's Icy Moons

The European Space Agency (ESA) launched a grand mission in 2023 to study and make observations of the planet Jupiter and its three largest moons – Ganymede, Callisto and Europa. It will make multiple flybys of Jupiter's three icy satellites and further orbit around Ganymede. Ganymede, the largest moon in the solar system, has a strong presence of underground oceans, possibly holding more water than on Earth's surface. It has its own magnetic field and the resultant oxygen atmosphere, raising intriguing questions about geophysical processes. Mission JUICE (JUpiter ICy moons Explorer) was launched on 14 April 2023, on the Ariane 5 Rocket. Utilizing the gravity assistance from Earth, Moon and Venus, JUICE will achieve an orbit around Jupiter after an eight-year journey in July 2031. With three years of extensive investigation, the mission will be completed after making an impact on Ganymede's surface.

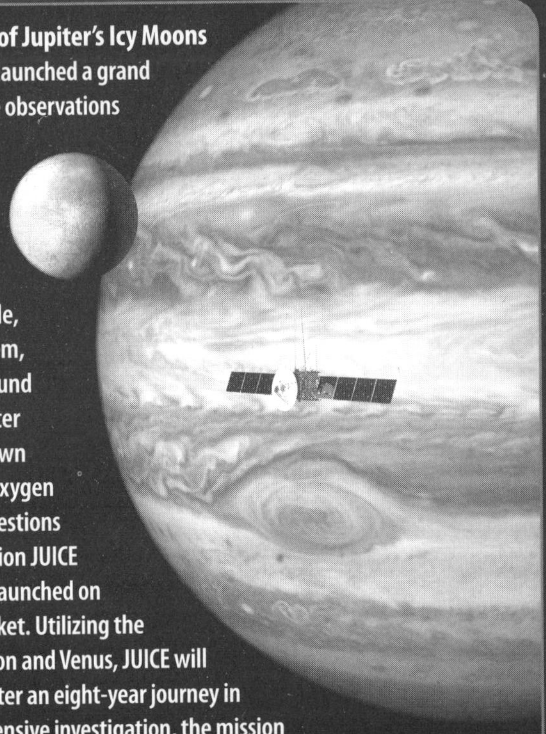

Euclid's Map of the Extragalactic Universe

After the success of the Hubble and James Webb Space telescopes, the Euclid mission launched by the ESA is a colossal attempt to create a 3-D map of the universe. It was launched by the SpaceX Falcon 9 rocket on 1 July 2023. Named after the Greek mathematician Euclid of Alexandria, the Euclid telescope is composed of two main instruments capable of measuring visible light and infrared light. This will help in collecting the shapes and distances of a billion galaxies by scanning almost one-third of the sky. Since light travels a long distance to reach our eyes, Euclid can give a view of galaxies from the perspective of 10 billion years before us. As part of the exploration of the 'dark' universe, an important target of this telescope is to detect dark matter (matter that does not absorb or reflect light) and dark energy, a force that has accelerated the expansion of the universe. After one month's travel to its destination, the Euclid telescope will join with the James Webb telescope and start collecting data.

DART Mission

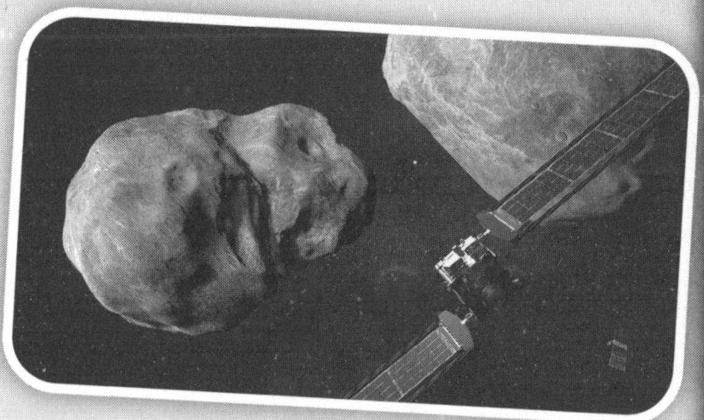

Imagine an asteroid is bound for an immediate collision towards Earth, and the only way to save the planet is to change its trajectory. This would have been looked at as unattainable and a feat for the remote future. But the flawless results of NASA's Double Asteroid Redirection Test (DART) showcase the possibility of safeguarding our planet from potential celestial collisions. While Earth doesn't face any immediate asteroid threat, scientists have been working on strategies to avert such catastrophes. The Kinetic Impact method is the most promising in which a spacecraft makes a high-speed impact and changes the path of the asteroid at a calculated angle. Demonstrated through NASA's DART mission, Dimorphos, the 160-m moon of the parent asteroid Didymos, was successfully impacted on 26 September 2022. The DART spacecraft was launched in November 2021. The investigation confirmed that the Dimorphos's orbit around Didymos has altered by 32 minutes. The DART mission's legacy will undoubtedly shape our approach to planetary defence and innovation.

MOXIE Celebrates Two Years

The Mars Oxygen In-Situ Resource Utilization Experiment (MOXIE) makes oxygen through a device called an electrolyzer, which skilfully collects CO_2 from the Martian atmosphere and then splits the molecules into methane (CO) and oxygen (O_2). It produces around 6 to 10 grams of oxygen per hour, the rate of an average tree on Earth. Proving its capability to make oxygen at any time of the Martian day and year, this small-scale mission has hopes for bigger goals. On 20 April 2023, MOXIE celebrated two years of its operation, successfully managing oxygen production runs without fail. NASA envisions a bold future as plans are underway of launching the next 'Big Moxie' that can produce 2,000 to 3,000 grams per hour amidst Martian storms.

Chandrayaan-3

On 14 July 2023, a new chapter in India's space exploration began as ISRO successfully launched the Chandrayaan-3 spacecraft from Sriharikota at 14.35 p.m. After orbiting the Earth in phases for a period of 15 to 20 days, it will enter the Moon's orbit and achieve landing between 23–24 August. Scientists have to reduce the speed of the rocket over the next few weeks to achieve soft landing. This must also coincide with the beginning of a lunar day, as the batteries of the Rover and the Lander can function only when charged with sunlight. The success of this mission would place India as the fourth country to achieve soft landing on the Moon. While the Chandrayaan-1 mission found the presence of water in 2008, and the Chandrayaan-2 mission in 2019 was partially successful, Chandrayaan-3 now aims to fulfil and surpass the goals of its predecessors. The spacecraft weighing 3,900 kg, with a 1,500-kg Lander called Vikram and a 26-kg Rover called Pragyaan is set to explore to South Pole of the Moon (surface area under shadow) where the possibility of finding water is speculated. The mission exemplifies ISRO's unwavering commitment to scientific discovery.

Chandrayaan-3: Launch vehicle lifting off from the Second Launch Pad (SLP) of SDSC-SHAR, Sriharikota

7 HISTORY

History is the study of what happened in the past, based on what has been written down or documented. Events before written records are generally considered prehistory. History is about our efforts to make sense of the past, by using information gained from what people remember, by discovering things and by interpreting all that we know about these events. Here are a few useful words related to history:

Annals: Historical accounts of facts and events ranged in chronological order, year by year.

Antiquarianism: Historical study focusing on the empirical evidence of the past, including manuscripts and archives, and archaeological and historic sites and artefacts. Now the term is used as a criticism to describe a narrow approach that excludes a historical context.

Antiquities: Objects or artefacts from ancient history, especially from the classical civilizations, the cultures of the Mediterranean region and the ancient Near East (modern Middle East).

Archaeology: The study of human history and prehistory through the excavation of sites and the analysis of physical remains.

Archive: A collection of historical documents and records.

Artefact: Any material object associated with a culture, such as a tool, clothing or food item.

Chronicle: A historical account of facts and events arranged in chronological order.

Chronology: The study of the sequence of past events.

Epigraphy: The study of ancient inscriptions.

Illuminated manuscript: A manuscript in which the text is supplemented by the addition of decoration.

Macrohistory: The study of long-term trends in world history to uncover patterns across diverse cultures.

Microhistory: The detailed investigation of a small unit (an event, a community or an individual) to cast light on broader historical issues.

Numismatics: The study of coins.

Phaleristics: The study of military orders, decorations and medals.

Presentism: Application of present-day ideas to interpretations of the past.

Primary source: Material from or directly related to the past. Documents and records of the period under study, such as diaries, letters, legal documents, accounts, photographs, news reports and artefacts.

WORLD: A BRIEF TIMELINE

5000 BCE
- Rise of the Sumerian Civilization in Mesopotamia in what is roughly present-day Iraq.
- First recorded settlements in the fertile valley of the River Nile in Egypt.

3500 BCE The wheel, the first written language and the use of bronze are located in this period. In the Indus Valley the first use of pottery is recorded.

2700–2600 BCE The Pyramids are built in Egypt.

2600 BCE The emergence of Mayan Civilization in the Yucatan Peninsula in South America. In 2620 BCE, Imhotep builds the first pyramid – the 'step pyramid' at Saqqara – as a tomb for the pharaoh Djoser, and Egypt begins its first era of remarkable monuments.

2500 BCE Building of the city of Mohenjo-Daro in the Indus Valley, the third oldest civilization after Mesopotamia and Egypt.

2500–2000 BCE First records of the Andean Civilization, the first of its kind in the Americas.

2300 BCE Civilization recorded in China. Astronomy appears as a science. This time also marks the Neolithic Age in Europe.

2250–1122 BCE Rise of the Chinese Civilization along the banks of the River Huang He.

2200 BCE First records of a civilization in the Malay Peninsula.

2000–1200 BCE The Iron Age civilizations discover the use of iron and start using it for various activities, both for practical purposes and craft.

2000 BCE
- The rise of Babylon in the Mesopotamian Civilization.
- King Hammurabi raises the first trained army in the world.
- The Bronze Age reaches Europe.
- Britain is invaded by the Scandinavian tribes for the first time.
- A civilization rises in Japan, soon after which Chinese and Korean groups invade it.

1500 BCE Rise of the Vedic culture in north India. The Rig Veda is compiled around this time.

1480 BCE Moses leads Israelites out of Egypt.

5000 BCE | 3500 BCE | 2500 BCE | 2000 BCE | 1500 BCE

1027 BCE The Chou Dynasty is established in China.

1000 BCE The decline of Egypt begins.

753 BCE The city of Rome is founded by Romulus.

660 BCE Birth of Zoroaster, the founder of Zoroastrianism in Media, Iran.

586 BCE Fall of Jerusalem to the Babylonians.

347 BCE Death of Greek philosopher Plato, disciple of Socrates and founder of the Academy, a school of philosophy in Athens, Greece.

336 BCE Accession of Alexander at the age of 22 to the throne of Macedon in south-east Europe. He will become one of the most successful conquerors of all time.

215 BCE Work begins on the Great Wall of China.

4 BCE–7 CE The birth of Jesus Christ (variously recorded).

44 BCE Julius Caesar is killed by Brutus and other conspirators.

1000 BCE | 500 BCE | 250 BCE | 0 BCE

264 BCE Ashoka is crowned, marking the start of the Golden Age in India.

73 BCE For the first time in history, slaves revolt against the Roman Republic in the Spartacus Uprising.

850 BCE *The Iliad* and *The Odyssey* are composed by Homer.

399 BCE Socrates, the Greek philosopher, is sentenced to death.

509 BCE Founding of the Roman Republic. The great architecture of Rome can be traced to this period.

55 BCE Julius Caesar conquers Britain, having already captured Gaul in present-day France.

560 BCE Gautama Buddha, founder of Buddhism, is born in Lumbini in present-day Nepal.

776 BCE The first Olympic Games are held in Olympia, Greece.

1431 Joan of Arc is burnt at the stake in France for allegedly practising witchcraft.

1492 Christopher Columbus discovers the Americas.

1504 The *Mona Lisa* is painted by Leonardo da Vinci.

1215 The Magna Carta, the historic charter of rights and laws in England, is signed.

1163 The University of Oxford is founded in England.

1776 Declaration of American Independence.

29 CE Jesus Christ is crucified.

570 CE Birth of Prophet Muhammad, the founder of Islam, in Mecca.

1666 London is engulfed by the 'Great Fire'.

1689 Constitutional monarchy is established in England.

0 CE | 1000 CE | 1500 CE | 1750 CE

1337 Beginning of the Hundred Years' War between England and France; ends only in 1453.

1756 Britain, Prussia and Hanover combine to battle Austria, France, Russia, Saxony, Sweden and Spain in the Seven Years' War.

1455 CE The War of Roses, a civil war in England, begins; ends in 1485.

64 CE A fire, which lasts for six days, destroys Rome.

1770 Captain James Cook discovers Australia.

1564 Birth of poet and playwright William Shakespeare in England.

1642 Civil war in England. King Charles I is in a feud with the Parliament, as they demand democratic powers. Eventually, he is executed in 1653.

1789 On 14 July, the French Revolution begins with the storming of the Bastille prison to free prisoners and end monarchy.

1854 Admiral Perry of the USA visits Japan and forces trade with the West.
- The Crimean War takes place between 1853 and 1856. Lord Cardigan leads the British cavalry against the Russians in what becomes known as 'The Charge of the Light Brigade'.

1860 Herman Hollerith invents an electronic tabulator for the US census. He starts a company that eventually becomes International Business Machines (IBM) Corporation.

1795 The Metric system of measurement is introduced in France.

1861–65 American Civil War; President Lincoln bans slavery; some states attempt to break the Union.

1812 On 24 June, Napoleon takes Moscow, but it is a hollow victory. The city is burned to the ground, yet the Tsar does not surrender. Napoleon and the French army retreat.

1848 Karl Marx and Friedrich Engels publish *The Communist Manifesto*.

1847 US troops, led by General Winfield Scott, enter Mexico City in September. A treaty ending the Mexican–American War is signed in February 1848.

1800 CE | 1825 CE | 1850 CE | 1875 CE

1815 On 18 June, Napoleon is finally defeated at Waterloo, Belgium, by the Duke of Wellington.

1859 Charles Darwin publishes *On the Origin of Species*.

1856 Louis Pasteur shows that diseases spread from tiny organisms. Modern-day germ theory is born.

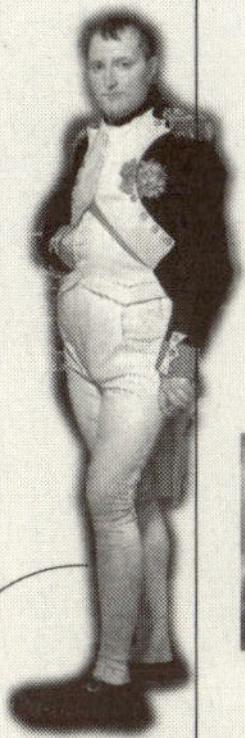

1814 The Battle of Trafalgar: The British fleet under the command of Horatio Nelson defeats a combined French and Spanish fleet.

1845–48 The Great Hunger (aka Potato Famine) in Ireland. More than 1.5 million die of starvation and disease.

1866 Prussia invades Austria.
- The United States and Europe are connected by a 4,000 km long telegraph cable.

1833 England outlaws slavery and frees more than 780,000 slaves.

1804 Napoleon Bonaparte is crowned emperor of France.

1838 On 24 January, Samuel Morse demonstrates the telegraph machine.

1901 Guglielmo Marconi sends the first transatlantic wireless radio signal.

1904 Russo-Japanese War: The Russians underestimate the modern Japanese fleet, which destroys most of the already depleted Russian Navy a year later. The Japanese use the new Marconi radios to keep track of the Russian Navy.

1905 While working as a patent clerk, Albert Einstein publishes his theory of relativity and also states energy equals matter ($E = mc^2$). He publishes four papers in one year. Three of them are Nobel Prize–winning material.

1898 The Spanish-American War starts. Reports of atrocities by the Spaniards against Cubans compel the USA to intervene.

1939 Hitler invades Poland on 1 September. The British Commonwealth and France declare war on Germany, starting the Second World War.

1930 The first FIFA World Cup starts: Lucien Laurent scores the first goal for France, against Mexico.

1876 Alexander Graham Bell patents the telephone.

1928 Scottish bacteriologist Alexander Fleming notices penicillin mould killing a staphylococcus culture. The 'antibiotics revolution' begins.

1875 CE | 1900 CE | 1915 CE | 1940 CE

1899-1902 Boer War: The descendants of the Dutch in present-day South Africa fight for independence from Britain.

1938 Adolf Hitler, Chancellor of Germany since 1933, launches *Kristallnacht*, the 'night of broken glass'. Hundreds of Jews are killed by Nazis.

1903 Orville and Wilbur Wright fly the first aircraft.

1912 The 'unsinkable' *Titanic* sinks with more than 1,500 passengers.

1918 On 11 November, the First World War ends.

1914 On 3 August, Germany declares war on France, starting the 'Great War' (First World War).

1941 On 22 June, Operation Barbarossa, the invasion of Russia by Germany, is launched 129 years (to the day) after Napoleon invaded Russia.
- On 8 December, the Japanese attack Pearl Harbour, effectively bringing the USA into the Second World War.

1883 The island volcano of Krakatoa in Indonesia erupts on 23 August. More than 36,000 people are killed. Its impact is seen as far away as London and New York. The sound of the explosion is heard 5,000 km away.

1917 The USA enters the First World War against Germany. Ten million people will die in the war.

1942 At the University of Chicago, USA, Enrico Fermi conducts the first nuclear reaction.

1944 The largest offshore landing in history, the invasion of Normandy, referred to as D-Day, starts on 6 June. This spells the end for Hitler's Third Reich.

1945 On 6 August, the USA drops an atomic bomb, 'Little Boy', on Hiroshima, Japan, killing an estimated 66,000 civilians. On 9 August, another bomb, 'Fat Man', is dropped on Nagasaki. Japan announces its surrender to the Allied powers on 15 August; it signs the Instrument of Surrender on 2 September.

1957 Russian-made Sputnik I becomes the first man-made satellite.

1961 On 11 April, Yuri A. Gagarin becomes the first human in space.

1969 On 20 July, Neil Armstrong lands on the surface of the Moon.

1990 Apartheid ends in South Africa.
● The First Gulf War begins when the USA attacks Iraq in response to Iraq's invasion of Kuwait.

1991 The Soviet Union dissolves, and with it, the Cold War with the USA.

1994 Rwanda is engulfed in a bloody civil war.

2001 On 11 September, terrorists in planes crash into the World Trade Center twin towers in New York, and the Pentagon in Washington DC.

2003 US and British forces invade Iraq. Saddam Hussein is caught, and executed in 2006.

2004 On 26 December, a huge tsunami kills thousands in Indonesia, Thailand, Sri Lanka, India, Maldives and Somalia.

2009 On 20 January, Barack Obama is sworn in as the first African-American president of the USA.

1950 CE | 1975 CE | 2010 CE | 2021 CE

1989 In Tiananmen Square, the Chinese army crushes a demonstration, killing hundreds of students.
● In November, the Berlin Wall that divided West Berlin from East Berlin is torn down. Germany is united for the first time since the Second World War.

2011 A democratic uprising in Egypt sets off similar civil uprisings, collectively called the 'Arab Spring', in Libya, Bahrain, Syria, Yemen, Algeria, Iraq, Jordan and Lebanon.
● On 1 May, Osama bin Laden, head of terrorist organization al-Qaeda, is killed in Pakistan by US Special Forces.

2014 In March, Russia annexes Crimea.

2017 The USA pulls out of the landmark Paris Climate Accord.

2018 Former cricketer Imran Khan of the Tehreek-e-Insaaf party becomes Pakistan's prime minister.

2019 Boris Johnson becomes UK prime minister after Theresa May resigns.

2020 COVID-19, a global pandemic, fans out from Wuhan, China, in December 2019, and is declared a Public Health Emergency of International Concern by WHO on 30 January 2020.
● The UK withdraws from the European Union (EU) on 31 January, a move popularly known as 'Brexit'.

2021 Democrat nominee Joe Biden begins his tenure as US president in January after defeating former president and Republican nominee Donald Trump. Vice President Kamala Harris becomes the first woman, first African American and first Asian American to hold the office.
● In August, the USA withdraws troops from Afghanistan, resulting in the Taliban taking over Kabul and more than two-thirds of the country.

2022 Russia invades Ukraine on 21 February. Much of the international community condemns Russia, and many countries implement economic sanctions against the country and its companies.
● Pakistan's prime minister Imran Khan is removed from office after losing a no-confidence vote on 4 April and replaced by Shehbaz Sharif, president of the Pakistani Muslim League.
● Boris Johnson resigns as British prime minister on 8 July.

ANCIENT INDIA TIMELINE

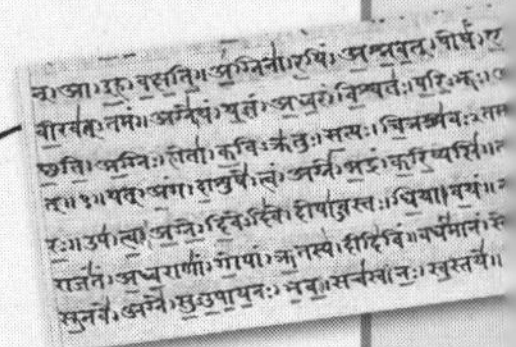

3000 BCE	The beginning of the Harappan (Indus Valley) Civilization.
2500 BCE	The establishment of the cities of Harappa and Mohenjo-Daro in the **Valley of the River Indus.**
2000 BCE	The decline of the Harappan Civilization.
1500 BCE	The people later referred to as the 'Vedic' people set up a recognizable Vedic culture in the Gangetic plains.
1100 BCE	With the discovery of iron, the Vedic people start using iron tools.
1800-1100 BCE	One of the earliest sacred scriptures of the Hindus, the **Rig Veda** (variously dated) is composed.
750 BCE	The Upanishads, a set of sacred texts of Hinduism, are composed.
600 BCE	Sixteen Mahajanapadas (Great States) are formed on the subcontinent.
543 BCE	King Bimbisara conquers the Magadha region in the east and becomes emperor of the Magadha Empire.
527 BCE	**Prince Siddhartha Gautama** attains Enlightenment, becomes the Buddha, and establishes Buddhism.
500 BCE	Prince Mahavira establishes Jainism in north India.
493 BCE	Bimbisara dies and is succeeded by Ajatashatru.
461 BCE	Ajatashatru expands the Magadha territory and dies shortly afterwards.
327 BCE	**Alexander of Macedonia** invades the Indus Valley on the Indian subcontinent, fights a famous battle with Puru (Porus).
304 BCE	Magadha king Chandragupta Maurya establishes the Mauryan dynasty with Pataliputra as the capital.
500–300 BCE	The Ramayana, the famous Hindu epic, is composed. There are various dates (between 500 and 300 BCE) put down for Valmiki's Ramayana.
300 BCE	The Chola dynasty establishes the first kingdom in southern India with its capital at Thanjavur.
290 BCE	Chandragupta's son Bindusara extends the Mauryan Empire to the Deccan region.
259 BCE	Mauryan emperor **Ashoka** converts to Buddhism.
220 BCE	The Mauryan dynasty expands to nearly all of India.
200 BCE	The famous epic, the **Mahabharata**, is composed. (Some sources put it down between 500 BCE and 200 BCE and others between 200 BCE and 200 CE).
184 BCE	The Mauryan dynasty ends and makes way for the beginning of the Sunga dynasty.

78 BCE	The Sunga dynasty declines.
50 CE	The first Buddhist stupa is built at Sanchi (now in Madhya Pradesh).
300 CE	The Pallava dynasty is established in Kanchipuram (now in Tamil Nadu).
350 CE	The Sangam is compiled in Tamil in the kingdom of Madurai. The Puranas are composed.
390 CE	**Chandragupta II** extends the Gupta kingdom to Gujarat.
450 CE	Kumaragupta, who succeeds Chandragupta II, builds the monastic university of Nalanda (in present-day Bihar).
499 CE	Mathematician Aryabhata writes the *Aryabhatiya,* a compendium of mathematics and astronomy.
500 CE	The beginning of the Bhakti cult in Tamil Nadu.
528 CE	The Gupta Empire sees a downfall due to continuous invasions.
550 CE	The **Chalukya kingdom** is established in central India with its capital at Badami.
606 CE	Harshavardhana rules the kingdom of Thanesar in north India and Nepal with its capital at Kannauj (in present-day Uttar Pradesh).

MEDIEVAL INDIA

761 CE	Muhammad bin Qasim battles Raja Dahir in Sind.
1000 CE	Invasion of Mahmud of Ghazni.
1017–30 CE	**Al-Biruni**, the scholar from Persia, travels in India.
1191 CE	The First Battle of Tarain is fought between Muhammad Ghori (from present-day Afghanistan) and Prithviraj Chauhan. Ghori is defeated by Prithviraj.
1192 CE	The Second Battle of Tarain is fought between Ghori and **Prithviraj Chauhan**.
1194 CE	Muhammad Ghori and Jaichandra, the Gahadavala king of Kannauj, fight the Battle of Chandawar.
1221 CE	**Genghis Khan** invades Punjab.
1310 CE	Alauddin Khilji's army occupies Devagiri, destroying the Seuna Yadava kingdom.
1336 CE	The **Vijayanagara Empire** is established by Harihara I and his brother Bukka Raya I in the Deccan.
1347 CE	Governor Hasan Gangu revolts against Muhammad bin Tughlaq, founding the Bahmani Sultanate.

1370 CE Bukka, the Vijayanagara ruler, and his son Kumara Kampana capture the entire Tamil-speaking region.

1407 CE Zafar Khan, governor of Gujarat, declares himself Sultan Muzaffar Shah, founding the Gujarat Sultanate/Muzaffarid dynasty.

1451 CE Bahlul Khan Lodi ascends the throne of the Delhi Sultanate, starting the Lodi dynasty.

1469 CE **Guru Nanak**, the founder of Sikhism, is born.

1486 CE **Sher Shah Suri**, founder of the Suri Empire, is born in Sasaram.

1490 CE Ahmadnagar declares independence, followed by Bijapur and Berar in the same year, thus breaking up the Bahmani Sultanate.

1497–99 CE **Vasco da Gama** makes his first voyage from Europe to India and back.

1503 CE The kingdom of Kochi is taken over by the Portuguese; this is the first European settlement in India.

1509 CE The Battle of Diu marks the beginning of the dominance of the Europeans in the Asian naval theatre.

1522 CE The Portuguese land on the Coromandel Coast.

MUGHAL ERA

1526 CE Sultan Ibrahim Lodi of the Delhi Sultanate angers local nobles, who respond by inviting Babur, the ruler of Kabul, to invade Delhi and Agra.

1527 CE **Babur** annexes Mewar.

1530 CE Babur completes his *Baburnama*. He dies, and is succeeded by his son Humayun.

1539 CE The Battle of Chausa is fought between Humayun and Sher Shah Suri. Humayun is defeated.

1540 CE The Battle of Kannauj: Humayun is defeated by the Afghans (Suri Dynasty), and spends 12 years in exile.

1552 CE **Humayun** regains the throne of Delhi.

1556 CE Humayun dies, and is succeeded by his son Akbar.

1556 CE The Second Battle of Panipat is fought between Hemu (Hem Chandra Vikramaditya) and Akbar.

1565 CE The Battle of Talikota results in the conquest of the Vijayanagara Empire by the Deccan sultanates.

1572 CE **Akbar** annexes Gujarat.

1574 CE Akbar annexes Bengal.

1586 CE Akbar annexes Kashmir.

1600 CE The East India Company is formed in England. It gets exclusive trading rights in India.

1605 CE	Akbar dies, and is succeeded by his son Jahangir.
1628 CE	Jahangir dies, and is succeeded by his son Shah Jahan.
1630 CE	Birth of **Chhatrapati Shivaji Maharaj**.
1658 CE	After completing the Taj Mahal, the Jama Masjid and the Red Fort, Shah Jahan dies. He is succeeded by his son Aurangzeb.
1674 CE	Forces led by Chhatrapati Shivaji Maharaj defeat Aurangzeb's troops, and establish the Maratha Empire.
1675 CE	Guru Tegh Bahadur, the ninth Guru of the Sikhs, is executed in Delhi on the orders of Mughal emperor Aurangzeb.
1680 CE	Chhatrapati Shivaji Maharaj dies at Raigad.
1681 CE	Aurangzeb invades the Deccan.
1699 CE	**Guru Gobind Singh**, the tenth Guru of the Sikhs, creates Dal Khalsa, a military force.
1707 CE	Aurangzeb dies, and is succeeded by his son Bahadur Shah I.
1708 CE	Guru Gobind Singh survives an assassination attempt in Maharashtra.
1719 CE	**Bajirao I** is appointed the Peshwa by Maratha emperor Shahu.
1735 CE	The annexation of Rajputana by Peshwa Bajirao I.
1737 CE	Bajirao I conquers Delhi; the Mughal emperor is spared and kept as a symbolic head.
1740 CE	Bajirao I dies, with the distinction of winning every battle he fought. He is succeeded by Balaji Bajirao.
1757 CE	The British East India Company's private army under **Robert Clive** annexes Bengal in the Battle of Plassey.
1760 CE	The Marathas comprehensively defeat the Nizam of Hyderabad; the Maratha Empire reaches its zenith.
1761 CE	The Afghans dominate in the Third Battle of Panipat, blocking Maratha expansion.
1766 CE	The Sikhs defeat Ahmad Shah Abdali; establish Sikh rule in Punjab.
	The First Anglo-Mysore War between Mysore's (now Mysuru) Hyder Ali and the East India Company.
1779 CE	Maratha Mahadji Shinde routs the British at the Battle of Wadgaon.
1782 CE	The First Anglo-Maratha War ends with the Treaty of Salbai.
1790 CE	The Marathas defeat the Rajputs of Jaipur and their Mughal allies at the Battle of Patan.
1799 CE	The Fourth Anglo-Mysore War ends with the death of **Tipu Sultan** and the restoration of the Wodeyar dynasty that had ruled Mysore earlier.

1801 **Maharaja Ranjit Singh** establishes Khalsa rule over Punjab, ruling from present-day Lahore.

1807 The East India Company signs the Treaty of Amritsar with Maharaja Ranjit Singh.

1818 The Third Anglo-Maratha War ends with the defeat of Bajirao II and the end of the Maratha Empire, leaving the British in control of most of India.

BRITISH RAJ

1853 First passenger train runs from Bori Bunder in Bombay to Thane in present-day Maharashtra.

1857 **Widespread uprising** in north India against British rule (the First War of Independence). It is crushed and the queen of England declares India a colony.

1858 The British Crown officially takes over Indian governance.

1877 The queen of England is proclaimed empress of India.

1885 The first meeting of the Indian National Congress.

1899 **Lord Curzon** becomes Governor General and viceroy of India.

1905 The first partition of Bengal takes place.

1906 The All-India Muslim League is formed.

1912 The capital of British India is shifted to Delhi from Calcutta.

1919 The **Jallianwala Bagh** massacre takes place in the wake of protests against the Rowlatt Act, which allows political cases to be tried without juries and suspects to be imprisoned without trial.

1920 Mahatma Gandhi launches the Non-cooperation movement.

1922 The violent Chauri Chaura incident takes place during the Civil Disobedience movement; Mahatma Gandhi calls off the protest.

1928 Simon Commission comes to India and is boycotted by all parties.

1930 **Salt Satyagraha**, which begins with the Dandi March, is launched as an agitation against the salt tax.

The First Round Table Conference takes place in London.

1931 The Second Round Table Conference takes place and the Gandhi–Irwin Pact is signed.

1934 The Civil Disobedience movement is called off.

1942 Gandhi meets the Cripps Mission; the Quit India movement is launched.

1943 Netaji Subhas Chandra Bose takes charge of the Indian National Army.

1947 **Lord Mountbatten** draws up plans for Partition of India.

Partition of India and independence from British rule, at midnight of 14/15 August.

MODERN HISTORY (POST-INDEPENDENCE)

1947–48	Thousands die in widespread communal riots during and after the Partition of India into two nations: India and Pakistan.
1948	On 30 January, Mahatma Gandhi, on his way to his daily prayer meeting, is assassinated by Nathuram Godse.
	The first conflict with Pakistan breaks out over the territory of Kashmir.
1951–52	The first general elections are held and the Congress party wins. **Jawaharlal Nehru** is elected prime minister (PM).
1962	India loses brief war with China.
1964	Prime Minister Jawaharlal Nehru dies. Lal Bahadur Shastri becomes India's second prime minister.
1965	The second war with Pakistan over Kashmir is fought.
1966	**Indira Gandhi**, Nehru's daughter, is elected prime minister.
1971	Third war with Pakistan over creation of Bangladesh.
	The Soviet Union and India sign a 20-year treaty of friendship.
1974	India's first underground nuclear test is carried out.
1975	Indira Gandhi declares Emergency in the country.
1975–77	Nearly 1,000 political opponents are imprisoned during the Emergency.
1977	Indira Gandhi loses the general elections.
1980	Indira Gandhi returns to power, heading a Congress party splinter group – Congress (Indira) – and winning by a huge margin.
1983	The Indian cricket team wins the (Prudential) World Cup for the first time, under the captaincy of Kapil Dev.
1984	Troops storm the Golden Temple in Amritsar, Punjab, the hideout of Sikh militants demanding self-rule.
	Prime Minister Indira Gandhi is assassinated by bodyguards, sparking off anti-Sikh riots in Delhi and across India. **Rajiv Gandhi**, her son, becomes prime minister.
	Toxic gas leaks at the Union Carbide pesticides plant in Bhopal. Thousands are killed and many more affected.
1987	India sends troops for peacekeeping operations in Sri Lanka's civil conflict with the Liberation Tigers of Tamil Eelam (LTTE).
1989	Congress is routed in the elections. V.P. Singh (Janata Dal) is PM.
1990	Indian troops are withdrawn from Sri Lanka.
1991	Rajiv Gandhi is assassinated by a suicide bomber.
1992	The Babri mosque in Ayodhya is demolished, triggering widespread communal violence.

1996	The Congress party suffers electoral defeat and the Bharatiya Janata Party (BJP) emerges as the largest single party.
1998	BJP forms a coalition government under Prime Minister **Atal Bihari Vajpayee**. This will be the first non-Congress government to complete a full term. India conducts five nuclear tests, closely followed by Pakistan.
1999	Vajpayee takes the new bus service to Pakistan to meet its prime minister, Nawaz Sharif, and sign the Lahore Peace Declaration.
2000	The billionth Indian citizen is born.
2001	Vajpayee meets President Pervez Musharraf of Pakistan in the first summit of the neighbours in more than two years. On 13 December, the Parliament is attacked by five terrorists from the Lashkar-e-Taiba and Jaish-e-Mohammed, leading to nine deaths, and a stand-off between India and Pakistan. The attackers are killed.
2002	Scientist **A.P.J. Abdul Kalam** is elected president of India.
2003	India and Pakistan resume flights between the two countries, which were banned after the December 2001 terrorist attack on the Indian Parliament.
2004	The United Progressive Alliance (UPA), with the Congress party as the largest member party, forms the government after the general elections. Dr Manmohan Singh becomes prime minister.
2006	President George W. Bush of the USA signs an agreement with Prime Minister Manmohan Singh to share nuclear technology.
2007	Pratibha Patil becomes India's first woman president.
2008	Terrorists from Pakistan terrorists **attack landmark spots** in Mumbai.
2009	India's unmanned lunar probe Chandrayaan-1 discovers water molecules on the Moon's surface.
2010	The Indian rupee gets a symbol: ₹ The Indian government initiates the Right of Children to Free and Compulsory Education Act to provide free and compulsory education to all children between six and 14 years of age. The 19th Commonwealth Games, are held in Delhi, from 3 to 14 October 2010.
2011	Mamata Banerjee's Trinamool Congress ends the 34-year rule of the Left coalition led by the CPI-M in West Bengal.
2012	Pranab Mukherjee is elected as India's 13th president. Hamid Ansari is re-elected as vice-president of India. Terrorist Ajmal Kasab is hanged for his role in the 2008 Mumbai attacks.
2013	The Criminal Law (Amendment) Act 2013 is passed after the 16 December 2012 'Nirbhaya' case.

2014	The National Democratic Alliance (NDA), led by the BJP, wins the general elections. Narendra Modi becomes the 15th Indian PM.
2016	The Goods and Services Tax (GST), the biggest tax reform since Independence, is launched on the midnight of 30 June. Ram Nath Kovind becomes the second Dalit president of India after K.R. Narayanan (1997–2002).
2018	The BJP wins the legislative assembly elections in Tripura, a Left stronghold for 25 years.
2019	The BJP wins the general elections with a thumping majority and **Narendra Modi** becomes prime minister for a second term. The government abrogates Article 370 of the Constitution, which gave special status to Jammu and Kashmir, and bifurcates the state into two Union Territories: Jammu and Kashmir, and Ladakh.
2020	Prime Minister Modi announces a 21-day lockdown throughout India, the largest in world history, to prevent the spread of COVID-19. National Education Policy 2020 (NEP 2020), a new policy on education, is approved by the Union cabinet. Prime Minister Narendra Modi performs *bhoomipujan* and lays the foundation stone of the Ram Temple in Ayodhya, Uttar Pradesh. Three Indian agriculture acts of 2020, referred to as the Farm Bills, are initiated by the Parliament of India in September 2020.
2021	For the first time in history, the Union budget is presented on an India-made tablet as a paperless budget. The contentious Farm Bills are repealed on 19 November. The Supreme Court permits women to take the National Defence Academy examination.
2022	Droupadi Murmu, a member of the BJP, becomes the 15th president of India on 25 July 2022, the first person belonging to the tribal community and the second woman after Pratibha Patil to hold the office.
2023	Prime Minister Narendra Modi inaugurated the new parliament building which is part of the Central Vista Redevelopment Project. Chandrayaan-3, the third and most recent lunar Indian space research exploration mission was launched from Sriharikota.

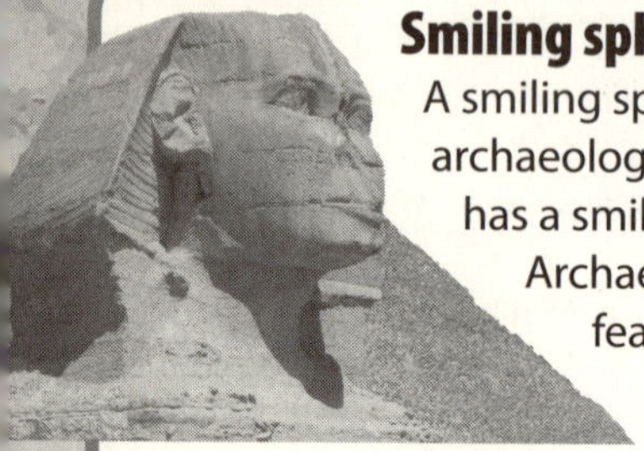

Smiling sphinx statue discovered in Egypt

A smiling sphinx-like statue has been unearthed by archaeologists in Egypt. The limestone structure has a smiley face with dimples on both cheeks. Archaeologists believe that the statue's features resemble that of Emperor Claudius, a Roman emperor who ruled between 41 to 54 A.D.Apart from the limestone statue, archaeologists have also discovered a mud-brick basin from Byzantine era and a Roman Stele(stone slab) with demotic and hieroglyphic inscriptions. The artefacts were excavated from a two-level tomb in the temple of Dendera, near the Hathor Temple.

21 royal Han tombs discovered in China

21 royal tombs, dating back to the 2000-year-old Han Dynasty were discovered by a group of archaeologists in the Chinese city of Changsha.The tombs were categorized according to their structures. Some had passages, while the others did not. The discovery of many luxurious artefacts and several paired tombs suggested that the tombs were an ancient royal burial site. More than 230 ancient artefacts were also discovered, most of which were earthenware and pottery in different forms. This discovery will further help in studying more about the Han Dynasty and their burial practices.

Dako sword unearthed in Japan

A giant, 2.3m long sword was excavated by a group of archaeologists from a 1,600-year-old ancient burial mound in the city of Nara, Japan. Experts believe that the 7.5-feet-long sword was not used for self-defense, but for protection against evil after death. The archaeologists also discovered a shield-shaped bronze mirror weighing more than 12 pounds that was covered in clay; the largest bronze mirror found till date. Both the discoveries have been marked as national treasures.

8 INDIA: STATES AND UNION TERRITORIES

TOP STATES/UNION TERRITORY STATISTICS

Largest by area: Rajasthan

Smallest by area: Goa

State with the longest coastline: Gujarat, with a mainland coastline of 1,600 km (approx.)

State with longest international border: West Bengal; 2,216.7 km long border with Bangladesh

State sharing borders with most states/UTs: Uttar Pradesh; shares borders with nine Indian states/UTs – Bihar, Chhattisgarh, Delhi, Haryana, Himachal Pradesh, Jharkhand, Madhya Pradesh, Rajasthan and Uttarakhand

Most populated: Uttar Pradesh

Least populated: Lakshadweep

Highest population density: Delhi

Lowest population density: Arunachal Pradesh

Highest literacy rate: Kerala

Longest railway network: Uttar Pradesh

Longest road network: Maharashtra

Best Smart State 2022: Madhya Pradesh

Best Smart UT 2022: Chandigarh

Best Smart Cities 2022: Indore (Madhya Pradesh) and Surat (Gujarat)

State with the most UNESCO World Heritage elements (Intangible, cultural, historical or other sites): Rajasthan (Hill forts, Jaipur city, Jantar Mantar, Keoladeo Ghana National Park, Kalbelia songs and folk dances) and Maharashtra (Ajanta, Ellora and Elephanta caves, Chhatrapati Shivaji Maharaj Terminus, Kumbh Mela (shared) at Nashik, and Victorian Gothic and art deco ensembles of Mumbai and [shared] Western Ghats)

UT with the most UNESCO World Heritage Sites: Delhi, with the Red Fort complex, Qutub Minar complex and Humayun's Tomb

Cities with UNESCO Heritage City status: Ahmedabad (Gujarat), Jaipur (Rajasthan) and Dholavira: a Harappan City

Highest Sustainable Development Goals Index Score 2021–22: State: Kerala: 75; UT: Chandigarh: 79

Cleanest City Award 2022: Indore (Madhya Pradesh) – six-time winner

States/UTs with most wildlife sanctuaries and national parks: Madhya Pradesh and the Andaman and Nicobar Islands: nine national parks each; Andaman and Nicobar Islands: 96 wildlife sanctuaries

* All information has been updated up to 1 August 2023

ANDHRA PRADESH

Capital: Amaravati

Location: South-eastern coast

Area: 160,205 sq. km

Population: 49,634,314

History: Formed in 1956; reorganized in 2014

Language: Telugu, Urdu

Literacy Rate: 67.02%

Governor: S. Abdul Nazeer

Chief Minister: S. Abdul Nazeer

Major Rivers: Godavari, Krishna

Industries: Textiles, shipbuilding, aquaculture, auto parts, cement, coal mining

Agriculture: Rice, cotton, maize

State Animal: Blackbuck

State Bird: Rose-ringed parakeet

ARUNACHAL PRADESH

Capital: Itanagar

Location: North-east

Area: 83,743 sq. km

Population: 1,382,611

History: Formed in 1987

Languages: Nisi, Dafla and others

Literacy Rate: 65.38%

Governor: Lt Gen Kaiwalya Trivikram Parnaik

Chief Minister: Pema Khandu

Major Rivers: Siang

Industries: Forest products, handloom, clay

Agriculture: Rice, potato, tea, apple, pineapple

State Animal: Gayal (Mithun)

State Bird: Great hornbill

ASSAM

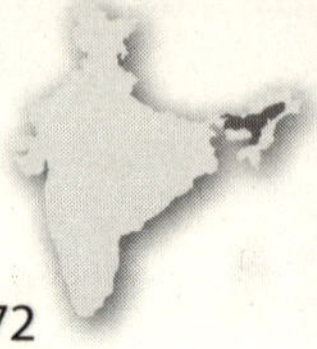

Capital: Dispur

Location: North-east

Area: 78,438 sq. km

Population: 31,169,272

History: Formed in 1947

Languages: Assamese, Bengali, Bodo, Karbi, Dimasa

Literacy Rate: 72.19%

Governor: Gulab Chand Kataria

Chief Minister: Himanta Biswa Sarma

Major Rivers: Brahmaputra, Barak

Industries: Tea, cement, textiles, sericulture, oil refining, coal mining

Agriculture: Rice, jute, tea, cotton

State Animal: Indian rhinoceros

State Bird: White-winged wood duck

BIHAR

Capital: Patna

Location: East

Area: 94,163 sq. km

Population: 103,804,637

History: Formed in 1936; reorganized in 2000

Languages: Hindi, Bhojpuri

Literacy Rate: 61.8%

Governor: Rajendra Vishwanath Arlekar

Chief Minister: Nitish Kumar

Major Rivers: Ganga, Gandak, Son

Industries: Food and beverages, plastic and rubber, tobacco, textiles, leather, dairy

Agriculture: Rice, wheat, maize, pulses, sugar cane, jute

State Animal: Gaur

State Bird: House sparrow

Background: Andhra Pradesh

CHHATTISGARH

Capital: Raipur
Location: East-central
Area: 135,194 sq. km
Population: 25,540,196
History: Formed in 2000
Languages: Chhattisgarhi, Hindi
Literacy Rate: 70.28%
Governor: Biswabhusan Harichandan
Chief Minister: Bhupesh Baghel
Major Rivers: Mahanadi, Indravati
Industries: Cement, mining, steel, aluminium, electricity
Agriculture: Rice, maize, wheat, niger seed, pulses
State Animal: Wild buffalo
State Bird: Hill mynah

GOA

Capital: Panaji
Location: West
Area: 3,702 sq. km
Population: 1,457,723
History: Formed in 1987
Languages: Konkani, Marathi
Literacy Rate: 88.7%
Governor: P.S. Sreedharan Pillai
Chief Minister: Pramod Sawant
Major Rivers: Mandovi, Zuari
Industries: Mining, textiles, tourism and hospitality, fisheries
Agriculture: Rice, millets, maize, cashew, coconut, bananas, sugar cane, pineapples, areca nuts
State Animal: Gaur
State Bird: Ruby-throated yellow bulbul

GUJARAT

Capital: Gandhinagar
Location: West
Area: 196,024 sq. km
Population: 60,383,628
History: Formed in 1960
Language: Gujarati
Literacy Rate: 78.03%
Governor: Acharya Dev Vrat
Chief Minister: Bhupendra Patel
Major Rivers: Narmada, Tapti, Sabarmati, Mahi
Industries: Fertilizers, textiles, petroleum, engineering, diamonds
Agriculture: Groundnuts, cotton, rice, wheat
State Animal: Asiatic lion
State Bird: Greater flamingo

HARYANA

Capital: Chandigarh
Location: North
Area: 44,212 sq. km
Population: 25,353,081
History: Formed in 1966
Languages: Hindi, Haryanvi
Literacy Rate: 75.55%
Governor: Bandaru Dattatreya
Chief Minister: Manohar Lal Khattar
Major Rivers: Yamuna, Ghaggar
Industries: Handloom, electrical appliances, automobiles, IT
Agriculture: Sugar cane, oilseeds, rice, groundnuts, maize, wheat, pulses, mustard
State Animal: Blackbuck
State Bird: Black francolin

Background: Chhattisgarh

HIMACHAL PRADESH

Capital: Shimla; Dharamshala (winter)

Location: North

Area: 55,673 sq. km

Population: 6,856,509

History: Formed in 1971

Languages: Hindi, Pahari

Literacy Rate: 82.8%

Governor: Shiv Pratap Shukla

Chief Minister: Sukhvinder Singh Sukhu

Major Rivers: Beas, Ravi, Chenab, Sutlej, Yamuna

Industries: Food and beverages, electronics, pharmaceuticals, hydroelectricity

Agriculture: Wheat, rice, maize, barley, fruits, olives, sugar cane

State Animal: Snow leopard

State Bird: Western tragopan

JHARKHAND

Capital: Ranchi

Location: East

Area: 79,714 sq. km

Population: 32,966,238

History: Formed in 2000

Languages: Hindi, Santhali

Literacy Rate: 66.41%

Governor: C P. Radhakrishnan

Chief Minister: Hemant Soren

Major Rivers: Damodar, Subarnarekha

Industries: Steel, locomotives, mining, sericulture

Agriculture: Rice, wheat, maize, pulses, mustard

State Animal: Indian elephant

State Bird: Koel

KARNATAKA

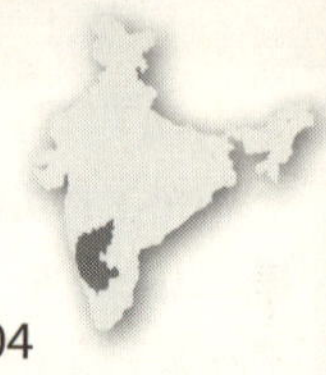

Capital: Bengaluru

Location: South-west

Area: 191,791 sq. km

Population: 61,130,704

History: Formed in 1956 as Mysore State; named Karnataka in 1973

Language: Kannada

Literacy Rate: 75.36%

Governor: Thaawar Chand Gehlot

Chief Minister: Siddaramaiah

Major Rivers: Krishna, Kaveri

Industries: IT, telecom, electronics, floriculture, silk

Agriculture: Rice, ragi, sorghum, pulses, pearl millet, coffee

Animal: Indian elephant

State Bird: Indian roller

KERALA

Capital: Thiruvananthapuram

Location: South-west

Area: 38,863 sq. km

Population: 33,387,677

History: Formed in 1956

Language: Malayalam

Literacy Rate: 94%

Governor: Arif Mohammad Khan

Chief Minister: Pinarayi Vijayan

Major Rivers: Periyar, Bharatapuza, Pamba, Chaliyar, Chalakudy

Industries: Handlooms and textiles, coir, marine products, agro-industries, electronics, tourism and hospitality, handicrafts

Agriculture: Coconut, rubber, tea, coffee, cashew, spices, rice, tapioca

State Animal: Indian elephant

State Bird: Great hornbill

 Background: Himachal Pradesh

MADHYA PRADESH

Capital: Bhopal
Location: Central
Area: 308,000 sq. km
Population: 72,597,565
History: Formed in 1956; reorganized in 2000
Language: Hindi
Literacy Rate: 69.32%
Governor: Mangubhai Chhaganbhai Patel
Chief Minister: Shivraj Singh Chouhan
Major Rivers: Narmada, Chambal, Betwa, Tapti
Industries: Automotive, electronics, cement, tourism, telecom, IT, forestry, textiles
Agriculture: Rice, wheat, millets, pulses, cotton, soyabean
State Animal: Barasingha
State Bird: Indian paradise flycatcher

MAHARASHTRA

Capital: Mumbai
Location: West
Area: 307,713 sq. km
Population: 112,372,972
History: Formed in 1960
Language: Marathi
Literacy Rate: 82.34%
Governor: Ramesh Bais
Chief Minister: Eknath Shinde
Major Rivers: Godavari, Wainganga, Penganga, Wardha, Bhima, Tapti
Industries: Textiles, engineering, pharmaceuticals, sugar, automotive, cinema, food products, breweries, printing and publishing
Agriculture: Rice, millets, sugar cane, pulses, oranges, mango
State Animal: Indian giant squirrel
State Bird: Yellow-footed green pigeon

MANIPUR

Capital: Imphal
Location: North-east
Area: 22,327 sq. km
Population: 2,721,756
History: Formed in 1972
Language: Manipuri
Literacy Rate: 76.94%
Governor: Anusuiya Uikey
Chief Minister: N. Biren Singh
Major Rivers: Barak, Imphal
Industries: Handloom, bamboo
Agriculture: Rice, wheat, maize, pulses, apricot, oranges
State Animal: Sangai
State Bird: Nongyeen

MEGHALAYA

Capital: Shillong
Location: North-east
Area: 22,429 sq. km
Population: 2,964,007
History: Formed in 1972
Languages: Garo, Khasi, Bengali, Assamese
Literacy Rate: 74.43%
Governor: Phagu Chauhan
Chief Minister: Conrad Kongkal Sangma
Major Rivers: Simsang, Umiam, Umtrew
Industries: Plywood, horticulture, agro-industries, cement, tourism handicrafts, sericulture
Agriculture: Rice, maize, oilseeds, tea, coffee, mushrooms, potato, fruits, including pineapple, betel nut
State Animal: Clouded leopard
State Bird: Hill mynah

Background: Manipur

MIZORAM

Capital: Aizawl
Location: North-east
Area: 21,087 sq. km
Population: 1,091,014
History: Formed in 1987
Language: Mizo
Literacy Rate: 91.33%
Governor: Dr Kambhampati Haribabu
Chief Minister: Pu Zoramthanga
Major Rivers: Tlawng, Tiau, Chhimtuipui, Tuirial, Tut, Tuivai
Industries: Handloom, bamboo, food processing, tea, sericulture
Agriculture: Maize, rice, sugar cane, tapioca, ginger, cotton
State Animal: Serow
State Bird: Hume's bar-tailed pheasant

NAGALAND

Capital: Kohima
Location: North-east
Area: 16,579 sq. km
Population: 1,980,602
History: Formed in 1963
Languages: Angami, Ao, Chang, Konyak, Lotha, Sangtam, Sema and Chakhesang
Literacy Rate: 79.55%
Governor: La Ganesan
Chief Minister: Neiphiu Rio
Major Rivers: Dhansiri, Doyang
Industries: Handloom, handicrafts, bamboo, food processing, forestry products
Agriculture: Rice, maize, millets, tea, bananas, pineapples, ginger
State Animal: Mithun
State Bird: Blyth's tragopan

ODISHA

Capital: Bhubaneswar
Location: East
Area: 155,707 sq. km
Population: 41,947,358
History: Formed in 1936
Language: Odia
Literacy Rate: 72.87%
Governor: Prof. Ganeshi Lal
Chief Minister: Naveen Patnaik
Major Rivers: Mahanadi, Brahmani, Baitarani, Subarnarekha, Salandi
Industries: Steel, aluminium, thermal power, cement, IT, petrochemicals, food processing
Agriculture: Rice, wheat, millets, oilseeds, coconut, cotton
State Animal: Sambar deer
State Bird: Indian roller

PUNJAB

Capital: Chandigarh
Location: North
Area: 50,362 sq. km
Population: 27,704,236
History: Formed in 1966
Language: Punjabi
Literacy Rate: 75.84%
Governor: Banwarilal Purohit
Chief Minister: Bhagwant Singh Mann
Major Rivers: Beas, Jhelum, Ravi, Sutlej, Chenab
Industries: Sugar, dairy, machine tools, textiles, sports goods
Agriculture: Wheat, rice, oilseeds, maize, sugar cane, cotton, pulses
State Animal: Blackbuck
State Bird: Northern goshawk

Background: Odisha

RAJASTHAN

Capital: Jaipur
Location: North-west
Area: 342,239 sq. km
Population: 68,621,012
History: Formed in 1949
Languages: Rajasthani dialects, such as Marwari, Mewari and others; Hindi
Literacy Rate: 66.11%
Governor: Kalraj Mishra
Chief Minister: Ashok Gehlot
Major Rivers: Banas, Luni, Sabarmati, Chambal, Mahi, Gambhir
Industries: Zinc and copper, cement, sugar, glass, semi-precious stones
Agriculture: Millets, pulses, maize, oilseeds, barley, cotton, chillies, rice
State Animal: Camel; Chinkara
State Bird: Great Indian bustard

TAMIL NADU

Capital: Chennai
Location: South
Area: 130,058 sq. km
Population: 72,138,958
History: Formed in 1956
Language: Tamil
Literacy Rate: 80.09%
Governor: Ravindra Narayan Ravi
Chief Minister: M.K. Stalin
Industries: Textiles, commercial vehicles, sugar, paper, electronic hardware, cement
Agriculture: Rice, sugar cane, cotton, coconut, cashew, tea, rubber, coffee
State Animal: Nilgiri tahr
State Bird: Emerald dove

SIKKIM

Capital: Gangtok
Location: North-east
Area: 7,096 sq. km
Population: 607,688
History: Formed in 1975
Languages: Nepali, Bhutia, Lepcha
Literacy Rate: 81.42%
Governor: Lakshman Prasad Acharya
Chief Minister: P.S. Golay
Major Rivers: Teesta, Rangeet, Takcham Chu, Ramphu Chu
Industries: Bamboo, handicrafts, handloom, carpet-weaving, floriculture, jewellery, tea, electronics
Agriculture: Oranges, cardamom, ginger, turmeric, cherry, pepper, baby corn
State Animal: Red panda
State Bird: Blood pheasant

TELANGANA

Capital: Hyderabad
Location: South-east
Area: 112,077 sq. km
Population: 35,003,674
History: Formed in 2014
Languages: Telugu, Urdu
Literacy Rate: 66.54%
Governor: Dr Tamilisai Soundararajan
Chief Minister: K. Chandrashekar Rao
Major Rivers: Godavari, Krishna, Musi
Industries: Sugar, textiles, IT, pharmaceuticals, cement
Agriculture: Rice, maize, millets, tobacco, sugar cane
State Animal: Jinka (spotted deer)
State Bird: Palapitta

Background: Rajasthan

TRIPURA

Capital: Agartala
Location: North-east
Area: 10,491 sq. km
Population: 3,671,032
History: Formed in 1972
Languages: Kokborok, Bengali
Literacy Rate: 87.22%
Governor: Satyadev Narayan Arya
Chief Minister: Dr Manik Saha
Major Rivers: Gomti, Khowai, Longai
Industries: Natural gas, food processing, rubber, tea, bamboo, handloom, handicrafts, sericulture
Agriculture: Fruits, cashew nut, jackfruit, coconut, tea, rice, rubber
State Animal: Phayre's leaf monkey
State Bird: Green imperial pigeon

UTTAR PRADESH

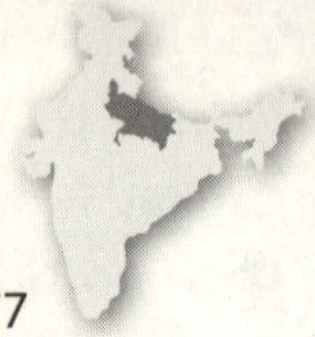

Capital: Lucknow
Location: North
Area: 240,928 sq. km
Population: 199,581,477
History: Formed in 1950
Language: Hindi
Literacy Rate: 67.68%
Governor: Anandiben Mafatbhai Patel
Chief Minister: Yogi Adityanath
Major Rivers: Ganga, Gomti, Yamuna, Ghaghara, Ken, Betwa, Chambal, Son
Industries: Sugar, textiles, mining, automobiles, IT, cement, handloom, fruits, forestry, food processing
Agriculture: Rice, wheat, pulses, sugar cane, barley, millets, potatoes, cotton, tobacco
State Animal: Barasingha
State Bird: Sarus crane

UTTARAKHAND

Capital: Dehradun (winter); Bhararisain/ Gairsain (summer)
Location: North
Area: 53,483 sq. km
Population: 10,116,752
History: Formed in 2000
Languages: Kumaoni, Garhwali, Hindi
Literacy Rate: 78.82%
Governor: Lieutenant General (Retd) Gurmit Singh
Chief Minister: Pushkar Singh Dhami
Major Rivers: Ganga, Yamuna, Alaknanda, Ramganga, Kali
Industries: Mining, forestry, hydel power projects, food processing, textiles, auto components
Agriculture: Rice, wheat, barley, millets, oilseeds, sugar cane, pulses
State Animal: Himalayan musk deer
State Bird: Himalayan monal

WEST BENGAL

Capital: Kolkata
Location: East
Area: 88,752 sq. km
Population: 91,347,736
History: Formed in 1947; reorganized in 1950 and 1956
Language: Bengali
Literacy Rate: 76.26%
Governor: Dr C.V. Ananda Bose
Chief Minister: Mamata Banerjee
Major Rivers: Hooghly, Teesta, Damodar, Rupnarayan
Industries: Steel, power, jute, tea, engineering, textiles, leather, aquaculture, coal mining
Agriculture: Rice, jute, maize, oilseeds, sugar cane, tea
State Animal: Fishing cat
State Bird: White-throated kingfisher

Background: West Bengal

UNION TERRITORIES

ANDAMAN AND NICOBAR ISLANDS

Capital: Port Blair
Location: Bay of Bengal
Area: 8,249 sq. km
Population: 379,944
History: Formed in 1947
Languages: Hindi, Bengali, Tamil, Telugu, Malayalam
Literacy Rate: 86.63%
Lt Governor: Admiral (Retd) Devendra Kumar Joshi
Industries: Handicrafts, fisheries, plastics, fibreglass, mild steel, tourism
Agriculture: Paddy, coconut, areca nuts, bananas, mangoes, pepper, clove, nutmeg, cinnamon
Official Animal: Dugong
Official Bird: Andaman wood pigeon

CHANDIGARH

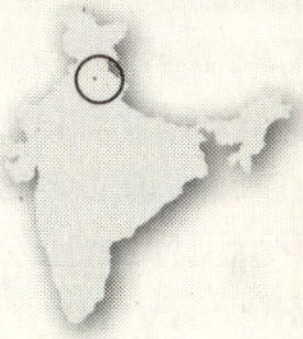

Location: Between Punjab and Haryana
Area: 114 sq. km
Population: 1,055,450
History: Formed in 1966
Languages: Hindi, Punjabi
Literacy Rate: 86.05%
Administrator: Banwarilal Purohit
Industries: Light engineering, electrical/electronic items, machine tools, pharmaceuticals, plastics
Agriculture: Wheat, maize, rice
Official Animal: Indian grey mongoose
Official Bird: Indian grey hornbill

DADRA AND NAGAR HAVELI AND DAMAN AND DIU

Capital: Daman
Location: Between Maharashtra and Gujarat
Area: 603 sq. km
Population: 586,764
History: Formed in 2020 by combining two Union Territories
Languages: Marathi, Gujarati, Bhili, Hindi
Literacy Rate: 81.67%*
Administrator: Praful Khoda Patel
Major Rivers: Daman Ganga, Bhagwan, Kalem
Industries: Tiles, chemicals, rubber, forestry products, animal husbandry, textiles and yarns, plastic, metal-based units, tourism
Agriculture: Rice, mango, sapota (chikoo), coconut

* Taken as an average of the two former UTs

JAMMU AND KASHMIR

Capital: Srinagar
Location: North
Area: 42,241 sq. km
Population: 5,350,811
History: Formed in 2019*
Languages: Kashmiri, Dogri, Urdu, Hindi
Literacy Rate: 67.16%**
Lt Governor: Manoj Sinha
Major Rivers: Jhelum, Chenab
Industries: Machinery, sericulture, handicrafts, horticulture
Agriculture: Paddy, wheat, fruit, saffron, cumin, fruits
Official Animal: Hangul (earlier)
Official Bird: Black-necked crane (earlier)

* Official date of creation announced as 31 October 2019;
**Before the division

Background: Andaman and Nicobar Islands

UNION TERRITORIES

LADAKH

Capital: Leh
Location: North
Area: 59,146 sq. km
Population: 290,492
History: Formed in 2019*
Languages: Ladakhi (Bhoti), Purki, Shina, Tibetan, Balti, Urdu, Hindi
Literacy Rate: 77.20%
Lt Governor: Brig. (Dr.) B. D. Mishra (Retd.)
Major Rivers: Indus, Zanskar, Shyok, Suru
Industries: Tourism, mountaineering
Agriculture: Barley, wheat, rice
Official Animal: Snow leopard
Official Bird: Black-necked crane

* Official date of creation announced as 31 October 2019

LAKSHADWEEP

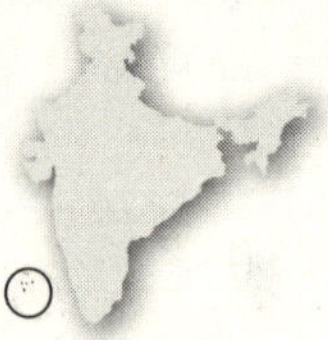

Capital: Kavaratti
Location: Arabian Sea
Area: 32 sq. km
Population: 64,429
History: Formed in 1956
Languages: Jeseri (Dweep Bhasha), Malayalam, Tamil, Urdu, Hindi
Literacy Rate: 91.85%
Administrator: Praful Khoda Patel
Industries: Coconut fibre, coir fibre, matting, fisheries
Agriculture: Coconut
Official Animal: Butterfly fish
Official Bird: Noddy tern

****WHAT ARE NCT AND NCR?**

The NCT, a Union Territory of India, is administered by the Union Government and the elected government of NCT. It includes the metropolitan area of Delhi as well as nine districts, 59 census towns and 300 villages. NCR stands for National Capital Region and includes regions around Delhi, such as cities like Gurugram and Faridabad (Haryana), and Noida and Ghaziabad (Uttar Pradesh), which are parts of other states. The NCR has been expanded to embrace Sonepat, Bahadurgarh and Meerut. However, the NCR is not a legal or electoral entity.

PUDUCHERRY

Capital: Puducherry
Location: South
Area: 483 sq. km
Population: 1,244,464
History: Formed in1954
Languages: Tamil, Telugu, Malayalam, French
Literacy Rate: 85.85%
Lt Governor: Dr Tamilisai Soundararajan
Chief Minister: N. Rangaswamy
Major Rivers: Ponnaiyar, Koringa
Industries: Textiles, computer products, electronics, leather
Agriculture: Rice, pulses, groundnuts, coconuts, spices, chillies
Official Animal: Indian palm squirrel
Official Bird: Asian koel

NATIONAL CAPITAL TERRITORY OF DELHI**

Location: North
Area: 1,484 sq. km
Population: 16,753,235
History: The Union Territory of Delhi was officially renamed the National Capital Territory of Delhi in 1991 under the NCT Act of the same year
Languages: Hindi, Punjabi, Urdu
Literacy Rate: 86.21%
Lt Governor: Vinai Kumar Saxena
Chief Minister: Arvind Kejriwal
Major River: Yamuna
Industries: Light machines, textiles, automobile parts, bicycles, leather, sports and consumer goods, IT
Agriculture: Wheat, maize, millets vegetables, pulses
Official Animal: Nilgai
Official Bird: House sparrow

SUPERLATIVES

Fastest Animal Blackbuck (Indian antelope) (speed: 80 km/h)

Largest Animal (land) Asian elephant (shoulder height: 2.4–2.75 m/ 7.8–9 ft; weight: 3,000–5,400 kg)

Largest Bird Great Indian bustard (length: 1.2 m/4 ft; weight: 15 kg)

Smallest Bird Pale-billed flowerpecker (length: 8 cm/3.1 in.; weight: 4–8 g)

Longest Bridge (railroad) Bogibeel Bridge, Assam (length: 4.94 km)

Tallest Building The 42, Kolkata, West Bengal (height: 268 m/879 ft)

Longest Canal Indira Gandhi Canal (length: 649 km)

Highest City Leh, Ladakh (altitude: 3,500 m/11,483 ft)

Largest City Delhi (area: 1,484 sq. km)

Most Populated City Mumbai, Maharashtra: 18,394,912 (as per Govt. of India data for Census 2011)

Longest Corridor Ramanathaswamy Temple, Rameswaram, Tamil Nadu (corridor length: 1,220 m/4,002 ft)

Largest Dam Bhakra Nangal Dam, Himachal Pradesh and Punjab (height: 226m/ 741 ft; length: 520 m/ 1,706 ft – on the River Sutlej)

Longest Dam Hirakud Dam, Odisha (length: 25.79 km – on the River Mahanadi)

Highest Dam Tehri Dam, Uttarakhand (height: 260.5 m/854.6 ft – on the Rivers Bhagirathi and Bhilangana)

Largest Delta Ganga–Brahmaputra, Bay of Bengal (Total area: 105,641 sq. km; 35,213.6 sq. km in India and 70,427.3 sq. km in Bangladesh)

Largest Desert Thar Desert (area: approx. 200,000 sq. km)

Biggest Dome (new architecture) World Peace Monument Dome, Pune, Maharashtra (diameter: 48.77 m/160 ft)

Biggest Dome (old architecture) Gol Gumbaz, Vijayapura, Karnataka (diameter: 43.89 m/144 ft)

Largest Island Great Nicobar Island, Bay of Bengal (area: 921 sq. km)

INDIA

Deepest Lake
Manasbal Lake, Jammu and Kashmir (average depth: 4.5 m/15 ft)

Highest Lake
Gurudongmar Lake, Sikkim (altitude: 5,425 m/17,800 ft)

Largest Lake (artificial)
Govind Ballabh Pant Sagar, Uttar Pradesh (active capacity: 8.9 billion cubic m)

Largest Lake (freshwater)
Kolleru Lake, Andhra Pradesh (area: 245 sq. km)

Tallest Minaret (freestanding)
Qutub Minar, Delhi (height: 72.5 m/238 ft)

Largest Lake (saltwater)
Chilika Lake, Odisha (maximum surface area – monsoon: 1,165 sq. km)

Largest National Park
Hemis National Park, Leh, Ladakh (area: 3,350 sq. km)

Coldest Place (region)
Siachen, Ladakh (average temp: – 50°C)

Hottest Place
Churu, Rajasthan (maximum recorded temperature: 50.3°C

Largest Port
Deendayal Port, by cargo handling capacity: 267.10 MTPA* (2020–21)

Longest Platform (railway)
Gorakhpur railway station, Uttar Pradesh (length: 1,366.33 m/4,482.7 ft)

Longest Railway Route
Vivek Express: Dibrugarh to Kanyakumari (length: 4,286 km)

Longest River
Ganga (length: 2,525 km)

Longest National Highway
NH-44 (length: 3,745 km)

Rainiest Spot
Mawsynram, Meghalaya (average annual rainfall: 11,873 mm/467 in.)

Largest Stadium
Narendra Modi Stadium, Ahmedabad, Gujarat (spread across 63 acres/25.5 hectares; seating capacity: 132,000)

Tallest Statue
Statue of Unity, Gujarat, (height: 182 m/597 ft)

Longest Tunnel (railway)
Pir Panjal Railway Tunnel, Jammu and Kashmir (length: 11.21 km)

Longest Tunnel (road)
Dr Syama Prasad Mookerjee Tunnel, Jammu and Kashmir (length: 9.2 km)

Longest Wall
Kumbhalgarh Fort, Rajasthan (length: 1,100 m/3,600 ft)

Highest Waterfall
Kunchikal Falls, Karnataka (height: 455 m/1,493 ft)

* Metric tonnes per annum

9 SCIENCE AND TECHNOLOGY

Science and technology, like space, have no frontiers! And this is clear from the kind of technologies coming up! Here are a few:

Drug cures a type of cancer: An experimental trial was conducted to test the effects of the drug Dostarlimab. The test was administered to 18 patients diagnosed with rectal cancer at the Memorial Sloan Kettering Cancer Center in New York, US. The trial lasted for six months. The results showed that Dostarlimab eliminated the tumours of all participants present in the study. It was the first time in the history of a cancer treatment alternative that a cancer drug has shown such extensive success. Taking this into consideration, Dostarlimab is now being tested for other forms of cancer treatment as well.

Special gel heals heart damage: Researchers at the University of Manchester, UK, have developed a special biodegradable gel that can repair damage incurred due to a heart attack. This gel is made up of chains of amino acids known as peptides and can be injected into the beating heart, to provide a safe support for damaged cells to grow new tissue. In the past, under other experiments, when cells have been injected straight into the heart, only 1 per cent have stayed in place and survived.

Scientists believe that this cell regenerative therapy can be a useful technique, which will allow heart patients to repair the fatal damage caused during a heart attack.

A step towards sustainability: In an effort to save valuable resources and practise sustainable development, a research team from Guwahati in Assam, India, has developed a bioelectrochemical device with the ability to generate green energy by treating wastewater. The device uses Microbial Fuel Cell (MFC), which allows it to have a dual function through which it generates bioelectricity and manages wastewater simultaneously.

The device uses microorganisms that release enzymes, converting organic substrates of wastewater into chemical energy. This chemical energy is later converted to electrical energy and put to greater use.

BRANCHES OF SCIENCE

Science is divided into four main branches: Natural Sciences, Social Sciences, Applied Sciences and Formal Sciences.

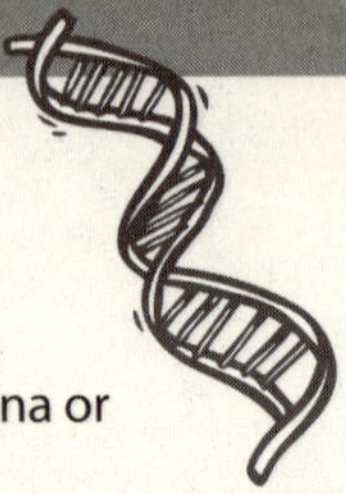

NATURAL SCIENCES involve the study of natural phenomena or the laws of the physical world.

- **BIOLOGY** is the study of living things, including their structure, origin, growth, evolution, function and distribution. **Botany** deals with plants, **zoology** with animals and **microbiology** with microscopic organisms.
- **CHEMISTRY** deals with the composition of substances as well as their properties and reactions. **Organic chemistry** is the study of carbon and its compounds. **Inorganic chemistry** is the study of the structure, properties and reactions of chemical elements and their compounds. **Biochemistry** studies chemical processes that occur inside living organisms.
- **EARTH SCIENCES** study the Earth, its composition and structure. **Geology** is about the Earth's inner rock formation. **Geography** is the study of the Earth's terrain. **Oceanography** focuses on ocean currents and habitats. **Meteorology** studies the weather, and **astronomy** is the study of objects and matter outside Earth's atmosphere.
- **ENVIRONMENTAL SCIENCES** are concerned with the relationship between organisms and their environment.
- **PHYSICS** is associated with the study of properties and interactions of time, space, energy and matter.

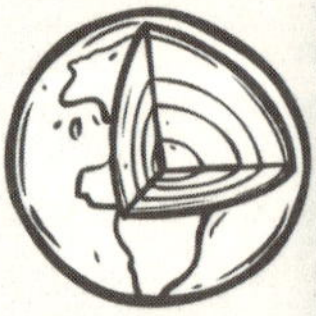

SOCIAL SCIENCES study human behaviour.

- **ANTHROPOLOGY** studies human physical traits, cultures and languages.
- **ECONOMICS** is the study of how money, goods and businesses affect people.
- **LAW** focuses on the rules of society, communities and nations.
- **POLITICAL SCIENCE** studies governmental processes and institutions.
- **PSYCHOLOGY** focuses on how the human mind functions.
- **SOCIOLOGY** analyses how humans behave in groups.

APPLIED SCIENCES involve the practical use of scientific knowledge.

- **BIOTECHNOLOGY** applies biological processes to make medicines and vaccines, and to enhance the quality of food and crops.
- **COMPUTER SCIENCE** focuses on computers and their functions.
- **ENGINEERING** is about the construction of machines and systems.

FORMAL SCIENCES form the category under which mathematics, statistics, logic and theoretical computer science fall. These disciplines, also called the 'formal' systems, have formal languages, based on logical reasoning, that contain strings of symbols and follow fixed sets of rules.

SCIENCE AND TECHNOLOGY

PHYSICS

Physics is the science that studies force, motion, heat, light, sound, electricity, magnetism, and changes that happen to these phenomena, not pertaining to chemical or biological changes.

MECHANICS AND MOTION

Mechanics is the field of physics dealing with the action of forces on solids, liquids and gases at rest or in motion. When forces act upon an object to make it change position with respect to time, it is known as motion. One of the ways to measure motion is to find out how much distance an object moves in one unit of time. This is known as speed, while velocity is speed in a definite direction. Velocities could increase or decrease in a given time period. The acceleration of an object is defined as its rate of change of velocity in one unit of time (usually measured in seconds).

NEWTON'S LAWS OF MOTION

In the 1680s, **Sir Isaac Newton**, an English physicist, worked on the idea of motion and formulated the three fundamental laws of motion.

THE FIRST LAW: This states that an object continues in its state of rest or of uniform motion unless an external force is applied to it.

THE SECOND LAW: The second law states that the acceleration of an object is dependent upon two variables – the force acting upon the object and the mass of the object.

THE THIRD LAW: The third law of motion states that for every action, there is an equal and opposite reaction. So if object A exerts a force on object B, then object B also exerts the same amount of force on object A.

HEAT

Heat is a form of energy caused by the motion of atoms and molecules in a body. When you increase the heat of a body, you are, in effect, increasing the amount of energy in its molecular system. When heat moves from one area to another, it is because millions of atoms and molecules are working together. The effect of heat on any atom leads to an increase in temperature and an expansion of volume (for example, railway tracks have expansion joints that let them expand and contract with temperature changes), or a possible change of physical state, like a solid turning to liquid, and a liquid turning to gas (as seen in the three states of ice, water and steam/vapour). This is known as a physical change.

LIGHT

Light is a form of energy that acts on the eye, illuminating objects. Light consists of electromagnetic (EM) waves that travel in straight lines. If you pass a ray of light through a glass prism, the colours split up into the 'spectrum' – the rainbow of colours in visible light when separated. What we call 'light' indicates only the light waves visible to us as human beings. There are different colours of light because of light waves that have different wavelengths: red light has the longest wavelength while violet light has the shortest. As far as we know, all types of light move at the same speed in a vacuum. The speed of light in a vacuum is 299,792.458 km/s. Funnily enough, light is used to measure really long distances, using a unit called a 'light year'. A light year is a unit of length equal to the distance light travels in a vacuum in one year. This distance is calculated to be 9,460,700,000,000 km (9.4607×10^{12} km).

> "At least 18 per cent of humans respond to bright lights by sneezing. This is called the photic sneeze reflex. It was first medically described in 1978. Initially, it was thought to be a reaction to heat. The disorder is actually caused by confused signalling from the trigeminal nerve, which is responsible for sensation in the face."

ELECTRICITY

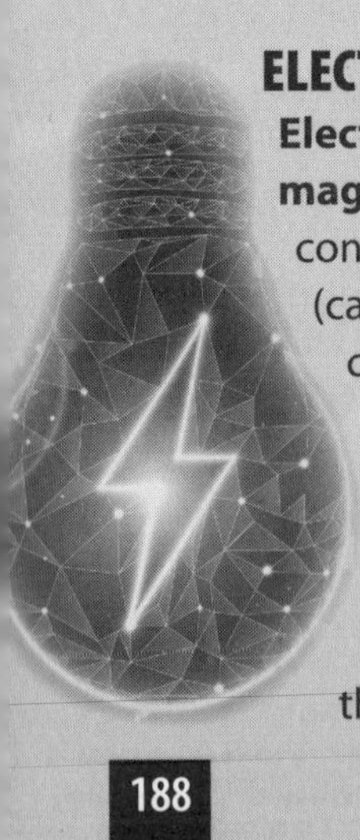

Electricity is a form of energy that produces heat, light, magnetic force and chemical changes. Objects around us contain billions of atoms, and each atom contains protons (carrying a positive charge) and electrons (carrying a negative charge). The protons are located in the centre of the atom, trapped in the nucleus. The electrons are in motion outside of the nucleus, and move to a positively-charged area. Currents are created when electrons move. We use chemicals to create an environment in which the electrons get charged enough to move, creating an electric current; this is how batteries can power electrical appliances.

MAGNETISM

Magnetism is the force by which a material attracts or repels other materials.
The space around a magnet, in which its power of attraction can have an effect on other objects, is known as its magnetic field. Magnetic poles are where the magnetic field lines begin, end and converge, at each end of the magnet. These poles have negative or positive charges. Positive poles attract the negative end of other particles and negative poles attract the positive end. Any object, small or large, may have magnetic fields. Earth, for example, has a huge magnetic field. Due to the high levels of iron in Earth's core, the magnetic field of our planet is very powerful. The North and South Poles are the magnetic poles of the Earth.

SOUND

Sound is a travelling wave that is an oscillation of pressure transmitted through a solid, liquid or gas, made up of frequencies within the range that can be heard. All matter is made up of molecules. Molecules can be tightly packed together as in a solid, or loosely packed as in a liquid or gas. When energy strikes molecules, it causes them to vibrate back and forth, producing a wave that transmits sound energy. It moves molecules in order to travel; that's why it's impossible for sound to move through outer space, where there are very few molecules. But sound does not have to move only through air – it can just as easily move through water or through metal.

SOUND AND LIGHT

Sound moves much more slowly than light. While light travels at 299,792.458 km/s, sound only goes at 1,220 km/h. That's why the Concorde airliner, with an average cruise speed of 2,140 km/h, was called 'supersonic' or 'faster than sound'. The difference in the speed at which light and sound travel is the reason why you often hear things long after you see them. For instance, you hear thunder several seconds after you see lightning in a storm, even though they may occur simultaneously.

TERMS THAT MATTER IN PHYSICS

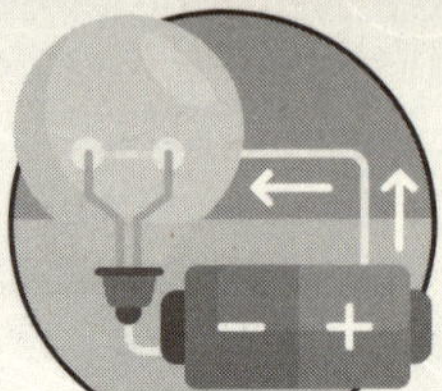

DENSITY: The density of a material is defined as its mass per unit volume. The symbol of density is ρ (the Greek letter *rho*).

ENERGY: In physics, energy is a physical quantity that describes the amount of work that can be performed by a force. Different forms of energy explain natural phenomena. These forms include (but are not limited to) kinetic, potential, thermal, gravitational, sound, light, elastic and electromagnetic energy.

ELASTICITY: It is the property of a substance that enables it to recover its original shape and size after an external force is applied to it.

FORCE: In physics, a force is that which can cause an object with mass to change its velocity. It has both magnitude and direction. A force acting on a three-dimensional object may also cause it to rotate or deform.

FRICTION: Friction is the force resisting the relative motion of solid surfaces, fluid layers or material elements in contact.

INERTIA: The property of a body to resist a change in its state of rest or of uniform motion is called inertia.

MASS: This is the quantity of matter that a body contains. A body of lower mass is accelerated less by the same force than a body of higher mass, if there is appreciable air resistance. Commonly, mass is used synonymously with weight. But, in physics and engineering, weight is the strength of the gravitational pull on the object. M (mass) = v (volume) x d (density).

MATTER: Matter is anything that has both mass and volume; it takes up space. Matter exists in five main states (or phases): solid, liquid, gas, plasma and the Bose–Einstein condensates.

MOMENTUM: The product of the mass and the velocity of a body, momentum is a measure of the quantity of motion in a body.

POWER: It is the measure of the rate of doing work.

VELOCITY: In physics, velocity is defined as the rate of change of position (or movement); both speed and direction are required to define it.

VOLUME: The quantity of three-dimensional space occupied by a liquid, solid or gas.

WAVE: A wave is a physical disturbance that transfers energy through time and space.

WEIGHT: Weight is a measure of the gravitational force acting on an object. Near the Earth's surface, the acceleration due to gravity is nearly constant, making an object's weight roughly proportional to its mass.
W (weight) = m (mass) x g (acceleration due to gravity).

BIOLOGY

Biology is the study of living things. Every form of life belongs to one of the five biological kingdoms:

A living thing is called an organism. All living organisms are made up of microscopic units called cells, which hold and carry all the biological equipment needed to keep an organism alive.

MONERA: This kingdom consists of very small, single-celled bacteria that don't have a nucleus. Some of these are able to move; others are not. Some of them can make their own food to live on, while others need to feed on things outside themselves.

FUNGI: These creatures have more than one cell, and their cells have nuclei. Fungi generally can't move. They must depend on a source outside themselves for food. This kingdom includes mushrooms, moulds and yeast.

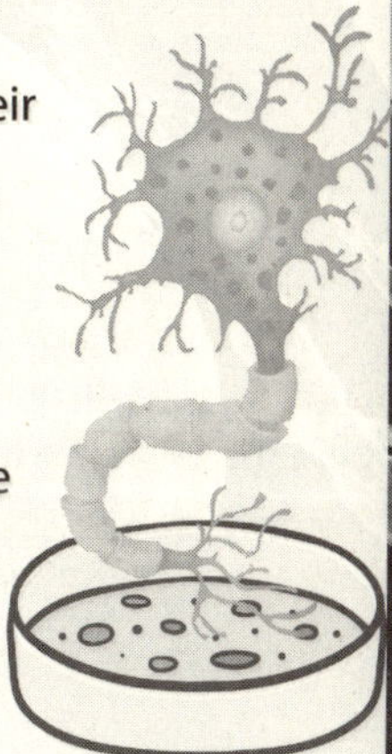

PROTISTA: The one-celled creatures of this kingdom share the same characteristics as those that belong to the Monera kingdom, except for the fact that they have a nucleus. Examples of protista are amoebas, paramecia and some one-celled algae.

PLANTAE: The plant kingdom consists of multicellular organisms that have nuclei, and remain in one place. They use sunlight and a substance called chlorophyll to produce their own food in a process called photosynthesis. Some plants produce flowers and fruit, while others don't. Examples of the plant kingdom are multicelled algae, ferns, mosses, shrubs, wildflowers, trees, fruits and vegetables.

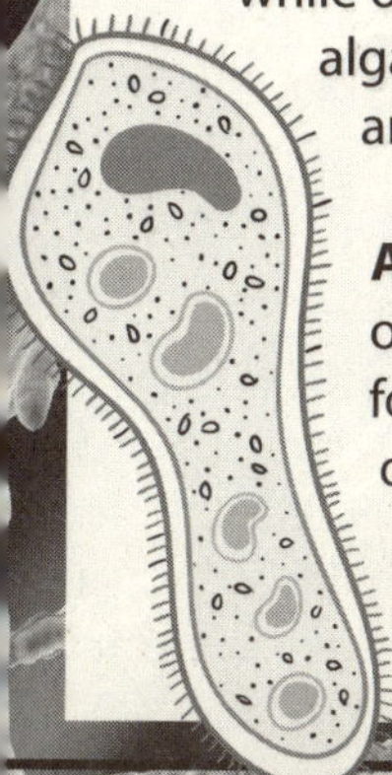

ANIMALIA: The animal kingdom comprises multicellular organisms that move and depend on outside sources for food. food. In general, they are the most complex creatures on Earth, and many members form social groups and communicate. Examples of animals include sponges, jellyfish, insects, amphibians, fish, mammals (including humans) and so on.

THE CLASSIFICATION OF LIVING THINGS

Scientists have divided and named every known living organism by a set of rules, called biological taxonomy. These names are called scientific names. For instance, scientists may say '*Canis familiaris*' for what you would call a 'dog'. The popular standard classification of living things is of seven groups. Each group has the characteristics of the level above it, but also has some of its own distinguishing features.

Kingdom: There are five main kingdoms: Animalia, which is made up of animals; Plantae, which is made up of plants; Protista, which is made up of protists (single-celled creatures invisible to the human eye); Fungi, which is made up of mushrooms, moulds, yeast and so on; and Monera, which is made up of bacteria.

Phylum: In the plant kingdom, phyla are often called 'divisions'. In the animal kingdom, the phylum Chordata, for example, refers to any animal with a backbone (fish, birds, mammals, reptiles, amphibians). Other phyla include Arthropoda (insects, spiders, crustaceans), Mollusca (snails, squid, clam), Annelida (segmented worms), Echinodermata (starfish, sea urchins) and many more.

Class: Phyla are further broken down into classes. The phylum Chordata includes classes like Aves (birds), Reptilia (reptiles), Amphibia (amphibians), Mammalia (mammals) and several others.

Order: Each class is made up of one or more orders. Mammalia is divided into Rodentia (mice, rats), Primates (Old- and New-World monkeys), Chiroptera (bats), Insectivora (shrews, moles), Carnivora (dogs, wolves, cats and weasels), Perissodactyla (horses, zebras), Artiodactyla (cows), Proboscidea (elephants) and many more.

Family: Orders are divided into families. The order Carnivora, for example, is broken down into *Canidae* (dogs), *Felidae* (cats), *Ursidae* (bears), *Hyaenidae* (hyenas, aardwolves), *Mustelidae* (weasels) and more.

Genus: The next division is the genus. The family *Felidae* (cats), for example, is divided into *Acinonyx* (cheetah), *Panthera* (lion, tiger), *Neofelis* (clouded leopard), *Felis* (domestic cats) and more.

Species: The next division is the species. The genus *Panthera* can be broken down to include *Panthera leo* (lion) and *Panthera tigris* (tiger). Subspecies, which differ slightly from each other, have evolved mostly due to geographical distribution or isolation: for example, *Panthera tigris sumatrae* is the Sumatran tiger. Usually, a species is called by its genus name (capitalized) followed by its species name (in small letters). A human being, for instance, is called *Homo sapiens* ('wise man' in Latin!).

Here's how these groupings apply to the animal called **'man'**:

Kingdom: Animalia
Phylum: Chordata
Class: Mammalia
Order: Primates
Family: *Hominidae*
Genus: *Homo*
Species: *sapiens*
Subspecies: *sapiens*

CHEMISTRY

Chemistry is the science concerned with the composition, behaviour, structure and properties of matter, as well as the changes it undergoes during chemical reactions.

WHAT IS MATTER?

Everything around you is matter, made of very tiny atoms and molecules. Anything that has mass, or takes up space, is known as matter. To date only five forms of matter have been found, though the possibility of there being more exists. The ones currently known are: solid, liquid, gas, plasma and Bose–Einstein condensates.

Changing States of Matter

Matter is constantly changing its form, depending on external forces acting upon it. Water is a common and good example of this. Whatever form it may be in, the compound is always two atoms of hydrogen and one of oxygen. The molecular structure of water will never change, whatever its state: gas, liquid or solid; or in other words: vapour, water or ice. Thus the physical state of a compound may change, but the chemical state always remains the same.

However, if you were to add an oxygen atom to water, that would constitute a chemical change, making hydrogen peroxide. Physical changes of a compound are about changing density, pressure, temperature and other physical properties, but the basic chemical structure does not change.

Solids, liquids, gases, plasmas and Bose–Einstein condensates are the different states of matter; all elements and compounds can move from one state to another state when special physical forces, such as increasing and decreasing temperatures, are introduced. Thus, when water reaches freezing point, it turns to ice, and when it reaches boiling point, it turns into steam. There are some other physical changes that may help cause a change in state, such as the application of pressure.

> **Tungsten has the second highest melting point (3,422°C), after carbon (3,550°C), of all the known elements.**

Physical changes are about energy and states of matter. Chemical changes happen at a

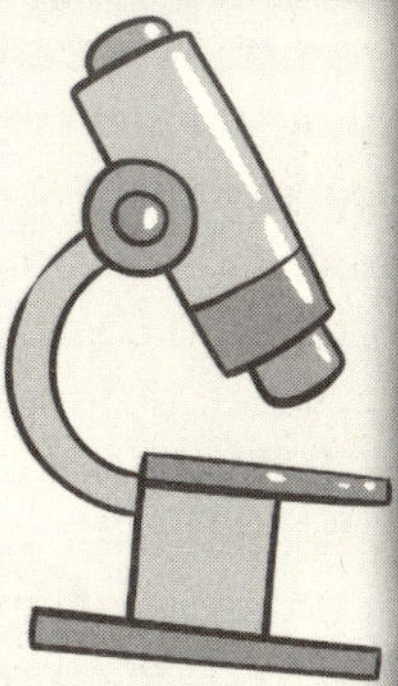

molecular level. When you step on a plastic bottle and crush it, you have forced a physical change. Chemical changes may happen on 'smaller' scales. While in some cases you can observe chemical changes such as a change in colour, most chemical changes occur at the molecular level, unseen to the naked eye. You can, for instance, see the chemical change in iron when it rusts over a long period of time; in fact, the change has occurred much earlier, but its visible manifestation happens later. Melting a sugar cube is a physical change, as you have not changed the chemical composition. However, when you burn it, the chemical bonds that held the sugar together are broken, making it a chemical change.

SOLIDS: Solids are hard as their molecules are tightly bound to each other. The tighter this bond, the harder the solid will be. This is not to say that the atoms and molecules of a solid are not always in motion. They may spin or rotate, but rarely change their positions.

LIQUIDS: Liquids are an in-between state of matter, found between solids and gases. When molecules of a gas, solid or liquid are dispersed and mixed with those of a liquid, the homogeneous mixture is called a liquid solution. A liquid has no shape of its own, and will fill up the shape of a container. Thus, if you pour water in a glass, a cup and a saucepan, the water will take the shape of each.

GAS: We are surrounded by gases. Our atmosphere is completely made up of gases. Gases are random groups of atoms. Their atoms and molecules are full of energy. Gases are used in various ways commercially, specifically because they fill a container of any size or shape. When you press down a bottle of deodorant, or open a bottle of cola, gases gush out. This is because gases are made up of free atoms and molecules, but in these cases they are packed under pressure in small spaces.

TERMS THAT MATTER IN CHEMISTRY

ACID: An acid is a chemical substance that donates protons or hydrogen ions and/or accepts electrons. Any chemical compound that, when dissolved in water, gives a solution with a hydrogen ion concentration greater than in pure water, that is, a **pH** value less than 7, is called an acid. The word 'acid' comes from the Latin words *acidus* or *acere*, which mean 'sour', since one of the characteristics of diluted acids is a sour taste – vinegar or lemon juice, for example.

ATOM: An atom is the basic unit of chemistry. It consists of a positively charged nucleus or core, containing protons and neutrons, and has a number of negatively charged electrons orbiting the nucleus.

BASE: Commonly speaking, bases are chemical compounds that, when dissolved in water, give a solution with a hydrogen ion concentration lower than that of pure water, that is, a pH value higher than 7. A soluble base is referred to as an alkali. Commonly, bases can be thought of as the chemical opposites of acids.

CATALYST: A substance that speeds up a chemical reaction without being used up in the reaction is called a catalyst.

COMPOUND: A compound is a substance that is formed by the union of two or more elements, in a definite ratio. Water, for example, is a compound with two atoms of hydrogen and one atom of oxygen.

ION: This is an atom or group of atoms that carries a positive or negative electric charge due to having lost or gained one or more electrons.

ISOTOPE: When an element has more than one possibility for the number of neutrons, it is called an isotope.

MOLECULE: A molecule is the smallest part of a compound, besides the atom. It has unique chemical properties, and undergoes certain well-defined reactions with other substances.

pH: This is a measure of the acidity or basicity of a solution, calculated on the basis of dissolved hydrogen ions, on a scale of 0 to 14, with 0 being the value of the strongest acids, and 14 being the value of the strongest bases. Distilled water is at 7, right in the middle, and, therefore, neutral.

SALTS: Salts are ionic compounds made of **cations** (positively charged ions) and **anions** (negative ions) so that the product is neutral. When acids and bases react with each other, they can form a salt and (usually) water. This is called a **neutralization** reaction.

SOLUTE: The substance (solid, liquid or gas) that dissolves in a solvent to produce a homogeneous mixture.

SOLVENT: The substance (solid, liquid or gas) in which a **solute** dissolves to produce a homogeneous mixture.

The Periodic Table of Elements

- Hydrogen
- Alkali metals
- Alkaline earth metals
- Transition metals
- Poor metals
- Non-metals
- Noble gases
- Rare earth elements

1 H																	2 He
3 Li	4 Be											5 B	6 C	7 N	8 O	9 F	10 Ne
11 Na	12 Mg											13 Al	14 Si	15 P	16 S	17 Cl	18 Ar
19 K	20 Ca	21 Sc	22 Ti	23 V	24 Cr	25 Mn	26 Fe	27 Co	28 Ni	29 Cu	30 Zn	31 Ga	32 Ge	33 As	34 Se	35 Br	36 Kr
37 Rb	38 Sr	39 Y	40 Zr	41 Nb	42 Mo	43 Tc	44 Ru	45 Rh	46 Pd	47 Ag	48 Cd	49 In	50 Sn	51 Sb	52 Te	53 I	54 Xe
55 Cs	56 Ba	La–Lu*	72 Hf	73 Ta	74 W	75 Re	76 Os	77 Ir	78 Pt	79 Au	80 Hg	81 Ti	82 Pb	83 Bi	84 Po	85 At	86 Rn
87 Fr	88 Ra	Ac–Lr**	104 Rf	105 Db	106 Sg	107 Bh	108 Hs	109 Mt	110 Ds	111 Rg	112 Cn	113 Uut	114 Fl	115 Uup	116 Lv	117 Uus	118 Uuo

*Lanthanides	57 La	58 Ce	59 Pr	60 Nd	61 Pm	62 Sm	63 Eu	64 Gd	65 Tb	66 Dy	67 Ho	68 Er	69 Tm	70 Yb	71 Lu
**Actinides	89 Ac	90 Th	91 Pa	92 U	93 Np	94 Pu	95 Am	96 Cm	97 Bk	98 Cf	99 Es	100 Fm	101 Md	102 No	103 Lr

A chemical **element** is a pure chemical substance consisting of one type of atom distinguished by its atomic number, which is the number of protons in its nucleus. Elements cannot be broken up into simpler substances, and in essence are the building blocks of everything around us. Common examples of elements are iron, copper, silver, gold, hydrogen, carbon, nitrogen and oxygen. In all, 118 elements have been observed as of 2012, of which 98 occur naturally on Earth.

The periodic table of chemical elements is a tabular method of displaying these elements. Although such tables existed earlier (including those by pioneering German chemist Lothar Meyer), the periodic table is usually credited to the Russian chemist Dmitri Mendeleev in 1869. He used the table to illustrate recurring ('periodic') trends in the properties of the elements.

The layout of the periodic table has been refined and expanded over the years as new elements have been discovered and added, and new theories presented to explain their chemical behaviour.

The only letter that doesn't appear in the periodic table is 'J'.

ARTIFICIAL INTELLIGENCE TIMELINE

1642–1644
◆ Blaise Pascal invents the first calculation machine.

1843
◆ Ada Lovelace publishes the first computer programme.

1943
◆ Warren McCulloch and Walter Pitts introduce the first neural network.

1950

◆ Alan Turing proposes the Turing Test to test a machine's ability to demonstrate human-like intelligence.

1956
◆ John McCarthy coins the term 'Artificial Intelligence'.

1958
◆ John McCarthy develops LISP, a ListProcessing computer language at MIT.

2002
◆ iRobot launches the most-awaited robot – a floor-cleaning, obstacle-avoiding, self-directing, battery-operated little helper called Roomba.

2005
◆ Stanford Racing Team's autonomous vehicle 'Stanley' wins the DARPA grand challenge by successfully driving across 211 km in under seven hours without human intervention.

2009
◆ Google introduces the first self-driving car for commercial services, thus launching Waymo.

2010
◆ The first virtual assistant, Siri, says hello as an app for iOS.

2011
◆ IBM's Watson Jeopardy's top two contenders in a $1M match.

2012
◆ Without ever being told what a cat is, Google's neural network cluster discovers what cats are within a week-long exposure to YouTube videos, exhibiting near-accurate self-taught recognition skills.

2013
◆ Boston Dynamics, maker of the four-legged robot BigDog, created Atlas, a bipedal humanoid robot.
◆ Google introduced a beta test version of Google Glass, a brand of smart glasses.

2014
◆ Eugene Goostman, a chatbot that simulates a 13-year-old Ukrainian boy, is deemed to have passed the Turing Test.
◆ Amazon releases a virtual assitant, Alexa, that is capable of shopping via voice interactions.

2015
◆ Elon Musk and Stephen Hawking were among the 3,000 people to sign an open letter requesting a ban on the development and adoption of autonomous weapons for war purposes.

2016
◆ Google DeepMind's AlphaGo beats legendary Go champion Lee Sedol by 4–1.
◆ Microsoft releases AI chatbot 'Tay'. It was designed to learn from and respond to Twitter conversations and had to be shut down within 16 hours because it began posting inflammatory and offensive tweets.

2017

◆ Nvidia debuts an AI that creates convincing fake photos of celebrities that do not exist.
◆ Google introduces AutoML, an AI designed to learn and create more AIs.
◆ Saudi Arabia grants citizenship to a social AI-based robot called Sophia.
◆ Mark Zuckerberg and Musk feud on Twitter about the pros and cons of a future ruled by AI.
◆ Robot Xiaoyi clears the Chinese National Medical Licensing Exam.
◆ iPhone X is launched with a neural engine.

2018

◆ DUPLEX by Google gets in trouble for being too convincing at its debut.
◆ Major companies like Amazon and Google suffer severe public and academic scrutiny for using AI in facial recognition and defence projects.
◆ OpenAI loses to professional DOTA 2 players.

SCIENCE AND TECHNOLOGY

1961
- First industrial programmable robot – an electronic arm that performs sequential actions – 'UNIMATE' lifts hot metal parts at the GM factory.

1964
- Joseph Weizenbaum creates ELIZA, a prototype chatbot that holds convincing therapy consultations with humans by focusing on keywords.

1966
- A robot that parses commands and decides subsequent actions, SHAKEY, is introduced by SRI.

1972
- Stanford University works on MYCIN, an early AI programme that provides a probable diagnosis with reasoning comparable to those of medical practitioners.

1974 TO EARLY 1980s
- AI winter as both interest and funding for R&D in AI wane because of excessive hype, slow results and low commercial viability.

1980
- Xcon (eXpert CONfigurer) is successful in automatically selecting computer system components based on customer requirements.

1982
- ACE, a system for Automatic Cable Expertise, is used to provide troubleshooting reports and management analyses using a conventional database management system.

1984
- A panel called 'The Dark Ages of AI — Can we avoid or survive them?' is held at the 1984 AAAI conference.

1987-1993
- Second AI winter as practical results fail to match public expectations.

1997
- DeepBlue, IBM's chess-playing supercomputer, is the first machine to defeat a Grand Master with a score of 3.5 to 2.5.

1998
- Cynthia Breazeal's KISmet, a robot that inetracts socially like a child with a caretaker, is able to identify and respond to emotions.

1999
- With over 3,000 sales in under 20 minutes, Sony launches its Artificial Intelligence roBOt dog (AiBO) that grows from a puppy to a dog and interacts with its human. You can still order one today!

2019
- OpenAI releases GPT-2, an AI that generates readable content based on a few lines fed into it intially.
- DeepMind trains AI to consider future consequences of decisions.

2020
- CovidScholar – a search engine that compiles and classifies all available studies on COVID-19 – launched.
- The first AI university, Mohamed bin Zayed University of Artificial Intelligence, is established in Abu Dhabi.

2021
- OpenAI launches DALL-E which generates images based on text.
- Facebook and NYU release an AI that predicts a COVID-19 patient's condition over the next four days.
- The European Commission poses restrictions over the use of AI.
- AI predicts the onset of Alzheimer's in patients with 97 per cent accuracy.
- AI helps identify hundreds of exoplanets.
- Google launches its pilot flood prediction system in India.

2022
- OpenAI introduces ChatGPT – an AI that answers queries and executes instructions given in prompts – for free use.
- Google DeepMind releases AlphaCode, a system that autonomously codes at competitive levels.
- DeepMind introduces GATO that performs various tasks, such as holding conversations, captioning images, playing video games and even moving robotic arms!

2023
- Amazon CodeWhisperer, a generative AI that suggests and completes codes in nearly 15 languages, is live and free for use.
- Google Bard available for both conversations and coding in over 40 natural languages.
- Gen AI and 'AI for all' are on the rise. AI will be integrated into most fields, ushering in the age of augmented working.

RIDING THE AI WAVE

The market for artificial intelligence (AI) today is valued at nearly $100 billion, and this number is expected to grow to $2 trillion by 2030, research predicts. According to a study by IIT Madras, 43 per cent of Indians believe that AI is the biggest emerging technology. But what is artificial intelligence and why has it become so important in our lives?

In 1950, Alan Turing – the 'father of computer science' – asked the question: 'Can machines think?' He proposed an experiment called the Turing Test, where a human interrogator tries to distinguish between textual responses that are produced by humans and by computers. Turing concluded that this question was too broad to merit consideration, but the quest for creating machines that can think like humans has followed us into the present. In AI today, research focuses on replicating many components of human intelligence, including perception, language use, learning, reasoning and problem-solving.

What types of AI exist?

Artificial intelligence can be classified under four types:

1 **Reactive machines** – These systems react to the data presented to them, but they cannot store memory. This prevents them from improving performance based on previous experiences. For example, IBM's Deep Blue AI, which defeated international champion Gary Kasparov in a chess game, was a reactive system.

2 **Limited memory** – These systems are more complex because they are able to store memories and use them to analyse new data. In this way, they 'learn' from their past actions. For example, self-driving cars use limited memory AI to make decisions based on their changing environment.

The first two types are what is called Artificial Narrow Intelligence (ANI) or 'weak AI'. It is used to train technology to perform specific tasks. All of the AI around us, including chatbots, autocorrect, virtual assistants like Siri or Alexa, personalized ads, Spotify curated playlists, Netflix recommendations and Google Maps, are uses of weak AI.

3 **Theory of mind** – This system only exists in theory. It posits an AI that is able to make reflective decisions based on gauging the emotions of external agents. For example, the AI Samantha in the film *Her* (2014) develops emotional intelligence.

4 **Self-awareness** – The final type of AI system would possess a sense of self and a conscious understanding of its existence. We are still miles away from understanding how to develop this kind of intelligent system, though they are scattered across science-fiction dystopias.

The last two types are called 'strong AI', made up of Artificial General Intelligence (AGI), which means a human-level intelligence; and Artificial Super Intelligence (ASI), which surpasses the ability of the human brain. These theories have led to the fear that robots will overpower humankind – even affecting the way AI is regulated today.

ChatGPT: Generating intelligent solutions… or impossible problems?

Generative AI is a deep learning model that has been making waves since 2022, when OpenAI launched ChatGPT for the public to test. Generative AI had been limited to numerical analysis until advances in deep learning made it possible to extend it to speech, images and other complex data types. This resulted in technologies like ChatGPT, which is a natural language processer that emulates human writing from essays to coding to poetry; DALL-E, which produces computer-generated images across art styles based on textual prompts; and Whisper, a speech recognition, transcription and translation software, among others.

After its release in November 2022, ChatGPT went viral, boasting 100 million active monthly users in January 2023 alone. The AI model was met with equal parts of enthusiasm and apprehension. From office workers to bored teenagers to techies, people rushed to explore its capabilities and limitations. ChatGPT was trained based on a massive amount of data consisting of human-written texts. It manufactures responses by writing a coherent summary of what it concludes is the most relevant information from across its database. While this makes it an incredibly efficient tool to supplement human work, it cannot replace human intelligence and creativity. Furthermore, the content it pulls from is wide, varied and imperfect, leading to answers that are frequently biased, harmful and factually incorrect. Since it basically crunches data, even creative forms of writing it turns out, like poetry, prose or lyrics, are formulaic and lack the meaningfulness of human experience. ChatGPT has brought about fears regarding the stability of writers' livelihoods, just as DALL-E has done for artists. The Writers Guild of America, which called for a strike beginning in May 2023, included in their list of demands a restriction on the use of AI to write scripts, as well as preventing the use of original scripts as training data for AI language models. Issues of copyright claims on original material have been thrown into confusion with the spread of generative AI. ChatGPT has also agitated the education sector, with students and teachers realizing that bots can be used to write tests and assignments. This has turned up a number of AI-response detectors, but with unreliable results – and it is unlikely that we will ever create a catch-all software to differentiate between AI and human content, especially as AI increasingly populates our world. From a journey that began with a single, intriguing question in 1950, our everyday lives are coming to resemble an unending and indecipherable Turing Test.

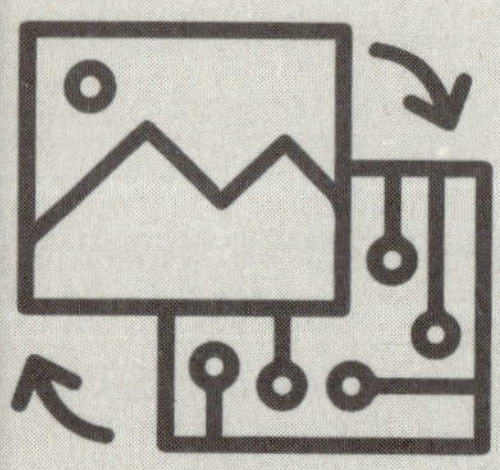

Future of AI

The first AI computers were built in the 1950s, and we have come a long way since then. Google, Amazon, Meta, Microsoft and others have poured billions of dollars into AI research. The AI market is expected to grow to $15.7 trillion by 2030, contributing to a 14 per cent increase to the global GDP. Further, over the next five years, India's AI market is expected to witness a 20 per cent growth, as a top talent pool for the industry.

SCIENCE AND TECHNOLOGY

A report by Goldman Sachs shows that one-fourth of all work being done could be replaced by generative AI – increasing efficiency and alleviating skill shortages across every industry.

Generative AI is a technology capable of producing new data from existing data and is being adopted in various fields at an unprecedented rate.

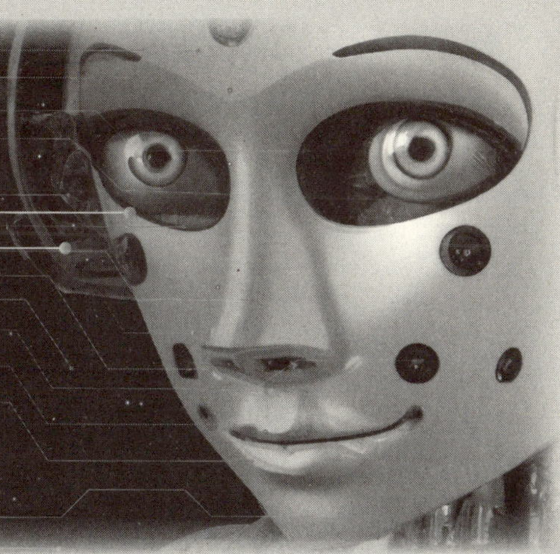

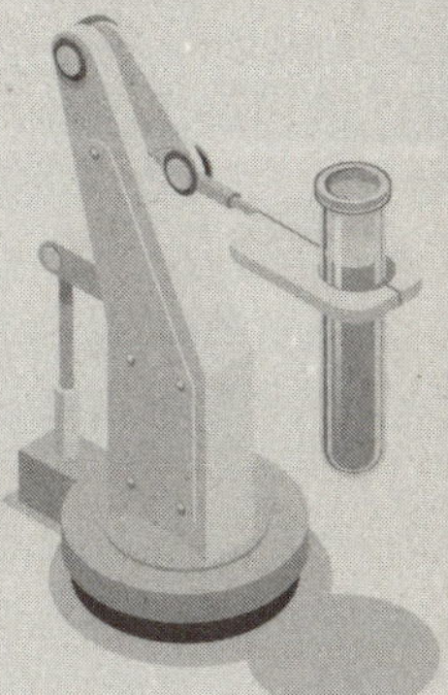

Healthcare: From scanning radiological images for early detection and predicting outcomes from electronic health records to producing more accurate diagnoses and enabling more personalized treatments.

Finance: From offering personalized customer experiences and efficient automation of processes to analysing vast volumes of data and preventing financial fraud.

Education: From automating administrative tasks and developing smart content to enabling students to easily access educational content in their native languages.

Fashion: From optimizing store layout planning to providing customized products for individual consumers at a large scale.

There's no doubt that AI will change the world of work, but to what extent is what remains to be seen.

SCIENCE NEWS

First X-ray of an Atom

In a study funded by the US Department of Energy, a team of scientists led by Saw Wai Hla have captured the first ever X-ray of a single atom. The smallest amount that can be detected by a conventional X-ray is an attogram, which is not less than 10,000 atoms. Using a synchrotron X-ray, this groundbreaking study will allow scientists to identify the exact materials which make up an atom.

New Phase of Matter

Scientists have discovered a new quantum state of matter called the Chiral Bose-liquid state. Apart from the three classical states of matter, which are solid, liquid and gas, new quantum states can emerge at atomic levels or very low temperatures. Tigran Sedrakyan from the University of Massachusetts led a team in building a device to induce kinetic frustration in electrons. Using a very strong magnetic field to measure the movement of electrons, a unique Chiral edge state which had been previously hidden was recorded.

3D Picture of Olfaction

Scientists at the University of California San Francisco have captured a 3D picture of how an odour molecule activates a human odorant receptor. Odorant receptors are proteins that bind odour molecules on the surface of olfactory cells. Using a type of imaging known as cryo-electron microscopy, the receptor OR51E2 was observed in its interaction with propionate, a molecule which contributes to the strong scent of Swiss cheese. The study is a big step towards deciphering our sense of smell.

Advanced Medical Microbots

A team of engineers at the University of Colorado Boulder have designed a new kind of microbot which holds great potential for medical use. Each one is only 20 micrometres wide and travels at the relatively rapid speed of 3 millimetres per second. They are made from biocompatible polymers, through a process similar to 3D printing. The team hopes to develop these microbots to fight illnesses like bladder disease by carrying prescription drugs through the body.

10 SPORTS

GENERAL

- On 9 October, **Prithvi Shaw** hit a double hundred in just 129 balls. He was playing for Northamptonshire in their One-Day Cup match against Somerset. He became only the third cricketer globally to hit a double hundred in the tournament's history.
- Australia retained the **Ashes** against England in 2023. The tournament's final score was 2-2.
- The **Khelo India Youth Games** took place from 30 January to 11 February 2023. Maharashtra topped the medal table with 56 gold medals, 55 silvers and 50 bronze. Haryana finished second. It won 41 golds, 32 silvers and 55 bronze.
- **Panjab University** won the Khelo India University Games 2023 (25 May–3 June). It won 69 medals: 26 gold, 17 silver and 26 bronze.
- Spain's **Carlos Alcaraz** won Wimbledon for the first time in 2023. At 20, he is the third youngest male champion after **Boris Becker** and **Björn Borg.**
- Germany won the 2023 **Men's Hockey World Cup.** Belgium was the runner-up. The tournament (13 January–29 January) was held in Bhubaneshwar in Orissa.
- **Jonas Vingegaard** from Denmark won the 2023 Tour de France. He won the cycling race in 2022 as well. The 110th edition started in Bilbao, Spain, on 1 July and ended at Champs-Élysées, Paris, on 23 July.
- The Indian men's hockey team defeated Malaysia 4-3 in the finals of the **Asian Championship Trophy.** They won all seven matches of the tournament. India rose to third in the FIH rankings following this triumph. India (2771.35 points) jumped one place to third. They went past England (2763.50 points) behind top-ranked Netherlands (3095.90 points) and Belgium (2917.87 points).

ASIAN GAMES

- **The Asian Games are also known as Asiad. Like the Olympics, they also take place every four years.**
- **More than 150 Indian athletes have qualified for the Asiads to be held in Hangzhou, China, in 2023. At the last edition, Jakarta 2018, India had sent 570 athletes to compete in 36 sports.**
- **Indians have qualified in archery, badminton, cricket, boxing, bridge, chess, diving, equestrian, e-sports, fencing, football, golf, gymnastics, handball, ju-jitsu, karate, rowing, sepaktakraw, shooting, skateboarding, squash, swimming, table tennis, tennis, triathlon, volleyball, weightlifting and wrestling.**

*Rankings updated by 1 July 2022

- The Indian basketball team defeated Indonesia 90–74 in the **FIBA Olympic Pre-Qualifier Asia Championship.** Before that, they defeated Syria 85–74.

ARCHERY

- India won four medals at the **Archery World Cup 2023 Stage 1** in Antalya, Turkey. India won two gold, one silver and one bronze. In stage 2 in Shanghai, China, India finished with three medals. At stage 3, in Medellin, Colombia, India won four medals – one gold and three bronze.

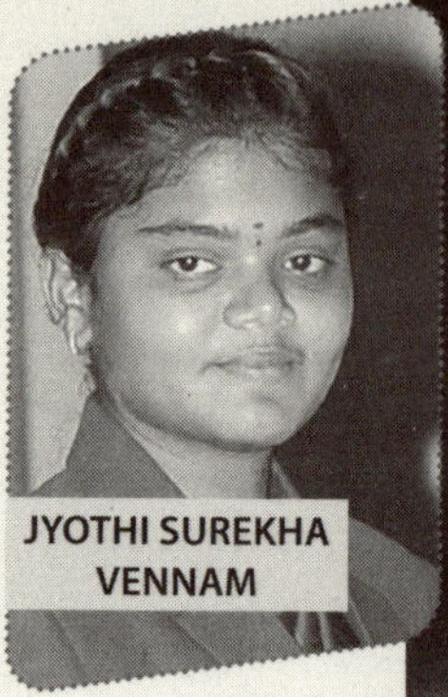

JYOTHI SUREKHA VENNAM

- India topped the medal tally with gold medals (three gold and one bronze) at the World Archery Championships 2023. **Aditi Gopichand Swami,** 17, became the youngest world champion.
- Indian women's compound team of **Jyothi Surekha Vennam, Aditi Swami** and **Parneet Kaur** won the gold medal by beating Mexico 235–229 in the final.

ASHES

- **The 73rd Ashes** series took place in 2023 in England. Australia won the first and second Tests. England won the third and fifth Tests. The fourth Test was drawn.
- Australia retained the Ashes because they had won the last time in **2022.**
- England's **Moeen Ali** and **Stuart Broad** retired from international cricket at the end of the tournament. Ali played for England for nine years and was only the 16th person to hit 3,000 runs and take 200 wickets in Tests. Broad took 604 wickets in Tests and 178 in one-day internationals.
- **Usman Khawaja** became the second Australian player to bat on all five days of a Test match. He achieved that feat at the first Test in Birmingham.

CRICKET

- **The World Cup** will take place in India in October–November 2023.
- India played Australia for the **World Test Championship** title in London in June. India lost by 209 runs. India lost the WTC final to New Zealand in 2022 as well.

- South African Hashim Amla, Australia's **Aaron Finch, Indian opener Murali Vijay**, and England's **Alex Hales** are some of the players who retired from international cricket this year.

- **The Board of Control** for Cricket in India announced that female cricketers will be paid the same match fee as their male counterparts.
- West Indies defeated India in the bilateral tournament that took place in the **Caribbean islands** in August. India lost the T20 series 3–2.
- **Chennai Super Kings** defeated the Gujarat Titans in the final by five wickets to win the 2023 IPL tournament. This was CSK's fifth IPL trophy.
- **Amol Muzumdar** was chosen to be the head coach of the Indian women's cricket team.
- Fifteen years after the **Indian Premier League,** the BCCI organized the **Women's Premier League** for the first time in 2023. Five teams were announced: Mumbai Indians, Delhi Capitals, Royal Challengers Bangalore, Gujarat Giants and UP Warriorz. Mumbai Indians beat Delhi Capitals in the final and won by seven wickets.
- The eighth **Women's T20 World Cup** took place in Cape Town, South Africa, in February. Australia defeated South Africa in the final by 19 runs. This was Australia's sixth and third consecutive title. India lost to Australia in the semi-finals.

Men's ODI Rankings

RANKS	TEAM	RATING
1	AUSTRALIA	118
2	PAKISTAN	116
3	INDIA	115
4	NEW ZEALAND	104
5	ENGLAND	101

Men's Test Team Rankings

RANKS	TEAM	RATING
1	INDIA	118
2	AUSTRALIA	118
3	ENGLAND	115
4	SOUTH AFRICA	104
5	NEW ZEALAND	100

Men's T20 Rankings

RANKS	TEAM	RATING
1	INDIA	264
2	ENGLAND	259
3	NEW ZEALAND	256
4	PAKISTAN	254
5	SOUTH AFRICA	253

Women's ODI Ranking

RANKS	TEAM	RATING
1	AUSTRALIA	165
2	ENGLAND	125
3	SOUTH AFRICA	119
4	INDIA	101
5	NEW ZEALAND	96

Women's T20 Ranking

RANK	TEAM	RATING
1	AUSTRALIA	299
2	ENGLAND	285
3	NEW ZEALAND	266
4	INDIA	236
5	SOUTH AFRICA	253

CRICKET WORLD CUP 2023

- India will host the **Cricket World Cup** for the third time. There will be **45 league stage** and three knockout (two semifinals and final) matches. This is the 13th Cricket World Cup.
- The world cup will be from **5 October to 19 November 2023**.
- Ten teams have qualified for the tournament: New Zealand, England, India, Bangladesh, Pakistan, Australia, Afghanistan, South Africa, Sri Lanka and Netherlands. Sri Lanka and Netherlands got the last two open spots.
- Ireland, Nepal, Oman, Scotland, UAE, USA, Zimbabwe and West Indies failed to qualify.
- For the first time, West Indies will not be featured in the tournament. They failed to qualify.
- **Nine ODI World Cup Games** have been rescheduled. Pakistan and England will have three of their games rescheduled. Dates of India's two games have also been altered.
- **World cup matches** will be played in Delhi, Kolkata, Mumbai, Ahmedabad, Hyderabad, Bangalore, Chennai, Lucknow, Dharamsala and Pune.

Table of India's Matches at the Cricket World Cup 2023

Match	Date	Time	Venue
India vs Australia	Sunday, 8 Oct	2:00 p.m.	MA Chidambaram Stadium, Chennai
India vs Afghanistan	Wednesday, 11 October	2:00 p.m.	Arun Jaitley Stadium, Delhi
India vs Pakistan	Saturday, 14 October	2:00 p.m.	Narendra Modi Stadium, Ahmedabad
India vs Bangladesh	Thursday, 19 October	2:00 p.m.	MCA Stadium, Pune

Match	Date	Time	Venue
India vs New Zealand	Sunday, 22 October	2:00 p.m.	HPCA Stadium, Dharamsala
India vs England	Sunday, 29 October	2:00 p.m.	Ekana Cricket Stadium, Lucknow
India vs Sri Lanka	Thursday, 2 November	2:00 p.m.	Wankhede Stadium, Mumbai
India vs South Africa	Sunday, 5 November	2:00 p.m.	Eden Gardens, Kolkata
India vs Netherlands	Sunday, 12 November	2:00 p.m.	M. Chinnaswamy Stadium, Bengaluru

FORMULA 1 RACING

- **Max Verstappen** from Red Bull has won 10 of the 12 races so far in 2023. The two-time defending champion already has 314 points this season.
- Red Bull currently has more than twice the points as second-place Mercedes in the constructor's standings. Verstappen has a 67-point lead on the point totals of **Lewis Hamilton** and **George Russell** combined.
- **The Red Bull team** now has the longest winning streak in F1 history. At 13 races, it has wins in every race so far this season.
- Mercedes's **Lewis Hamilton** won his 104th pole position at the Hungarian Grand Prix. It was his first pole position in 33 races. But he did not win the race.

LEWIS HAMILTON

- **Michael Schumacher's** 2002 Australian Grand Prix-winning Ferrari F2001b is being auctioned. It is one of the very few cars to have always finished on the podium. The car is expected to fetch six million pounds.

Formula 1 Rankings

RANK	DRIVER	TEAM	POINTS	WINS	PODIUMS
1	MAX VERSTAPPEN	RED BULL	57	54	178
2	SERGIO PÉREZ	RED BULL	66	53	176
3	FERNANDO ALONSO	ASTON MARTIN	32	34	92
4	LEWIS HAMILTON	MERCEDES	16	23	61
5	CHARLES LECLERC	FERRARI	12	17	49

CHESS

- Grandmaster(GM) **Vidit Gujrathi** drew against GM **Etienne Bacrot** of France to advance to the fifth round of FIDE World Cup 2023. GM **Arjun Erigaisi** is the only other Indian who advanced to the pre-quarterfinals.
- Norway's world no. 1 **Magnus Carlsen** won against **R Praggnanandhaa**, the youngest international master in history, at the FIDE World Cup 2023. The final tie-breaker score was a draw to Carlsen.
- In the women's tournament of the FIDE World Cup, among the top favourites, **Aleksandra Goryachkina** and **Polina Shuvalova** qualified for the next round. **Ju Wenjun** and **Elisabeth Pähtz** will decide the winner on the tiebreaks. India's **Koneru Humpy** won her second game against **Georgia's Bella Khotenashvili.**
- Two players from the top 10 rating-wise were eliminated in the tiebreaks of round 3 at the open section of the World Cup. **Nijat Abasov** knocked out **Anish Giri**, while **Jaime Santos** defeated **Teimour Radjabov.**

DOMMARAJU GUKESH

- Grandmaster **Dommaraju Gukesh** has now become India's top-ranked chess player. He surpassed India's first GM **Viswanathan Anand** in live ratings. This comes after the 17-year-old Gukesh qualified for the third round of the FIDE Chess World Cup. Gukesh beat Azerbaijan's GM **Misratdin Iskandarov** to secure a live rating of 2755.9, narrowly beating Anand's 2754.0.
- FIDE-rated player **Kandi Santosh Sai Karthik** clinched the HCC First Invitational Classic Chess title in Secunderabad. Sai Karthik, with 5.5 points from six rounds, secured top spot. **Andabatla Satvik** finished runner-up with 4.5 points, while **Natura Bethi**, with four points, took the third place.
- Eleven-year-old **Adhiraj Mitra** of Jamshedpur is in the title race of the FIDE rating chess championship with a thumping victory over **Kishan Kumar** of Bihar.

TENNIS

NOVAK DJOKOVIC

- Australia's **Nick Kyrgios** has pulled out of the US Open In order to focus on his recovery from injury.
- **Carlos Alcaraz** defeated seven-time champion **Novak Djokovic** to claim his first Wimbledon title. World No. 1

Alcaraz recovered from dropping the first set and saving a set point in the second. He won 1–6, 7–6 (8/6), 6–1, 3–6,6–4 after four hours and 42 minutes on Centre Court.

- **Novak Djokovic** won the French Open for the third time this year. He defeated 7–6(1), 6–3, 7–5. He also won the Australian Open in January for the 10th time against **Stefanos Tsitsipas** 6–3, 7–6 (4), 7–6 (5).
- **Iga Świątek** defeated **Karolina Muchova** 6–2, 5–7, 6–4 to win the 2023 French Open. **Markéta Vondroušová** defeated **Ons Jabeur** in the final 6–4, 6–4 to win the first Wimbledon title. **Aryna Sabalenka** defeated **Elena Rybakina** 4–6, 6–3, 6–4 in the final to win the Australian Open grand slam in 2023.
- Former champion **Rafael Nadal** did not play in 2023 French Open or Wimbledon because of a hip injury and surgery. He will not be playing in the US Open either.

- India's **Rohan Bopanna** reached the semifinals of the men's doubles at Wimbledon. His partner was Australia's **Matthew Ebden.** They lost 5–7, 6–4, 6–7 (5) to **Wesley Koolhof** (Netherlands) and **Neal Skupski** (England).

Men's Rankings

RANK	NAME	POINTS	CHANGE
1	CARLOS ALCARAZ	9,225	0
2	NOVAK DJOKOVIC	8,795	0
3	DANIIL MEDVEDEV	6,360	0
4	STEFANOS TSITSIPAS	5,090	+1
5	CASPER RUUD	4,985	-1
6	HOLGER RUNE	4,825	0
7	JANNIK SINNER	3,815	0
8	TAYLOR FRITZ	3,605	0
9	FRANCES TIAFOE	3,085	0
10	KAREN KHACHANOV	2,900	0

Women's Ranking

RANK	NAME	POINTS	CHANGE
1	IGA ŚWIĄTEK	9,590	0
2	ARYNA SABALENKA	8,746	0
3	JESSICA PEGULA	5,480	+1
4	ELENA RYBAKINA	5,465	+1
5	ONS JABEUR	4,747	0
6	CAROLINE GARCIA	4,685	0

RANK	NAME	POINTS	CHANGE
7	CORI GAUFF	3,760	0
8	MARIA SAKKARI	3,585	+1
9	PETRA KVITOVA	3,341	-1
10	MARKÉTA VONDROUŠOVÁ	3,106	0

2023 COMMONWEALTH YOUTH GAMES

- **The seventh Commonwealth Youth Games** took place on the Caribbean islands of Trinidad and Tobago between 4 and 11 August 2023. Over 1,000 athletes from 71 Commonwealth nations and territories participated. These games are meant only for under-18 athletes. They started in 2000 and this year, they made a return after six years.
- Medals were offered in seven sports – athletics, beach volleyball, cycling, netball fast 5, rugby sevens, swimming and triathlon. India, however, only fielded sportspersons in cycling, triathlon, swimming and athletics. The **Indian contingent** had 24 athletes – eight in athletics, six each in cycling and swimming, and four in triathlon.

- India won **five medals** and was number 17 on the medals tally. Australia topped the list with **64 medals.**

Indian winners at the Commonwealth Youth Games

Athlete	Sport	Event	Medal
Shoan Ganguly	Swimming	Men's 400m individual medley	Silver
Asha Kiran Barla	Athletics	Women's 800m	Silver
Anupriya Valliyot Sasi	Athletics	Women's shot put	Bronze
Pooja	Athletics	Women's high jump	Bronze
Arjun	Athletics	Men's javelin throw	Bronze

FIFA WOMEN'S WORLD CUP

- The women's football world cup is taking place in **Australia** and **New Zealand**. The 2023 tournament is the first to feature 32 teams from the previous 24. The opening match took place between New Zealand and Norway in Auckland.
- **Two-time champion USA** was eliminated in the round of 16. They

lost to Sweden on penalties. Two-time world champion Germany was eliminated in the group stage. This was their first time in the history of the tournament.

- Of the 32 countries that qualified, 20 competed at the previous tournament in 2019. Haiti, Morocco, Panama, the Philippines, Portugal, the Republic of Ireland, Vietnam and Zambia made their debuts at the 2023 world cup. This tournament is the first ever **FIFA tournament** for the **Philippines**.
- The top two players in the race for the **Golden Boot trophy** are: Hinata Miyazawa, Japan (5 goals) and Kadidiatou Diani, France (4 goals).

WORLD UNIVERSITY GAMES

- India finished seventh in the medals tally at the **World University Games** 2023 in Chengdu, China. India won 26 medals–11 gold, 5 silver and 10 bronze.
- China claimed the pole position with **103 gold medals**. It won a total of **178 medals**. Japan came second with **21 golds** from **93 medals**. The Republic of Korea finished third with **17 gold** medals from a total of 58.
- Close to 230 Indian athletes participated at the **2023 World University Games**. Fourteen of the 26 medals were won by India's shooting contingent. They won eight gold, four silver and two bronze medals.
- Rifle shooter **Aishwary Pratap Singh Tomar** was the most successful Indian athlete with four medals. He won gold medals in men's 10m air rifle and 50m rifle 3 positions. He was also a part of the gold medal-winning men's 10m air rifle team. He also won a bronze with the men's 50m rifle 3 positions team.
- **Manu Bhaker** bagged gold medals in the women's 10m air pistol individual and team events. **Sift Kaur Samra** won gold in the women's 50m rifle 3 positions.
- Archers **Avneet Kaur** and **Sangampreet Singh Bisla** won individual gold medals in women's and men's compound events. **Aman Saini** and **Pragati** won a gold medal in the mixed compound team event.

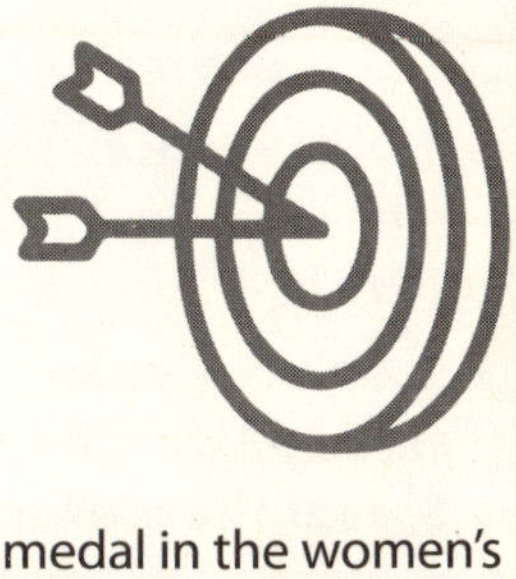

- **Priyanka Goswami** got a bronze medal at the 20-km race walk. **Jyothi Yarraji** clocked a new national record at 12.78 seconds to win the bronze medal in the women's 100m hurdles. **Amlan Borgohain** (men's 200m) and **Bhavani Yadav** (women's long jump) also won bronze medals.

RUGBY WORLD CUP

- **The Rugby World Cup 2023** begins on 8 September with France taking on New Zealand. The final will be played on 28 October. South Africa was the winner of the last tournament in Japan in 2019 when they defeated England in the final.
- All the matches will be played in **France** across nine cities – Paris, Marseille, Lyon, Lile, Bordeaux, Saint-Étienne, Nice, Nantes and Toulouse.
- A total of **20 teams have qualified** for the world cup. These teams have been split into four groups of five. Each pool has one team from five 'bands'. Band one featured the four highest-ranked teams (South Africa, New Zealand, England, Wales). Band two has the next four highest-ranked teams (Ireland, Australia, France, Japan), and band three the four after that (Scotland, Argentina, Fiji, Italy).

- Each side in the **first three bands qualified** for the tournament automatically because of their world ranking. The final two bands comprise the sides who qualified for the tournament (Samoa, Georgia, Uruguay, Tonga, Namibia, Romania, Chile and Portugal).
- The 2023 will be the last for Fiji rugby legend **Nemani Nadolo**. Known as the Flying Fijian, Nadolo's 15-year-long career has seen him flatten defenders and score tries in England, France, Japan, New Zealand and Australia.

KHELO INDIA UNIVERSITY GAMES 2023

- **Panjab University won the Khelo India University Games 2023.** They reclaimed the title after three years. Panjab University won the inaugural Games title back in 2020. It won a total of 69 medals – 26 gold, 17 silver, and 26 bronze.
- **Amritsar's Guru Nanak Dev University came in second.** They won 68 medals – 24 gold, 27 silver and 17 bronze. Karnataka's Jain University got 16 gold, 10 silver and 6 bronze medals (32 medals total).
- Swimmer **Siva Sridhar** topped the men's section with a total of 11 medals, including eight golds. **Shrungi Bandekar**, also a swimmer, won nine medals in the women's section, including five golds. Both represented Jain University.

Khelo India University Games 2023 medals tally

RANK	UNIVERSITY	GOLD	SILVER	BRONZE	TOTAL
1	PANJAB UNIVERSITY, PUNJAB	26	17	26	69
2	GURU NANAK DEV UNIVERSITY, AMRITSAR	24	27	17	68
3	JAIN UNIVERSITY, KARNATAKA	16	10	6	32
4	PUNJABI UNIVERSITY, PATIALA	12	14	8	34
5	GURU KASHI UNIVERSITY, TALWANDI SABO, PUNJAB	9	10	9	28

BADMINTON

- The 2023 BWF World Championships will be held at the end of August in Copenhagen, Denmark.
- **Satwiksairaj Rankireddy** and **Chirag Shetty** won India's second gold medal in the Badminton Asia Championships in April in Dubai. They beat Malaysia's eighth seeds Ong Yew Sin and Teo Ee Yi 16–21, 21–17, 21–19. This was India's second gold medal in the Asian Badminton Championships after **Dinesh Khanna** bagged the men's singles gold in 1965.
- **Satwiksairaj Rankireddy** and **Chirag Shetty** also won a historic men's doubles title at the Indonesia Open. They become the first doubles pair from India to claim a Super 1000 event. They defeated **Aaron Chia** and **Soh Wooi Yik** of Malaysia 21–17, 21–18.
- China's **Li Shifeng** defeated compatriot **Shi Yuqi** in the men's singles final at the 2023 All England Open to claim his first BWF Tour Super 1000 title. He won 26–24, 21–5. **An Se-young** from Republic of Korea became the All England women's singles champion with victory over **Chen** Yufei of China. She won 21–17, 10–21, 21–19.
- India's **Lakshya Sen** lost in the semi-finals of the Japan Open in July. He went down to world number nine **Jonatan Christie** 15–21, 21–13, 16–21.
- **H.S. Prannoy** and **Lakshya Sen** made significant advancements in the BWF world rankings. Prannoy climbed one spot to secure the ninth position, and Sen improved two places to claim the 11th spot.
- **Anupama Upadhyaya** and **Rutaparna Panda/Swetaparna Panda** won the Tajikistan International Series 2023 in August.

BOXING

- At the IBA World Women's Boxing Championship in March, **Nitu** (48kg category), **Lovlina Borgohain** (75kg), and **Saweety Boora** (81kg) also won gold medals. This was India's best haul in terms of gold medals since the World Championships in 2006, which was also held in New Delhi.
- Irish boxing legend **Bernard Dunne** has become the new director of high performance for Indian boxing. Dunne was in charge of the Irish boxing team from 2017 to 2022. He helped Irish pugilists win European, world and Olympic gold medals.
- India finished with three bronze medals at the 2023 IBA Men's World Boxing Championships in May. **Deepak Bhoria** (48–51kg), **Mohammed Hussamuddin** (54–57kg) and **Nishant Dev** (67–71kg) emerged victorious.
- **Ashish Raman Sethi** became the first Indian boxer ever to win a Bangla boxing stadium belt. Bangla Boxing Stadium is a prominent Muay Thai arena in Phuket known for hosting real Thai Boxing matches.

FOOTBALL

- Portuguese legend **Christiano Ronaldo** joined the Saudi Arabian club Al-Nasser from Manchester United. Paris Sant-Germain and Brazilian footballer **Neymar Jr** has been reported to join Saudi Arabian club Al-Hilal.
- England's **Harry Kane** also moved from Tottenham Hotspur to German club Bayern Munich. He played for Tottenham for over 10 years. In other transfer news, Argentina's **Lionel Messi** also changed clubs. He moved from Paris Saint-Germain to American club Inter Miami.

SPORTS NEWSMAKERS

CARLOS ALCARAZ **In the news for:** Winning the men's Wimbledon singles titles for the first time in 2023; **Where:** Wimbledon, England ▸▸ On 16 July, Spain's Carlos Alcaraz defeated seven-time winner and defending champion Novak Djokovic of Serbia. The five-set match lasted four hours and 42 minutes. Djokovic would have equalled Roger Federer's eight Wimbledon titles had he won.

SUNIL CHHETRI **In the news for:** Captaining the Indian football team to win the Inter-continental Cup and SAFF Championship; **Where:** India ▸▸ On 18 June, India became the champion of the Inter-continental Cup after defeating Lebanon by 2–0 in the final. Along with Lallianzuala Chhangte, Sunil Chhetri also scored two goals to become the joint-top scorers of the tournament. On 4 July, India defeated Kuwait in the final of the 2023 Bangabandhu SAFF Championship 5–4 in penalties. Chhetri was again the tournament's top scorer with five goals.

SUNIL CHHETRI

MURALI SREESHANKAR **In the news for:** Bagging a silver medal in the Asian Athletics Championships; **Where:** Bangkok ▸▸ On 15 July, long jumper Murali Sreeshankar qualified for the 2024 Paris Olympics after bagging a silver medal in the Asian Athletics Championships. The qualification mark for the Paris games is 8.27m and Murali produced a final round jump of 8.37m. This is his career's second-best jump. He will be competing in his second Olympics.

NIKHAT ZAREEN **In the news for:** Become the world champion in the 50kg category at the IBA World Women's Boxing Championship; **Where:** India ▸▸ In March, Nikhat Zareen defeated Vietnam's Nguyen Thị Tam and won the bout by a unanimous verdict. The scores from the five judges read: 28–27, 28–27, 28–27, 29–26 and 28–27. Tam is a two-time Asian champion. Nikhat became only the second Indian after M.C. Mary Kom to win this tournament twice.

MAHENDRA SINGH DHONI **In the news for:** Not retiring; **Where:** India ▸▸ The former India cricket captain was said to retire after IPL 2023. However, after leading the Chennai Super Kings to their fifth IPL title, Dhoni announced that he may not retire from the IPL. He has already retired from all other forms of cricket.

MAHENDRA SINGH DHONI

ANUPAMA UPADHYAYA **In the news for:** Becoming the new world number 1 in the latest BWF world junior women's rankings; **Where:** India ▸▸ Anupama won the Polish Open 2022 in March 2023. Before that she won a juniors international title in Uganda earlier this year. The Polish Open was Upadhyaya's maiden seniors' title. The 17-year-old rose to the top spot in the junior badminton world rankings with 18,060 points from 18 tournaments. She replaced compatriot Tasnim Mir, who became the first Indian junior woman to achieve the world number 1 rank earlier in 2023.

LIONEL MESSI **In the news for:** Winning the FIFA World Cup for Argentina and moving to Inter Miami from Barcelona; **Where:** Qatar ▸▸ Messi led Argentina to lift the FIFA World Cup for the first time in 36 years. He scored two goals in the final against France. After the world cup, Messi decided to leave Paris Saint-Germain and moved to US's Inter Miami club. He rejected offers from Saudi Arabian clubs to play in America.

LEBRON JAMES **In the news for:** Becoming NBA's all-time leading scorer; **Where:** Los Angeles ▸▸ In February, LeBron James became the all-time leading scorer in the National Basketball Association. He surpassed a record held by Kareem Abdul Jabbar since 1984. James, who plays as a forward for the Los Angeles Lakers, reached the mark in the third quarter with a fadeaway jumper over two defenders against the Oklahoma City Thunder. He scored his 38,388th point in the process. He has a career average of 27.2 points, 7.5 rebounds and 7.3 assists from 1,409 games over a 20-year career.

HARMANPREET KAUR **In the news** for: Being banned for two matches; **Where:** Dhaka ▸▸ Indian women's cricket team captain Harmanpreet Kaur was by the ICC for violating the Code of Conduct in a recent ODI against Bangladesh. She criticised the umpiring during the match after she was dismissed. Harmanpreet will miss the first two matches of the Asian Games cricket tournament in Hangzhou in September-October.

HARMANPREET KAUR

NOVAK DJOKOVIC **In the news for:** Winning a record 23rd Grand Slam at the French Open; **Where:** Paris ▸▸ By winning the 2023 French Open Djokovic broke the tie between him and Rafael Nadal for most Grand Slam titles. In the all-time list, Djokovic is now tied with Serena Williams (23) and only one behind Margaret Court (24). He also became the first man in history to have won each of the four Grand Slams at least three times.

INDEX

INDEX